GLOBALIZATION

Viewed as a destructive force or a inevitability of modern society, Globalization is the focus of a multitude of disciplines. A clear understanding of its processes and terminology is imperative for anyone engaging with this ubiquitous topic. *Globalization: the Key Concepts* offers a comprehensive guide to this cross-disciplinary subject and covers concepts such as:

- Homogenization
- Neo-Liberalism
- Risk
- Knowledge Society
- Time-space compression
- Reflexivity

With extensive cross-referencing and suggestions for further reading, this book is an essential resource for students and interested readers alike as they navigate the literature on globalisation studies.

Annabelle Mooney is a Lecturer at Roehampton University. Her research interests include marginal religious movements, the semiotics of law, HIV and quality of life.

Betsy Evans is a Research Associate at Cardiff University. Her research interests include language variation and change and attitudes to varieties of language.

ALSO AVAILABLE FROM ROUTLEDGE

Economics: The Basics
Tony Cleaver
0-415-31412-7
978-0-415-31412-1

Politics: The Basics
Second Edition
Stephen Tansey
0-415-30329-X
978-0-415-30329-3

Sociology: The Key Concpets
Edited by John Scott
0-415-34406-9
978-0-415-34406-7

Fifty Major Economists
Second Edition
Steven Pressman
0-415-36649-6
978-0-415-36649-6

The Routledge Companion to Global Economics
Edited by Robert Benyon
0-415-24306-8
978-0-415-24306-3

GLOBALIZATION

The Key Concepts

Edited by
Annabelle Mooney
and
Betsy Evans

Routledge
Taylor & Francis Group

LONDON AND NEW YORK

Mohawk Valley Community College Library

First published 2007
by Routledge
2 Park Square, Milton Park, Abingdon, Oxon OX14 4RN

Simultaneously published in the USA and Canada
by Routledge
270 Madison Ave, New York, NY 10016

Routledge is an imprint of the Taylor & Francis Group, an informa business

© 2007 Annabelle Mooney and Betsy Evans

Reprinted 2008
Typeset in Bembo by
Taylor & Francis Books
Printed and bound in Great Britain by
MPG Books Ltd, Bodmin

All rights reserved. No part of this book may be reprinted or reproduced or utilised in any
form or by any electronic, mechanical, or other means, now known or hereafter invented,
including photocopying and recording, or in any information storage or retrieval system,
without permission in writing from the publishers.

British Library Cataloguing in Publication Data
A catalogue record for this book is available from the British Library

Library of Congress Cataloguing in Publication Data
A catalog record for this book has been requested

ISBN13: 978-0-415-36859-9 (hbk)
ISBN13: 978-0-415-36860-5 (pbk)
ISBN13: 978-0-203-09883-7 (ebk)

Ref
JZ
1318
.G5b45
2007

CONTENTS

KEY TO CONTRIBUTORS

AC Andrew Curtis
Roehampton University

CM Dr Christopher Marlowe
Faculty of Media and Humanities, University of Lincoln

CW Dr Christopher White
Department of Politics and International Relations, University of Reading

DM Dr David Machin
Department of Media and Communication, Leicester University

FO Dr Mag. Florian Oberhuber
Research Centre "Discourse Politics Identity," University of Vienna, Austria

GW Dr Glynne Williams
School of Social Sciences, Cardiff University

HB Hywel Bishop
Centre for Language and Communication Research, Cardiff University

JH Jan Harris
Lecturer, Department of Media and Communications, University of Swansea

JJ Dr John Jewell
Tom Hopkinson Centre for Media Research, School of Journalism, Media and Cultural Studies, Cardiff University

MG Professor Max Gillman
Business School, Cardiff University

NC Dr Nancy Cook
Sociology Department, Brock University

NH Dr Nikolas Hammer
Centre for Labour Market Studies, University of Leicester

RC Dr Ravi de Costa
Institute on Globalization and the Human Condition, McMaster University, Canada

RF Dr Raffaele Marchetti
European University Institute, Florence

RM Dr Ruth McManus
School of Sociology and Anthropology University of Canterbury New Zealand

SL Dr Sarah Lawson
Head of Ethnic Minority Achievement, Rokeby School

TB Dr Tammy Boyce
Cardiff School of Journalism, Media and Cultural Studies, Cardiff University

ACKNOWLEDGEMENTS

This book would not have been possible without the generous funding of the Leverhulme Trust (grant no. F/00 407/D project on Language and Global Communication). Our colleagues Hywel Bishop, Sarah Lawson, David Machin, Klas Prytz, and Lowri Griffith have been indefatigable in their work and generosity. We consider ourselves incredibly fortunate to have worked with such talented individuals. We would also like to thank Theo van Leeuwen for his continuing enthusiasm and support in this and all our work. Our contributors have been extremely generous in patience and time. Not only have they written entries, but also helped enormously in clarifying the range and purpose of this exploration into globalization. Their expertise has been indispensable in this project. We would also like to thank the anonymous reviewers for their very helpful recommendations.

INTRODUCTION

Globalization is a buzzword of the moment, within universities, government and society. The power of the word itself, and all that it brings with it, is immense (e.g. Bourdieu 1999). Some tell us that globalization is inevitable, that it entails specific events and others that it is something that should be defeated.

In academic circles, there are many definitions of and approaches to globalization simply because it is not a field of study that is restricted to any one discipline. Globalization scholars belong to fields as diverse as cultural studies, sociology, economics, international relations, political theory, art and linguistics. This cross-disciplinary nature of globalization is perhaps one of its defining features. Hence, it is a field that borrows a significant number of terms and concepts from existing lexicons. The result is that what globalization means is always in dispute. In the end, globalization concerns a field of inquiry defined more by the questions it asks and its object of study: the world as a whole and parts of it in relation to this whole.

Among nonacademics, however, recent research indicates something of a consensus as to the meaning of globalization (Garrett, Evans and Williams, forthcoming). When asked what "globalization" made them think of, respondents tended to focus on economic issues including capitalism, money, big business, and the expansion of large corporations. The prominence of multinational corporations as increasingly present and powerful players in contemporary society was often noted.

Why this is one of the most salient features for the general public is a question we can't answer here. This does, however, highlight the difference in conceptualization of globalization that exists among lay persons and scholars. Globalization studies point squarely at the difficulty of understanding and theorizing our present stage of history.

This book is intended to help navigate the labyrinth that is the literature about globalization studies. The sophistication of the key concepts speaks to the enormity and complexity of issues in the field.

Because the meaning of globalization is constantly disputed, and because it is a subject visited by scholars from an immensely wide range of disciplines, our task here is not an easy one. Naturally it has not been possible to include within this book every concept in globalization studies and the entries are necessarily concise. This book attempts to identify some of the key terms and concepts within the field and outline the discussion and the central debates that different scholars raise. The terms that we have chosen emerged from consultation of influential texts in the field of globalization as well as the specialist suggestions of our contributors. Some terms that may be central to a small number of theorists might not be found here. We have tried to identify terms that, while emanating from a particular discipline, have more general currency in the field of globalization. In short, we have considered how much a term is used in the current debates. We have also not included terms that we understand as fundamental to a discipline, unless they have been the focus of specific attention in globalization studies. Thus some entries presuppose an understanding of basic categories of various fields. On the other hand, if a fundamental term is being used outside of its "home" discipline in a way that is related to globalization studies, we have included it. Most importantly, this text aims to provide a point of departure for the reader.

The widespread adoption of a discourse and perspective of globalization also means that what globalization means will vary contextually. Therefore the reader must bear in mind that although one scholar may use a term in a particular way, this does not mean that other scholars will do the same. That is, it is entirely possible that the reader will encounter the terms from this book used in different ways elsewhere.

Thus, for example, we have included entries on Marx, modernism and panopticon. These, and other terms, existed before the appearance of globalization studies as a field. And yet because globalization as a field of study involves reexamining the primary categories of thinking and the bases of disciplines, such terms are relevant. This reexamination exemplifies the reflexivity that is considered by some to be central to globalization.

We hope that the concepts, descriptions, and sources provided within this book provide readers with a solid, basic understanding of this complex field.

LIST OF KEY CONCEPTS

Abstract systems
Active citizens
Alien culture
Americanization
Anarchism
Anticipation of pleasure
Antiglobalization
Anti-imperialism
Asymptotic progression
Atomization
Aura (of cultural phenomenon)
Automobility
Autonomization (of an
  institution)
Autonomization (of culture)
Axial period
Axial principle
Balance of power
Basic needs
Biculturalism
Bio-politics
Bio-power
Biospheric politics
Bodily display
Bretton Woods institutions
Bureaucracy
Capitalism
Centrism
Chaos theory
Choice (discourse of)
Citizenship
Civil inattention

Civil society
Clash of civilizations
Cleft countries
CNN effect
Coca-colonization
Coevolution
Cognitive reflexivity
Collectivism
Colonialism
Commodification
Commodity biographies
Commodity candidacy
Commodity chain
Commodity fetishism
Commodity flows
Commodity phase
Common Agricultural Policy
  (CAP)
Communicative rationality
Communities of fate
Communities of limited liability
Community participation
Complexity theory
Confluent love
Constructive postmodernism (or
  integralism)
Consumerism
Consumption rituals
Contextual universalism
Contingency theory
Contracting out
Convergence thesis

Core–periphery model
Corporatism
Cosmocracy
Cosmopolis
Cosmopolitan democracy
Cosmopolitanism
Counter-culture
Counter-hegemony
Counter-narratives
Creolization
Cultural autonomy
Cultural capital
Cultural convergence
Cultural defence plea
Cultural dumping
Cultural economy
Cultural entrepreneurs
Cultural fate
Cultural heritage
Cultural imperialism
Cultural integration
Cultural landscape
Cultural storage
Cultural synchronization
Cultural tourism
Culturalism
Culture industry
Culture of civility
Cyberactivism
Debt relief
Decisionism
Decolonization
Decommoditization
De-governmentalization
Democracy
Dependency theory
Developmental state
Diaspora
Digital divide
Digital nomads
Direct action
Disconnected contiguity

Discrepant cosmopolitanism
Disorganized capitalism
Distant proximities
Divergence/convergence
Divided self
Downsizing
Economic liberalization
Ecotourism
Embedded journalists
Embedding
Embodiment
Empire
Enclave
Enclaved commodities
End of history
Epistemic communities
Epistemic violence
Essentialism
Ethnic diversity
Ethnic tourism
Ethnocentrism
Ethnocide
Ethnolinguistic
European Union (EU)
Europeanization
Exchange value
Experts/expert systems
Export processing zone (EPZ)
Extra-legal economy
Fair trade/free trade
False consciousness
False needs
Family wage (decline of)
Feminism
Feminization of the workforce
Fetishism Theory
Financialization
Foreign Direct Investment (FDI)
Formal/informal economies
Fragmentation (social)
Fragmented State
Free trade

Fundamentalism

Futurist/futurology/future studies

G7/G8

GATT

GDI (Gender Development Index)

GEM (Gender Empowerment Measure)

Gemeinschaft

Genealogies (of globalization)

Genoa

Geopolitical rationality

Global capitalism

Global cities

Global Commodity Chain (GCC)

Global elite

Global English

Global fluids

Global governance

Global health policy

Global labor market

Global managerial class/global elite

Global media

Global politics

Global social policy

Global sub-politics

Global Union Federations (GUFs)

Global village

Globalism

Globality

Globalization from below

Glocal/glocalization

Governmentality

Habitus

Hard/soft power

Hegemony

Heritage tourism

Heterogeneity

High modernity

Homogenization

Human capital

Human rights

Hybridity/hybridization

Hyperglobalist thesis

Hypermasculinity

Hyperreality

Identity politics

Identity thinking

Ideological State Apparatus

IFA (International Framework Agreements)

IGO (Intergovernmental Organizations)

Imaginative hedonism

Imagined communities

IMF (International Monetary Fund)

Imperialism

Income polarization

Incorporation theory

Index of Social Progress

Indigenization

Indigenous culture

Individuation

Industrialization

Informal economies

Information age

Infotainment

INGO (International Non-Governmental Organization)

Inhuman hybrids

Institutional reflexivity

International Financial Institutions

Internationalization

Internet

Kin country rallying

Kitsch

Knowledge society

Kyoto

Language rights
Legitimation crisis
Liberal democracy
Liberal humanism
Liberalization
Lifestyle
Lifestyle enclaves
Lifeworld
Liminal/liminality
Liquid modernity
Localization
Macroanthoropology
Marginalization/centralization
Market segmentation
Marx/Marxism
Mass media conglomerates
Master concepts
Materialism
McDonaldization
Media imperialism
Metaculture
Microglobalization
Microstate
Migration
Mobility
Modernism
Modernity
Monetarization
Montage
Moral economy
Multicultural/ism
Multinational corporation
  (MNC)
Nation-state
Nation-state, decline of
Nationalism
Nationalization/nationalized
  industries
Neoconservatism
Neoliberalism
Network society
New Labour

New public management
NGO (Non-Governmental
  Organization)
Non-Aligned Movement
  (NAM)
Non-modern
North/south divide
OECD (Organization for
  Economic Co-operation and
  Development)
Offshoring
One world paradigm
Open society
Organization of Petroleum
  Exporting Countries (OPEC)
Orientalism
Panopticon
Particularlism
Perfect knowledge
Performative citizenship
Placeless geography
Pluralism
Pluralist paradigm
Policy agendas
Policy cycle
Policy evaluation
Policy programs
Political globalization
Postcolonialism
Post-Fordism
Post-information age
Post-materialism
Postmodernity/postmodernism
Post-tourist
Primitive accumulation
Privatization
Protectionism (economic)
Psuedo events
QUANGO
Racialization (of governmental
  processes)
Radical modernity

Rationalities of risk
Realist paradigm
Re-embedding
Reflexive modernization/
  modernity
Reflexivity
Reform (political)
Relativism
Re-localization
Revitalization movement
Risk
Seattle
Semi-periphery countries
Service work
Simulacrum
Skeptics
Social capital
Social movements
Societies of control
Soft power
Sovereignty
State
Statist paradigm
Structural Adjustment Programs
Structuration
Subaltern
Subsistence perspective
Supermodernity (or
  hypermodernity)
Surplus value
Sustainable development
Sweatshop
Symbolic analysts

Symbolic capital
Territorialization (de- & re-)
Third Way
Third World War (WWIII)
Time-space compression
Tobin tax
Traditionalist
Transnational
Transnational Corporation
  (TNC)
Transnationalist Capitalist Class
  (TCC)
Trust
United Nations (UN)
Universal civilization
Universal human rights
Universalism
Urbanism, transnational
Wage earner welfare states
War of position
Welfare state
Westernization
Work rich/work poor
World Bank
World cities/global cities
World culture theory
WHO (World Health
  Organization)
World hegemony
World polity theory
World systems theory
World Works Council
WTO (World Trade Organization)

GLOBALIZATION

ABSTRACT SYSTEMS

A general term covering **expert systems** and symbolic tokens particularly used by the sociologist Anthony Giddens. Abstract systems refer to the collection of rules and procedures that we increasingly rely on in order to calculate and negotiate **risk**. These systems are not accessible as such to the individual and are often very opaque. Whereas in traditional societies we might have relied on local experienced individuals, now we tend to rely on principles and rules administered by groups of experts (anything from psychologists to weather forecasters) and bureaucracies.

Expert systems and symbolic tokens are disembedding mechanisms. Symbolic tokens allow interaction and exchange between and among everyone. An excellent example is money, which allows "enactment of transactions between agents widely separated in time and space" (Giddens 1991:24). Such symbolic tokens need some authority to stand behind them such that they retain exchange value as they have no intrinsic value (for an example of money as symbolic, see the work of J.S.G. Boggs, who trades "art" money for commodities).

Further reading: Giddens 1990, 1991; Weschler 2000

ACTIVE CITIZENS

Active citizens are individuals who participate in public life. They see themselves as having a role to play in and are agents for social change. Active citizenship is a way of defining what it takes to be a good citizen, a notion that has been debated since Aristotle. Active citizens are linked to globalization literature in at least two ways. One way is to see active citizenship as an effect of and response to globalization. The globalization of economic markets is seen as a challenge to **democracy** because it undermines the authority and influence of **nation–states** and established ways of defining citizenship. The response to the democratic threat posed by globalization is to turn to, and revitalize civic culture. Encouraging active citizenship is a way to regenerate civic culture. Active citizenship is now seen as a central mechanism for ensuring and achieving democracy during a period of unprecedented social upheaval. The concept of active citizen is used to marshal certain targeted groups of people into behaving and thinking about themselves as self-governing and therefore able to regulate themselves towards good citizenship behaviors. The link between active citizen and globalization is different in this view. Instead of active citizenship being an effect of and response to the massive social transformations associated with globalization, active citizenship is a strategy that is part of the tangled bundle of practices, techniques and mentalities through which the geopolitical rationality called globalization gets configured and enabled (Larner and Walters 2004b).

See also: **choice (discourse of), community participation, geopolitical rationality, global sub-politics**

Further reading: Dean 1995; Giddens 1998

RM

ALIEN CULTURE

A term used in opposition to "native culture" to refer to practices or things introduced to (or embedded in) another culture. This term suggests that the new practice has been imposed on the other culture. Tomlinson (1991) claims that it is more usual for other cultural practices to be adopted willingly, incorporated and **re-embedded** than for them to be seen as imposed and "alien."

See also: **cultural imperialism**

AMERICANIZATION

This term dates from 1860, meaning strictly to become American (in language, habits or professions) especially for migrants to the USA. The term has a particular meaning with regard to globalization in that it encompasses anything from an alleged **cultural imperialism** by the United States, to stimulating changes in local patterns of behavior and consumption because of the dominance of free-market economics.

The cultural imperialist view is clearly pejorative and relates to the increased presence of "American" products (fast food, clothing labels, soft drinks, Hollywood films) in foreign markets. In many cases, especially when used by social activists against economic globalization, Americanization is used to mean the changing nature of

4

political and economic systems to fall in line with US administrative polices of **free trade** and **democracy**.

There is a question, though, of what counts as "American." Some practices and products are thought of as American because of a symbolic link. So, for example, **neoliberal** trade practices are considered American when really they are common throughout the world (though the US was a major force behind the shape and detail of **Bretton Woods institutions**). Others (e.g. Featherstone 1990 and Giddens 1990, 1991) stress the critical reception of products and practices as well as their **hybridization** and embedding into local contexts. Note that Gienow-Hecht (2000) refers to Americanization as "American cultural transfer."

See also: **homogenization, McDonaldization**

Further reading: Plender 2003

ANARCHISM

Also known as libertarian–socialism and anarcho–communism. While anarchy is a technical term describing a particular kind of political system and organization, anarchism is relevant to globalization in the way it has been used to categorize those who are also known as antiglobalizers. Anarchism in a strict sense is a theoretical or actual society which rejects the imposition of authority. A common misconception is that anarchism promotes anarchy, that is violence, chaos and social upheaval. Generally, however, anarchism is the political belief that everyone should be allowed to choose the relations they have with others (including representatives in government) and *intentionally* enter into relationships with other people for mutual benefit and social goals. That is to say, there is nothing inherently unorganized about the order that anarchism envisages. Rather, it is based on the actual individual making real choices as opposed to developing systems that people are then forced to inhabit. Thus, anarchism does not require that there are no representatives of people. It is the way in which such representation occurs and is established which is at issue.

Anarchism, or more usually anarchists, is an important feature of globalization discourses. Anarchists are not generally esteemed figures. Anarchism is not supportive of the neoliberal, "democratic" systems which are typical of and valorized in contemporary society. Often, as a result of a very imprecise use of language and incorrect representation of those involved, anyone speaking or demonstrating against globalization and capitalism is labeled anarchist.

See also: **antiglobalization, neoliberalism**

Further reading: Miller 1984; Ward 2004; Woodcock 1986

ANTICIPATION OF PLEASURE

Concept coined by John Urry (1990) in relation to consumption of products and experiences, particularly related to the tourist experience. The pleasure anticipated is based on representations of a yet to be had experience (in the media, tourist brochures and the like). Thus people "seek to experience 'in reality' the pleasurable dramas they have already experienced in their imagination" (1990: 13). Imaginative travel contrasts with corporeal (actual physical) travel. It may form part of the anticipation process prior to corporeal travel. Imaginative travel is elicited by the media in, for example, travel guidebooks, TV travel programs, brochures and the **internet**. By reading material or watching programs about their destination, potential tourists begin to imagine themselves already on holiday and to anticipate the holiday experience.

See also: **cultural tourism, lifestyle**

SL

ANTIGLOBALIZATION

Antiglobalization is an umbrella term used to refer to a diverse set of stances against the current form of globalization and the perceived negative impact that it is said to be causing. Members of the antiglobalization movement see the global order as being largely shaped by the interests and for the benefits of an elite minority of the world to the general detriment of the rest of humanity, especially those in the Third World. The globalization process is said to be the major cause of environmental destruction and to be leading to a growth in inequality, both across and within nations, and to the erosion of democratic processes.

There is no real consensus about exactly when the antiglobalization movement first came into being. One defining moment was the indigenous uprising of the Zapatistas in the Chiapas region of Mexico, which occurred on New Years Day, 1994 to symbolically coincide with the implementation of the North American Free Trade Agreement (NAFTA). Another key event was the now infamous "Battle of Seattle" both of which have achieved an iconic status within the movement. However, resistance to globalization is not a new phenomenon and protests against the **Bretton Woods institutions**, and structural adjustment policies have been reasonably regular occurrences within the global South since at least the mid-1970s.

Within the West the movement initially focused principally on the unethical practices of large multinational corporations, which were seen as one of the principle driving forces behind the reorganization of the global economy that characterizes globalization. For instance, in the mid-1990s the movement, which was increasingly gaining momentum, focused on the issue of "sweatshops" and the exploitative practices that these entailed with corporations such as Disney and Nike being held to account and seen as largely responsible for the conditions under which their goods were manufactured. Through such campaigns international coalitions were formed and recent years have witnessed a growing mobilization leading to a number of large demonstrations outside the meetings of the world's political and economic elites such as that in **Seattle**, Prague, Quebec City and Genoa amongst others. These mass protests were largely aimed at highlighting the negative aspects of the current global order and to bring to wider public attention the exploitative, unequal and coercive logic of globalization. As well as protests the movement coheres around a number of large events. The most prominent of these being the World Social Forum (WSF), which began in January 2001 in Porto Alegre, Brazil as a deliberate counter-summit to the elite World Economic Forum held in Davos, Switzerland. The WSF has grown into a very large event and now attracts well over 100,000 people to discuss different aspects of globalization and its alternatives.

In many ways the "antiglobalization" label (apparently initially coined by the US media) is misleading and indeed many activists reject the label entirely. The movement is not against globalization per se and despite criticism to the contrary an abundance of political and economic alternatives and remedies to the current problems associated with globalization have been proposed. Many have called for the complete cancellation of Third World Debt or at least a substantial reduction to it. There is also widespread belief that the three major financial institutions (the **World Bank**, **IMF** and World Trade Organization (**WTO**)) of **global governance** either need to be substantially reformed or scrapped altogether and replaced with more accountable, democratic and transparent institutions capable of regulating global capital flows, especially the activities of multinational corporations. Others have argued for a return to more locally (be they local, regional or national) based economies which, it is believed, would alleviate many of the problems associated with economic globalization. While for many within the movement this is seen as a way of offering, amongst other things, protectionism to poorer countries, this mode of thinking also represents a more conservative thread of antiglobalization sentiments. This mode of thought is fearful that globalization is leading to the loss of national self-determination and largely blames recent immigrants for the deterioration and erosion of national cultural traditions and lifestyles.

See also: **global capitalism, legitimation crisis, protectionism (economic), social movements, transnational corporations (TNC)**

Further reading: Brecher *et al.* 2000; Held and McGrew 2002; Kingsnorth 2003; Klein 2002; Notes from Nowhere 2003

HB

ANTI-IMPERIALISM

A movement of the political left that would be understood by some to be the same as antiglobalization. Critique of imperialism has its roots in Marxist theory which sees the first world as economically exploiting the third world. In globalization discourses, this exploitation stretches to culture, language and local practices and products.

See also: **Americanization, cultural imperialism, homogenization, Marx/Marxism**

ASYMPTOTIC PROGRESSION

Related to epistemology and generally attributed to Popper's (1959, 1982, 1983) writings on the progress of science. An asymptote is a value (usually mathematical though it can be considered a place) that is progressively approached but never actually reached. In the case of epistemology, the asymptote can be understood as "truth." Thus, while we may advance towards "truth," constantly refining our facts and terms and understanding, we never actually reach it. For science, although truth might be the ultimate goal, it is never attainable. The rhetorical value of the concept is great, as it retains the concept of a positive goal and progression towards it.

See also: **abstract systems, epistemic communities, experts/expert systems, knowledge society, risk**

Further reading: Castoriadis (1991, 1997)

ATOMIZATION

Generally meaning fragmentation, or dividing into small pieces. In the globalization debate it is usually employed to mean a negative distance between individuals and their society, what might be called 'estrangement' by others. Massive social and economic change, especially of a **neoliberal** kind, leads to the destruction of communities thus people begin behaving individually rather than socially. Atomization is thus problematic from the point of view of political action. Calls to collective action are attempts to reverse the effects of atomization.

It is connected to **homogenization**, insofar as people are understood as relating to global concerns (or very private concerns) rather than to local communal ones.

See also: **active citizens, global sub-politics, individuation**

AURA (OF CULTURAL PHENOMENON)

A quality that Walter Benjamin ([1936] 1968) attributes to original works of art. He argues that technologies of reproduction (that is, mechanical reproduction) mean that this aura is potentially lost. Benjamin writes, "even the most perfect reproduction of a work of art is lacking in one element: its presence in time and space, its unique existence at the place where it happens to be" – this element is the aura which only the original has, however, "technical reproduction can put the copy of the original into situations which would be out of reach for the original itself" (Benjamin 1968: 220). The aura is created partly by distance; when there is only one original which is prized, it is literally kept away from the masses, or at least consumed at a distance. Reproduction of art collapses this distance and brings art to the masses; in a manner which parallels arguments about the collapse of time and space in a period of globalization. Indeed, the question of whether originals even exist is one pertinent to globalization and to postmodern thought.

See also: **postmodernism, simulacrum, time-space compression**

AUTOMOBILITY

The term was coined by Sheller and Urry (2000) and refers to six features which, in combination, produce a certain culture of, and attitude towards and reliance on the automobile in modern times. Automobility is a complex hybrid.

See also: **hybridity/hybridization**

AUTONOMIZATION (OF AN INSTITUTION)

From the work of Castoriadis (1997) who describes an autonomized institution as one which "possesses its own inertia and its own logic, that, in its continuance and in its effects, it outstrips its function, its 'ends', and its 'reasons for existing'" (1997: 110). Habermas (1987b) refers to the same process as a "decoupling of system and life world." Autonomization is a process that results in money and power, not communicative intervention, being the sole guiding principles. Others see autonomization as synonymous with corporatization, giving public bodies freedom to behave like corporations. Thus autonomization when applied to the public sector means moves towards internal and external contracting out. **Privatization** is the most extreme (though increasingly common) form of this.

See also: **McDonaldization, offshoring**

AUTONOMIZATION (OF CULTURE)

Featherstone, drawing inspiration from Weber, describes the shifting autonomy of the cultural sphere, that is, how independent "knowledge and other symbolic media" (1995: 15) are or can be from the market, economic and consumer fields. Featherstone suggests that we need to understand the shifting relationship "between those sectors that seek to achieve greater autonomy (high culture) and those sectors that are more directly tied to production for the popular markets in cultural goods (mass consumer culture)" (1995: 32). As Featherstone points out, culture is a continuum and cultural goods include not only art but other leisure activities and artifacts (such as attending the theatre or purchasing books). While those who consider themselves artists may want to claim an autonomy, that is, independence from (and indifference to) economic spheres, this is only possible in certain times and places. The artist has material needs her/himself, at least at the level of human survival.

In recent years artwork has become an investment for some as much as an aesthetic experience, indicated by explicit investment information compiled and made available by large auction houses. Given this **commodification** of art, high culture, if not independent of, at least intersects with the economic field and the more popular scene of the celebrity, personality and indeed mass produced articles (such as postcards, posters and other ephemera).

See also: **consumerism, enclaved commodities, postmodernism, symbolic capital**

Further reading: Albrow 1996; Douglas and Isherwood 1979

AXIAL PERIOD

Coined by Karl Jaspers (1953) to identify a particular period in history (from approximately 800 to 200 BC) when radical changes occurred all over the world. These were predominantly religious and civilizational and remained well in place until the Enlightenment period.

The rise of **capitalism** (and thus what some understand as the beginning of globalization) is sometimes seen as a second axial period insofar as this too represents a radical change in the way we see and interact with the world. In fact Jaspers also considered the modern age as a second axial period characterized by modern science and technology, a craving for freedom, the emergence of the masses in the political arena (nationalism, democracy, socialism, social movements), and globalization.

Also known as axial age.

See also: **axial principle, reflexive modernization/modernity, risk**

AXIAL PRINCIPLE

A principle that underlies or causes an axial change or period. Bell (1973) and Bell and Kristol (1971) argued that knowledge would be the axial principle of the postindustrial age; however, the prominence that they accorded to universities and the academy as generally linked to this has become questionable. However, Albrow (1996) argues that there is no single axial principle underlying global institutions. Beck (1992) defines risk societies as those who have **risk** as its axial principle of social organization.

See also: **axial period**

BALANCE OF POWER

A key term in international relations relating to the relative powers of states in relation to each other. It is of particular centrality to realist accounts of international relations which see power as the driving force of politics and the conduct of states and countries (as opposed to the way individuals behave). Balance of power is related to international and regional security and can be understood as a driving analytic and political concept for military action, trade arrangements and alliances in both fields. Thus economic, military and regional alliances (such as the **EU**, NATO, etc.) are crucial in the managing of power balances. Balance of power can also refer to the power possessed by a small concern which shifts its support from one position to another. For example, swinging voters in a marginal election will hold the balance of power.

In the context of globalization, discussion centers on how balance of power might be shifting. For example, with economic globalization and changes in global and national governance, some argue that the global balance of power has shifted toward private interests such as multinational corporations (as opposed to public interests, that is government). The most crucial aspect of balance of power in the globalization context is who the holders of power are. Traditionally, and certainly post-WWII and during the Cold War, power was most significantly held by **states**. During this period, global institutions such as the **WTO**, while consolidating the power of some states (the allies in particular) also contributed to a shift in the way states operate.

Many argue (Monbiot 2000; Korten 2001) that the balance of power presently is actually held by corporations, which either bypass national governments or work with them. Given that economic stability and development is fundamental to a state's power, this should not be surprising. The increasing tendency of governments to work in part-nership with private companies means that even global institutions of governance (especially such as the **WTO**) are driven more by capi-talist concerns. While realist theory sees states as *akin* to firms (though directed towards power rather than pure economic profit), governments can be seen as becoming firms in the way they make decisions, whether notionally "economic" or "political."

See also: **realist paradigm**

BASIC NEEDS

Basic needs is a theory relating to how human "basic needs" are assessed and subsequently how they are provided and raises issues of development and human rights. While basic needs requires some attention to economic disparities, it is also vital to remember that simply raising the income of the poor will not necessarily lead to basic needs being met. Some needs such as clean water, sanitation and health, can only be provided by people or infrastructures. While strictly speaking basic needs could be considered commodities, they cannot simply be bought when one needs them. Psychologist Abraham Maslow can be seen as the originator of the phrase, but in that case it is used in contrast to "transcendental needs" and "growth needs" (1970). However, the phrase "basic needs" does have a certain transparency, and it is important more in terms of how such needs are assessed, supplied and then eval-uated. It is a theory focused on "what is being produced, in what ways, for whom and with what impact" (Hicks and Streeton 1979: 577) rather than looking at GDP or other national economic indicators.

Further reading: Gasper 1996

See also: **subsistence perspective**

BICULTURALISM

Someone who exists in two cultures is considered to be bicultural. The term stems from work by Park (1928) and Stonequist (1935) for people who live in two cultures and can claim allegiance to both. It has been suggested that the state of biculturalism leads to psychological problems, termed double-consciousness by DuBois (1961). This can be conceived as dual identity or cultural literacy in two different (and perhaps competing) cultural repertoires. The life of the bicultural person is challenging exactly when two cultures intersect competitively. Bicultural people are also called "marginal people" (Goldberg 1941; Green 1947), gesturing towards the tendency of the term to be applied to minorities (numerically or in terms of status) and very often to indigenous people seeking to maintain traditional ways of life.

As with bilingualism, there are many ways of accommodating bicultural individuals. While assimilation and acculturation models were the norm at one time, these valorize and value one culture over another. Alteration, multiculturalism or fusion approaches may in fact be more successful in terms of individual well-being and identity and social harmony.

In the globalizing world, one would expect to see more and more bicultural and even multicultural individuals as people migrate for various reasons. While the so-called "global citizen" might be said to have the *world* as his/her home, in practice, people have a number of cultures that are primary to them.

Naturally, biculturalism is a political and social issue in **postcolonial** terms and then not only at an individual level. Whole countries and regions struggle with something akin to the issues often associated with being bicultural.

See also: **hybridity/hybridization, multicultural**

BIO-POLITICS

Bio-politics can be treated as an extension of the notion of **biopower**. Implicit in Foucault's analysis of bio-power as an invention of the nineteenth century was the recognition that the disciplinary bio-political formulation was in decline ([1976], 1990).

In the nineteenth century human bodies had been subject to meticulous, constant discipline, and coerced into productivity. Under consumer capital the body and its functions undergo an apparent liberation; sexuality becomes a subject open for discussion and experimentation, women reclaim their bodies from labor, new discourses concerning health and exercise emerge: in short the body becomes a field of active political contestation.

But this apparent emancipation is quickly followed by insidious forms of "control," which rather than regulating the body through institutions, operate at the level of the individual, within their very subjectivity's relation to their body. Here advertising and the representation of the body play a crucial role; they infiltrate and persuade each member of society to "produce" a body, to regulate and maintain it in accordance with an ideal. At the level of the bio-politics of populations, a range of transnational organizations take some of the powers of the state, supplying the materials of life and exploiting the destitution of one population to stimulate the physical health of another.

Bio-politics then can be understood as the analysis of the body as a political field, as the site of new apparatus of control and regulation and also as a source of new resistance and alternatives.

See also: **commodification**

Further reading: Hardt and Negri 2000

JH

BIO-POWER

Bio-power is a concept put forward by the French philosopher and historian Michel Foucault. Foucault ([1976], 1990) was concerned with the nature of power and maintained that power underwent changes in its nature and expression in different historical periods. Bio-power, a power over "life" and its reproduction, designates a new system of power and regulation which emerged in the nineteenth century. Prior to this, power was generally expressed through the imposition of death and physical punishments. More specifically, the rituals of punishment created a spectacle of death (e.g. public execution and torture) the aim of which was to guarantee the force of law (in straightforward terms of deterrence).

Bio-power was mediated through institutions (schools, prisons, the military and the factory) that disciplined and regulated the lives of individuals. Through the structure of these institutions, the human body was subject to a meticulous regime, which controlled and monitored its operation and function, and in this fashion the human body became the center of a new form of governance.

Bio-power was a bipolar system; at one pole a *bio-politics of the population*, understood in terms of the overall control of populations by a range of regulations, registers of birth, marriage, death, public health programs etc., and at the other an *anatomo-politics of the human body*. The latter consisted of tactics that disciplined the individual body, drills and routines that optimized its functioning and converted it into a reliable socioeconomic machine. Foucault maintained that bio-power was an essential component of capitalism; it produced the laboring body that would work in the factory, and by seizing the "life" of the population turned it into an economic field.

See also: **capitalism, Marx/Marxism, societies of control**

JH

BIOSPHERIC POLITICS

Jeremy Rifkin (1991) argues that biospheric politics should replace geopolitics. This is because of the modernist goal that seeks "to enclose the natural world as a vain quest for freedom from environmental dangers." The consequences of this are climate change and global warming as well as exhaustion of earth's resources.

See also: **reflexive modernization/modernity, risk**

BODILY DISPLAY

A term often related to tourism, it refers to how the human body may be used to show certain values or qualities, be they related to ethnicity (e.g. costume or dance) or status (e.g. the tanned body in certain cultures). The body comes to represent culture in such performances.

When "culture" is displayed in this way, for example when certain dances or rituals are performed for the tourist, it is perceived by the viewer as authentic, even though this may be only staged for the purpose of entertaining tourists and no longer a current part of the culture.

See also: **cultural tourism, heritage tourism**

Further reading: Desmond 1997, 1999, 2000

BRETTON WOODS INSTITUTIONS

Those bodies established at a 1944 conference in Bretton Woods (New Hampshire, USA), notably the **IMF** and the International

Bank for Reconstruction and Development (now part of the **World Bank**). This meeting also established the valuing of national currencies against a gold standard which lasted for nearly 30 years. Because of the establishment of these international financial institutions, the Bretton Woods conference is regarded as a watershed both in terms of international relations and globalization studies. This is despite the centrality of **nation-states** in the Bretton Woods agreement. Arguably the start of a new period of globalization occurred in the immediate post-WWII environment.

BUREAUCRACY

First coined in the early nineteenth century referring to a type of administration that is structured around a hierarchical authority of departments with specialized functions that are staffed with non-elected officials who follow fixed procedures. It was generally a pejorative term until Max Weber's (1954) more descriptive work. It is a significant concept for globalization in as much as most Western democracies function through bureaucracies of some sort. The central criticism of bureaucracy is that these officials often enjoy permanent positions of power and are unelected. With increasing **offshoring**, bureaucracies may become smaller, though no less powerful for this. Further, as governments model themselves on corporate modes of governance, bureaucracies may tend to function more like businesses than governments. This is particularly troubling for those who value a **welfare state** model.

Further reading: Albrow 1970

CAPITALISM

Capitalism can be defined simply as exchange within markets. Capitalism in conjunction with globalization is more varied in its usage.

Globalization through capitalism is a phrase that has been used to refer to many disparate phenomena. Some use it to describe environmental degradation and lesser worker rights. Some use it to describe the threat to their own cultural identity. And some use it simply as a name for the world economy. What is clear is that there are many dimensions to its meaning, depending on the context in which it is being used.

Mohawk Valley Community College Library

Perhaps a fundamental basis of capitalism globally is the existence of private property rights, internationally, and the freedom to trade such property rights. Of course, property rights and the freedom for exchange are also the basis for markets. Such rights can be held in respect of land, financial capital, natural resources, and one's own labor. Naturally the output of any firm, or company, whether products or services, also can be openly traded. Markets can only operate on a global scale with open, free and transparent trading, guided and protected by a system of international trade law.

The effects of capitalism depend largely on how open the societies are that are involved. Problems usually attributed to global capitalism can also be viewed as problems of the individual countries, particularly that their more localized markets have not been fully articulated. Put differently, using a fundamental definition of capitalism as exchange based on the establishment of property rights, problems may arise if property rights are not rigorously or justly defined. For example, a nation may not define within its laws the ownership of natural resources in a way that the populace accepts as fair. Workers (who exchange their own labor) may perceive the wages they receive from international companies as insufficient. Indeed, consumers at the other end of the commodity chain may argue that wages and conditions are unjust. Or small family shops and farms may be driven out by international competition which is seen as causing changes in culture that are not acceptable.

In these cases, the problem is not the international markets per se, but the "externality" of property rights that are not well defined. Natural resources may well have societal benefits that are not being reflected in their market price, or in their usage, because the nation's government has not built the full societal values into its laws regarding the use and exchange of property rights with respect to the natural resources. The international company that is paying low wages, and is not providing health care, education, and other local public benefits, may be exerting undue power over the working conditions because the nation's laws do not ensure that firms supply such broader public benefits. And the demise of small family business, and small farm life, may result because the government does not incorporate the need to protect certain cultural institutions within its laws.

At the same time, **nation-states** may be, or may perceive themselves to be, unable to amend laws and property rights in order to protect these goods not factored into market economics. This may be because of pressure from large corporations, because of conditions imposed by the **IMF**, because of a particular economic strategy or out of the self-interest of the powerful few.

Capitalism of this kind, in a free-trade sense, is basically what Adam Smith was advocating in his *Wealth of Nations*, written in 1776 and marking the beginning of modern economy theory. He advocates against legislation that restricts trade for spurious reasons. Smith writes against the Corn Laws of Great Britain, which were enacted to restrict the import of corn and the export of gold. These restrictions were part of what was called "mercantilism"; this doctrine argued that gold needs to be kept in the home country. Today, free trade advocates argue instead for flexible exchange rates. Allowing the international price of a nation's currency to be freely set in international markets means that no gold, or "international reserves" need flow into or out of a country. Such flow of gold, dollar, or yen reserves, which a country keeps in its Treasury, are not required to equilibrate markets as long as the supply and demand for international currencies can be adjusted by a freely set price of these currencies, as established with floating exchange rates. Trying to set the price of a currency, with a fixed exchange rate, typically leads to many more laws that restrict trade, so that the international reserves do not change too much. Also, most international financial crises, such as the collapse in East Asia and Russia in the late 1990s, were due to fixed exchange rates that were suddenly adjusted, rather than gradually changing, because of concern over large changes in international reserves.

Moving to a flexible exchange rate system, in increasingly more countries across the globe, has largely ended the worry about the flow of a nation's international reserves. This process began in earnest with the demise of the Bretton Woods fixed exchange rate system in the early 1970s, in which the US dollar's price of gold was set at a constant value in order to provide the basis for the fixed exchange rates. The advent of flexible exchange rates, in turn, has opened up the international markets to a regime of less restrictions on trade, globally. Global trade agreements, and international trade organizations such as the **World Trade Organization**, have hastened the establishment of global free trade. Organizations such as the **World Bank** and the **International Monetary Fund** play a much more subsidiary role, compared to the establishment of free-trade regimes. These bank-like organizations allow for elements of the market system to be taught to nations with little experience in global markets.

Free trade, with freely set prices for goods, labor, and financial capital including international currencies, is what make global trade possible. Problems arise because many nations have entered the global markets with insufficient institutions established that can define localized property rights so as to reflect societal values. Thus the entry of some nations into global markets can be viewed as causing harm to a nation as a whole, if trade occurs for commodities in ways that do not reflect a reasonable social value of the goods.

Capitalism at a global level is a largely positive, and irreversible, evolution of open societies. Care needs to be taken as to how resources are allowed to be engaged within international markets, so that property rights are well established over valuables that affect everyone in society, such as the old trees of a rainforest. Nations can take different strategies in this regard. Russia has been exerting strong state policy over the ownership of oil and gas, while restricting non-governmental international organizations. China continues to restrict societal interaction, while still fixing its exchange rate at undervalued levels, so that it is importing one of the largest international reserve hoards in the world. The United States has organized many international free-trade agreements, while at times supporting dictatorships in the interest of short-run global stability. As free trade within open markets continues to spread to all the corners of the world, the establishment of institutions that can define property rights that reflect societal values will continue to be paramount to the success of global capitalism.

See also: **Bretton Woods institutions, common agricultural policy (CAP), free trade, global capitalism, Marx/Marxism**

Further reading: De Soto 2000; Norberg 2003; Sachs 2005

MG

CENTRISM

From the early to mid-twentieth Century "centrism" has meant taking the middle road, the path between extremes. While this can be applied to anything, it is usually used in relation to politics. Thus as political extremes are described in terms of "left" and "right," the middle view would be "centrism" which seeks moderation, integration of both left and right and implementing the best from each side. Centrism, or more usually "radical centrism" or "radical middle" is increasingly used to mean something more like a departure from left/right politics. The same terms appear also to be used for what was previously identified as the "floating" or "swinging" voter (the "Vital Center").

Some claim that radical centrism is equivalent to the **Third Way**. The emergence of the radical middle is connected with disenchantment with the political party system and the values that both left and right are increasingly in agreement over.

In Marxist tradition, centrism is an ideological stance between revolution and reformism; that is reform at once and revolution eventually. This kind of centrism usually emerges when there are ideological or economic crises in the middle classes.

In short, the use of "centrism" or "middle" is polysemous. It has a positive value attached to it (being the opposite of "extreme") but in the Marxist tradition means something specific. In terms of globalization, the Third Way is the most likely incarnation.

Centrism is also used as a suffix used to indicate an implicit orientation to a particular group. For example, ethno–centrism takes as given the importance of one's own ethnic or cultural position, and anglo–centrism foregrounds the point of view of Western (or Anglophile) values.

See also: **Marx/Marxism**

Further reading: Giddens 1998

CHAOS THEORY

Chaos theory has its roots in the fields of mathematics and physics but has become popularized by accessible science experts such as Gleick (1993). The essential insight of chaos theory is that while some systems (for example ecosystems, environmental patterns and so on) might look unpredictable (that is, "chaotic" in the lay sense) they are in fact deterministic; it is just a question of which parameters are examined and at what times.

Chaos theory shows that even small variation in initial conditions can lead to large changes in the long run. This is often known as the butterfly effect:

> The flapping of a single butterfly's wing today produces a tiny change in the state of the atmosphere. Over a period of time, what the atmosphere actually does diverges from what it would have done. So, in a month's time, a tornado that would have

devastated the Indonesian coast doesn't happen. Or maybe one that wasn't going to happen, does.

(Stewart 1990: 141)

Chaos theory, because it deals with complex systems, differs from classical mechanics where cause and effect are related in a linear fashion. It seeks to find order in apparent chaos and in certain systems succeeds. Perhaps the most startling aspect of chaos theory is that it explains natural systems such as the weather, heart beats, and plant growth.

In the field of globalization the appeal of chaos theory as an analogical explanatory device is indisputable as it allows social scientists in particular to include factors that might not usually be considered because of the traditions of their discipline. The interconnectedness that is typical of chaotic systems is also parallel to aspects of globalization such as flows and networks and the shifting and collapsing of time and space. Chaos theory may be referred to as "**complexity theory**," even though *complexity theory* includes the study of other complex systems. Urry (2002b) asks whether complexity theory is able to "generate productive metaphors for analyzing various 'post-societal' material worlds" particularly in relation to September 11th. Urry, drawing on Latour (1999) suggests that complexity and chaos theory offer a way to think about influences which are neither micro nor macro (the categories of classical sociology and social history).

See also: **experts/expert systems, knowledge society, network society, risk, time–space compression**

CHOICE (DISCOURSE OF)

The *discourse* of choice emphasizes that "choice" is a site of struggle and a medium for the exercise of power. The discourse of choice is linked to globalization in multiple ways. It is associated with neo-liberal agendas as "choice" is a political rhetoric that emphasizes the libertarian principle of freedom from constraints over and against the social democratic principle of equality. This translates into political support for free trade, small noninterventionist states and the global expansion of the market. Social theorists tend to focus on how "choice" has come to define our sense of who we are as people. For instance Anthony Giddens (1991) links the discourse of choice to globalization in his account of how social and technological changes have affected our self–identity.

For Giddens, globalization is a phase of modernization marked by **time–space** distanciation, a result of technological-communication advances and a particular attitude to life marked by **risk**. Western society has "de-traditionalized" and life has become "doubly reflexive." Double **reflexivity** demands of late-modern individuals that they perceive their cultures and societies as socially constructed, and proactively reflect on the choices and social world around them. The realm of politics has shifted from emancipatory politics to "life politics" which is "a politics of identity as well as of choice" (Giddens 1994b: 9).

Choice is an advanced liberal conception of subjectivity and technology of the self (Rose 1999: 45). Explaining how advertising technologies developed techniques to present goods as having the power to transform purchasers into particular kinds of people having particular kinds of (desirable) lives, Rose explains how individuals "play their own part in the games of civilization as they shape a style of life for themselves through acts of choice in the world of goods" (Rose 1999: 86). Now we have come to understand and enact our life in terms of choices we have personally made. This encourages us to understand our lives in terms of success or failure to acquire the skills and make the choices to actualize or fulfil oneself.

See also: **governmentality, neoliberalism, risk, structuration theory**

RM

CITIZENSHIP

What citizenship means depends on the prevailing political organization of a particular area. In the past, citizenship was linked primarily to national identity as ratified in some way by a state. Despite the claim that the **nation–state** is at an end, and that the concept of the citizen is shifting, citizenship is still required for some rights to exist or to be upheld by the state. In the context of globalization studies, citizenship cannot be exhaustively defined but rather discussed and problematized. While the majority of people are legal citizens of at least one nation-state, this does not tell us much about how people construct their own identities or how they live their lives.

Delanty (2000) sees citizenship as classically having four components; rights, responsibilities, participation and identity. Rights, for example, have in theory been protected by the nation-state of which one is a citizen. More recently, they are also protected by other bodies, such as the European Council, the **UN**, international law and even other nation-states (especially when crimes against humanity have been alleged). The nature of rights has also developed, at least theoretically, with collective rights being added to individual rights, and the emergence of cultural, minority, social and economic rights.

See also: **active citizens, civil society, cosmopolitanism, democracy, global sub-politics, human rights, migration, nationalism, nation-state**

CIVIL INATTENTION

This concept was coined by the sociologist Irving Goffman (1963) referring to the way in which a person notices another's presence, but does not engage with them. The situations in which this occurs are most likely to be culturally based, though Goffman notes that civil inattention will usually operate in elevators, near-empty bars and with cabdrivers. As Bauman (1993: 155) reminds us, Helmut Plessner (1974) calls this "civil indifference" and thus the concept can be read as concerned with maintaining and respecting privacy. Bauman (1993) reads the "mismeeting" central to civil inattention as a form of **risk** management. In Goffman's terms, Bauman's reading would be called "unfocussed interaction." The risk occurs at the moment one wants to move from unfocussed to focussed interaction. There is **trust**, however, in the continuance of this civil inattention insofar as people rely on others not to go too far. In a sense, civil inattention is a "live and let live" attitude which is essential to tolerance and the sustaining of heterogeneous communities. At the same time, if there is too much civil inattention, that is, if there is no focussed interaction at all, a community can become fragmented and individuals can experience alienation.

See also: **cosmopolitarism, culture of civility, social capital**

CIVIL SOCIETY

We owe the concept of "civil society" to Aristotelian philosophy which distinguished the private realm of the household from the public sphere where equal citizens participate in ruling and being ruled. With the advent of political modernity, i.e. the formation of bureaucratically organized, large-scale territorial states, the meaning of the concept changed: "society" and "state" came to be conceived as separate spheres, and thus political philosophers of the eighteenth and nineteenth centuries used the term civil society to refer to a set of institutions *outside* state or government.

In the twentieth century, the language of civil society has largely been forgotten, and only recently has it come to a notable revival, namely in two contexts: (a) the collapse of the Soviet bloc and the subsequent problems of transition of the states of Central and Eastern Europe to **democracy**; and (b) the proliferation of a network of **non-governmental organizations** (**NGO**s), movements and institutions sometimes referred to as international or global civil society.

In the years leading up to the revolutions of 1989, "civil society" meant a perspective of autonomy and self-organization of citizens outside direct state control and the organization of collective life. Totalitarian regimes had left no room for private initiative and had repressed civil rights and liberties. The transition to democracy, it was understood, presupposed rebuilding a vital civil society, i.e. citizens freely articulating and organizing their interests, scrutinizing political elites and participating in public life. Conceptually, such understanding of the term "civil society" goes back to Hegelian political philosophy which introduced it as referring to the realm of intermediate associations that stand between the individual and the state and which had been characteristic for European societies since the Middle Ages (e.g. corporations, guilds). Thinkers of pluralist and communitarian persuasion have emphasized that it is such meso-level social units that sustain a liberal society by empowering people for having a say, protecting civil liberties and investing into community life. Robert Putnam, for instance, in his book *Bowling Alone* (2000), has argued that Americans have increasingly become disconnected from family, friends, and democratic institutions (see **social capital**). In the same vein, scholars of transition have called for building up structures of civil society in the newly democratic states.

A second strand of civil society discourse is an even more recent phenomenon, responding to the enormous spread of NGOs working on the international scene, and to the changing political situation after the end of the Cold War. The ideological sources of this discourse are heterogeneous and its claims ambiguous or even contradictory. Some draw on ideas from liberal evolutionism and hope that the globalization of free markets will bring about a peaceful and civil world society. Others join with classical idealism in calling for the establishment of global democratic institutions or the development of efficient "**global governance**." At the more concrete level, international civil society is often understood as a global public conscience made possible by modern means of mass communication: citizens all over the world protest against war or donate for victims of natural disasters. Indeed, such phenomena demonstrate that the Earth has become a small place, where feelings of solidarity – but also of hatred, envy and resentment – transcend local communities. The discourse of international civil society tends to highlight the light side of this state of affairs, while ignoring its dark side.

See also: **citizenship, internationalization, liberal democracy, social capital**

Further reading: Cohen and Arato 1992; Iriye 2004

FO

CLASH OF CIVILIZATIONS

The term "civilizational paradigm" was first used by Lewis (1990) in the field of international relations to account for and predict relationships between nations. It was brought into broader usage by the historian Huntington (1993). It is used in international relations to refer to a way of interpreting **balance of power** and potential **risks**. With the Cold War over (which was essentially based on a clash of political ideologies), Huntington argues that in the future international relations will be explicable in terms of cultural (or civilizational) clashes.

"The clash of civilizations will dominate global politics. The fault lines between civilizations will be the battle lines of the future" (1993: 24). Civilizations will clash because (1) they are real and basic; (2) the world is getting smaller; (3) economic and social change is alienating people from their local identities (which weakens ties to **nation–states** and often brings religion to the fore); (4) the dual role of the West, "A West at the peak of its power confronts non-Wests that increasingly have the desire, the will and the resources to shape the world in non-Western ways,"; (5) culture is less malleable; and (6) economic regionalism is increasing.

The emphasis on civilizations does not mean that nation–states are no longer players in Huntington's model. Rather, the differences between civilizations will be central in defining conflicts and their motivating issues. The civilizational groupings may well draw on "common objective elements, such as language, history, religion, customs, institutions, and [the] subjective self-identification of people" (1996: 43). Obviously, these elements are also commonly associated with nation–states. Indeed, these elements may lead to identifying with a civilization in the first place, especially if these elements are felt to be under threat.

Given that the study was written in 1993, well before events of 2001, Huntington's work is prophetic. "This centuries-old military interaction between the West and Islam is unlikely to decline. It could become more virulent." (1993: 31).

See also: **cultural imperialism, fundamentalism**

Further reading: Huntington 1996

CLEFT COUNTRIES

Cleft countries refers to countries where significant numbers of the population belong to different civilizations, that is, different cultures, though ethnicity is often a factor. This term is different from "torn countries" where leaders are attempting to (or have tried to bring about) a new civilizational paradigm, e.g. Turkey, Russia and Australia according to Huntington (1993). Cleft countries can be related to Huntington's civilizational paradigm (1993). Cleft countries and the concept of civilizations acknowledge that **nation–states** do not have homogenous or continuous cultures/civilizations. Cleft countries may be in danger of violence from or secession by some groups. This is essentially because nation–states have traditionally been about (or conceived to be about) singular identity, that is, the ideological foundation of the nation was something that all citizens ostensibly have in common.

CNN EFFECT

Also known as the "CNN curve" or "CNN factor." The term is used in two distinct fields, politics and economics, though both are related to a theorized effect on government and the public of the Cable News Network (CNN) and similar real-time news services. Both meanings appear to originate with the first Gulf War (1991) and to be connected to foreign conflicts in particular. The first, and to our mind the primary meaning, is that described by Livingston (among others) and referring to the effect of real-time news coverage on foreign policy and diplomacy, especially that of the USA.

The CNN effect has been attached to a number of specific scenarios about the way live news can influence political policy and public opinion. Live news crews can, especially in conflict situations, provide more up-to-date information than the state is able to procure through its normal intelligence sources. In this sense, the immediacy of the media may enable political and military decisions to be made quickly, or at least for policy to be developed pending confirmation of media reports through sanctioned channels. As McCorquodale and Fairbrother (1999) point out, this is problematic because of the relatively sparse concentration of CNN personnel. In 1997, CNN had only 23 foreign bureaux and 50 overseas journalists. "Decisions based on CNN coverage, as many are, including those made during the [first] Gulf War, may be made on insufficient or insufficiently objective, information." (McCorquodale and Fairbrother 1999: 760).

Livingston points out that real-time media coverage may work as an accelerant, an impediment or an agenda setting agency. The first, coverage working as an accelerant, refers to the effect mentioned above, shortening the time in which the state can respond to events. Impediments to "operational security" and to policy objectives generally are also evident. Media coverage may undermine public backing of a military engagement, or of particular responses. The agenda setting agency of the media works in a number of ways. It can be argued that the way in which an event is covered will influence public opinion, to the benefit of the state or those with a stake in the media. On the other hand, and more akin to the impediment factor (at least as far as the state is concerned) public opinion may put pressure on the government to respond to situations.

The second Gulf conflict saw much debate about the freedoms of the press and how much this might conflict with "security" considerations. The use of embedded journalists can also be theorized in this connection as there were fears about the objectivity of such embedded journalists as well as possible threats to military security. Brookes *et al.* (2005) show that while there was some attempt at censorship, it was primarily the journalists themselves who decided what kinds of images were appropriate for British television. In terms of objectivity and reliability, the new "genre" of news reporting seems no different to current forms.

The second meaning is current in economic circles and refers to the tendency of people to stay at home and watch CNN (or other similar news programs) during any crisis, typically a war. The result of this, at least in part, is a downturn in consumer spending. The earliest citation available, however, suggests that the conflict persuaded people not to travel overseas (Shapiro 1991).

See also: **global media**

Further reading: Alleyne 1995; Livingston 1997

TB

COCA-COLONIZATION

Coca-colonization refers to a form of **cultural imperialism** specifically economic, and specifically American. The term derives from Wagnleitner (1994) who argues that the consumer culture "exported" from the US is not in fact American culture as experienced there, but the commodification of the American dream.

See also: **Americanization, homogenization**

COEVOLUTION

This term, drawn from biology (Kauffman 1993), refers to the way in which species inhabiting the same ecosystems (especially plants) interact and influence the continuing development of self and neighbor. The term has been used in globalization studies to refer to the way in which social actors interact and change each other, for example, the changes in the **cultural landscape** because of global flows.

This term may also refer to Deacon's (1997) concept of language and the brain coevolving.

COGNITIVE REFLEXIVITY

See: **Reflexivity**

COLLECTIVISM

In political science terms, collectivism at one time was a term in **anarchism** (particularly that developed by the anarchist Bankunin)

29

such that the collective (which was freely formed and self governing) was the primary unit (politically, economically and morally) of organization. It has come to mean anything for the "public," however some so-called "antiglobalizers" are pro-collective.

Further reading: Storey and Bacon 1993

COLONIALISM

Colonialism in its normal sense refers to the period from about 1500 onwards where Western nations expanded their empires throughout the world. Foreign territories were occupied, often economically exploited and brought within the political control of the empire nations. This colonization was carried out in a number of ways, from commercial colonization to claiming lands.

In globalization studies "colonialism" is present in two primary ways. The first is as a synonym for imperialism, whether cultural, linguistic or economic, and involving a Western nation(s) or corporation as the colonizer. This finds expression in other terms such as **Americanization** and **Coca-colonization**. The second is in the context of postcolonialism which, like colonialism, is a field of study in itself. Postcolonialism refers to both a period of time (that is, since colonial powers withdrew) and is also a way of describing the changes within and since that period. Such changes may include political structures, especially in relation to independence and democratization, policies in relation to language, culture and social welfare and how identity is constructed or recovered.

Colonialism can refer to the colonization process itself, the period of colonization or the effects of the colonization. It is essential to understand the basic process of colonization in order to understand how the world today might be seen as different from the past. It is, for example, possible to argue that globalization is not a new phenomenon but merely a new form of colonialism. It is impossible to adequately cover all aspects of colonialism here as it is a field of study itself (see *Further reading*).

Postcolonialism is also used to refer to a mode of literature, especially that emerging from former colonies, and the textual interpretative strategies that have been developed to interpret and discuss such texts.

See also: **core-periphery model, homogenization, subaltern, world systems theory**

Further reading: Bhabha 1994; Césaire 1972; Dirlik 1998; Johnson 2004; Memmi 1965

COMMODIFICATION

A concept which refers to the process by which products, services, or any form of human activity are transformed into commodities. Once turned into commodities these then acquire an exchange value (as opposed to being principally of use-value to the producer) and can thus be sold on the market for profit. While **Marx** did not use the term himself he saw the process expressed by the concept of commodification as a central ingredient of capitalist social relations and as an essential element through which **capitalism** develops.

Contemporary globalization is said to have intensified the commodification process as the logic of the market extends into ever more spheres of life. For instance, recent years have witnessed an increased **privatization** of services which were previously supplied by governmental agencies such as education, health care and public transport. While many of these were once supported by tax revenue and delivered to the public free of charge, a growing number have now been taken over by private companies with members of the public now having to pay to access them.

Commodification is also observable with respect to information and knowledge as in recent years we have witnessed the growth of what is referred to as the knowledge economy. Through things such as patents, copyright and intellectual property rights, the control of information and knowledge is increasingly being placed in the hands of an ever-decreasing number of multinational corporations. Many are concerned about the effects of this arguing that it will impede intellectual progress and lead to such information as well as the findings of scientific research being largely used to serve commercial rather than human and social interests. This is especially true in the realm of biotechnology. There is considerable concern that patents on biological material such as seeds and human genetic information (e.g. DNA) are leading to the commodification of both the human body and of life itself. The academic and environmental activist Vandana Shiva (1997) has referred to the patenting and private ownership of genetic information as biopiracy. Such information and knowledge is said to be the common heritage of the whole of humanity and thus the appropriation of these natural and collective resources for private profit and gain is seen as a form of theft from us all.

The commodification of the body is also very much apparent in the growing market for a host of human biological materials including human organs, blood, semen and ova and even babies through surrogacy arrangements. This has provoked considerable debate over the ethics of treating such things and relationships as marketable commodities as much of this trade involves people in poor countries selling their body parts to those in rich countries.

The process of commodification is also said to have extended to that of culture and nowhere is this more apparent than with respect to tourism. Within the field of anthropology there has been much discussion of the effects of tourism on different cultures around the world. Tourism is said to have resulted in the debasement of cultural heritage and a loss of authenticity as cultural rituals and traditions are repackaged for consumption by tourists. A number of theorists have criticized this perspective arguing that it rests on a number of highly debatable assumptions. For instance, it depicts other cultures as having lived in spaces of enclosed cultural purity, in which they are protected from contamination from outside influences. Furthermore, critics have argued that the notion that cultural commodification through tourism has resulted in a loss of "the real" is based on an oversimplified dichotomy between non-commodified authentic, and hence real, cultures made up of "deep" and meaningful exchanges and commodified simulations, which consist of little more than "shallow" and largely meaningless exchanges.

See also: **capitalism, consumerism, cultural tourism, human capital, knowledge society, lifestyle enclaves, postmodernity/postmodernism, privatization**

Further reading: Appadurai 1986; Frow 1997

HB

COMMODITY BIOGRAPHIES

Commodity biographies is another term for **commodity chains** used primarily in cultural studies.

Further reading: Lyons (2005)

COMMODITY CANDIDACY

This phrase, coined by Appadurai (1996), refers to an object's qualifications as a commodity. Such qualifications are not stable and depend on availability, social values, legislation and the like.

See also: **commodity phase, Global Commodity Chain (GCC)**

Further reading: Cohen 1993; Kopytoff 1986

COMMODITY CHAINS

A commodity chain is comprised of all stages of the production of an item such as design, materials, manufacture, and marketing. It can be thought of as tracing all stages and processes of where a product comes from. The approach distinguishes between producer driven and buyer driven commodity chains. Producer driven chains tend to be technology and capital intensive (cars and aircraft for example); buyer driven chains tend to be labor intensive (clothes and toys). Producer driven chains make money from volume, scale and technological advances thus making them capital intensive. Such producer driven industries have high entry costs and tend to be oligopolies.

Buyer driven chains are characterized by having no direct involvement in the manufacture of their goods. Nike, for example, will design and sell its footwear but it does not actually own any factories. While entry to these markets is not so capital intensive in terms of acquisition of means of production, it is highly competitive and thus entry barriers are non-tangible. Developing a viable global competitor to Coca Cola for example would require intense investment in research and marketing. To find a gap in the market where a new product may succeed is also expensive. Theories about commodity chains try to account for the way corporations work in a global context. Some critics of global trade, however, trace commodity chains in order to draw attention to low wages, worker exploitation and how products are made in an attempt to raise awareness of social injustice and the disparity between production and product image (Klein 2001).

See also: **Transnational Corporation (TNC), Global Commodity Chains (GCC), human rights, wage–earner welfare state, World Systems theory**

Further reading: Gerreffi and Korzeniewicz (1994), Lyons (2005)

COMMODITY FETISHISM

Marx introduces this term in *Capital* (1867). At the time, fetishism was mainly used about primitive religions. It refers to the way in which people in capitalist societies tend see their social relations only in terms of things (i.e. commodities). People are not seen as individuals but rather in relation to their production use and consumption value. This leads to alienation from social life and political structure. Commodity fetishism means that people are unaware of the way they are used by the system. Thus rather than knowing or thinking about the production value of an object (how much and what kind of labor produced it) people orient towards objects and people in terms of exchange value.

Jean Baudrillard, a post-structuralist theorist, also theorized commodities in terms of four values in his work *System of Objects* (1996). His four values are the functional, the exchange, the symbolic (the value an object has in relation to another person), and the sign exchange (the value of an object in relation to other similar objects).

It has also been used to mean the way in which people imbue commodities with meaning. Articles of clothing, for example, may have prestige value, index identity claims or signal **lifestyle** choices.

See also: **cultural capital, exchange value, false consciousness, false needs, social capital**

COMMODITY FLOWS

Commodity flows refers to the movement of goods, particularly their vectors of movement.

See also: **commodity chain**

COMMODITY PHASE

When something has **commodity candidacy** it is said to be in its commodity phase. The "phase" highlights the unstable nature of the candidacy.

See also: **commodity chain**

Further reading: Appadurai 1996; Kopytoff 1986

COMMON AGRICULTURAL POLICY (CAP)

This policy was established by the Treaty of Rome (which established the **EU**) in 1957 for the support of the agricultural industry in the European Union, to ensure local food production and a reasonable standard of living for farmers. The CAP can also provide grants for modernization. For foodstuffs, "target prices" are set below which imported food cannot be sold. Further, if prices fall below the target (to "intervention prices") the EU buys surplus stock. This is sometimes sold cheaply to less developed countries and impacts badly on their own production industries. In 1988, due to overproduction, farmers across the EU were paid to leave land fallow. It is an expensive policy, accounting for up to two-thirds of EU expenditure. It is also controversial, especially at world trade summits and negotiations. At the time of writing, British Prime Minister Tony Blair was calling for a complete reconsideration of the program.

COMMUNICATIVE RATIONALITY

Communicative rationality is a way of speaking with, thinking about and making decisions with other people. In formulating this theory (though really a blueprint for behavior), Habermas (1987) seeks to find a way of arriving at decisions which is fair, transparent and human. Thus communicative rationality is intersubjective and dialogic. It is a "central experience" of and inherent in human life. It is inherent because it is unavoidable. It is social, unforced agreement oriented towards action. This concept and mode of action can be seen as a way of dealing with **risk**.

For communicative rationality to take place requires discourse ethics, essentially procedural ground rules with five principles: (1) of generality, everyone involved in the issue should be involved in the communication; (2) autonomy, all should be able to offer and contest views; (3) ideal role taking, those involved must be willing to empathize with other points of view; (4) power neutrality, such that power differential has no bearing on the way or kind of consensus that is reached; and (5) transparency, openness without strategic argument.

In short, communicative rationality is a framework that would facilitate the building of well-founded, ethical and workable relationships and communities. It is an imperative rather than being descriptive, but is potentially useful in **civil society** and governance.

See also: **active citizens, democracy, experts/expert systems, global sub-politics, postmodernity/postmodernism, social capital**

COMMUNITIES OF FATE

Because actions and events in one place concerning some people will eventually affect all people, we can be said to be living in the same communities of fate. In other words, because events have global consequences, all people share at least some **risks**. This is most apparent in the case of environmental issues, however economic and political events are also involved.

Further reading: Held *et al.* 1999; Marske 1991

COMMUNITIES OF LIMITED LIABILITY

"Limited liability" in the context of communities pertains to obligations that people in a community have (or feel they have) to others. It is a term from Fischer (1991) though can be traced earlier to Janowitz (1967). "Limited liability" is said to be typical of cities and urban areas; however, whether one can speak of 'communities' of limited liability also depends very much on how community is defined. It is relevant to globalization insofar as people are more likely to live in cities and may have no lasting connection with a place because of mobility. Simply, because of the collapse of time and space connected to globalization, "community" may become less meaningful or decoupled from conventional space relations, becoming for example, more virtual.

It should not be forgotten that some groups are seeking to actively establish communities of responsibility, through direct action, petitioning government or through alternative lifestyles.

"Limited liability" is more usually used in relation to companies and money, referring to the fact that certain types of companies can be established which protect shareholders or owners by limiting their personal liability for losses the company may suffer.

See also: **active citizens, antiglobalization, civil inattention, citizenship, digital nomads, direct action, global village, placeless geography, social capital, time–space compression**

COMMUNITY PARTICIPATION

Community participation is associated with the idea of active communities and **active citizens** and is linked to new democratic practices associated with the impact of globalization. There is much debate over the gap between the rhetoric and practice of community participation. Usually the rhetoric stresses proactive participation when communities are given the opportunity to participate in identifying their own problems, devising and implementing their own solutions. The logic of community participation is that a community knows best what its needs, problems and available resources and networks are. Community participation is linked to globalization as it marks the move away from national center driven policy decision-making processes and is a way for **nation–states** to offset the difficulties while decreasing their role and level of responsibility. In practice, community participation is often seen as tokenism or "co-opted" participation. Community participation, originally developed as a preventive health strategy, has shifted into the fabric of governing practices and has come to define the new social democracy practices associated with the **Third Way**.

See also: **active citizens, racialization (of governmental processes)**

Further reading: Giddens 1998, Partnerships and Participation

RM

COMPLEXITY THEORY

Complexity theory defines and describes "complex systems." This theory originates in the fields of mathematics and natural science and is treated as synonymous or as a hyponym of **chaos theory**. Chaos and complexity theory are often borrowed by those working in the field of globalization to explain social, cultural or natural processes.

Complex systems are not just complicated, they are defined by a set of features. The key feature is that of emergence, which means that the system behaves as it does because of relationships between the elements, which are more like networks than simple cause and effect. In complex systems some outcomes cannot be predicted on the basis of the elements' properties.

More needs to be said about these relationships to understand why they are so significant. The relationships are nonlinear and thus part of networks (see **chaos theory**); they contain feedback loops, that is, effect impact on future possible effects and thus the system transforms. Because of this, complex systems have a history. How elements will behave in relation to each other depends on their history, not just their physical properties. Complex systems are open, receiving and outputting energy and information. This means that it is difficult to identify boundaries of the system. At the same time, there are complex systems within complex systems, that is, they are nested.

Further reading: Byrne 1998

CONFLUENT LOVE

This concept was introduced by Giddens (1992) and is connected to his theories about the move from traditional to modern societies. The changing gender roles that the move from traditional society has brought means that the framework of confluent love is more realistic and workable. Giddens writes, "Confluent love is active, contingent love, and therefore jars with the 'forever', 'one-and-only' qualities of the romantic love complex" (1992: 61). Confluent love is reflexive and present in a "pure relationship" which is driven and sustained by intimacy and equality. It is free from the gender imbalance and expectations inherent in romantic love. Confluent love is also linked to sexual emancipation (especially of women) and the separation of sex from reproduction. Indeed, sexual activity and identity are themselves negotiated in the context of confluent love. Giddens calls this "plastic sexuality" to refer to its malleable, shifting character rather than to suggest that it is artificial. Indeed, confluent love, the pure relationship and plastic sexuality are all argued to be democratic and (potentially at least) emancipatory.

This does not mean that romantic love no longer has any influence or currency. Indeed, confluent love and the "pure relationship" which grows out of it always contingent. Such uncertainty is at odds with both the concept of romantic love and what many people desire. The desire for "romantic love" may be a desire or need for the kind of commitment which traditionally (and for many, practically) allows having and raising children (emotionally and financially).

Rather, Giddens is pointing out that changing social norms, including those relating to gender, marriage and relationships generally, mean that new relationships (and ways of being in relationships) are possible.

See also: **feminism, reflexive modernization/modernity, risk, trust**

Further reading: Brown 2005; Langford 1999

CONSTRUCTIVE POSTMODERNISM (OR INTEGRALISM)

A popular and populist view of **postmodernism** is that it is nihilistic and that it has nothing to offer particularly in relation to political action and debate. Many argue that this is a misunderstanding of postmodernism. Constructive postmodernism accepts that the foundations of knowledge (and indeed "truth") are contingent and contextual and it argues for the value and utility of **pluralism**.

The phrase "constructive post-modernism" is also used as a banner by those who look to use and promote religious explanations of knowledge and the world.

Further reading: Habermas 1987; Schiralli 1999

CONSUMERISM

The term consumerism is used in two distinct ways. The first definition (more commonly used in the US) refers to consumerism as an organized social and political movement designed to protect consumer rights and interests. The second, and by far the most commonly used, refers to the cultural ideology whereby our sense of self, personal fulfillment and happiness are seen as being intimately interlinked with the products and services that we use and consume. A number of social theorists see this form of consumerism as one of the hallmarks of contemporary globalization as more and more areas of social life, such as education and health care, are seen as being transformed by a consumerist ethos. Consumerism initially arose in Europe and the US during the period of industrialization but it was not until the 1960s that consumerism emerged as a way of life and spread, albeit unevenly, across the globe. A key component in the global spread of consumerism has been the growth of the mass media and advertising, which has been accompanied by the exponential rise of global brands, which now extend to most of the populated world. Through advertising, consumers are urged to buy into and align themselves with the identities, values and **lifestyles** that a given commodity expresses. There has been substantial debate about whether the growth of global consumerism spearheaded by predominantly Anglo-American owned multinational corporations such as Coca-Cola, Nike and McDonalds leads to global **homogeneity** or an increase in diversity and choice, thus giving rise to a growing debate over the desirability of consumerism.

See also: **aura (of cultural phenomenon), autonomization (of culture), lifestyle, postmodernity/postmodernism, simulacrum, transnational corporations**

Further reading: Bocock 1993; Lee 2000; Miles 1998

HB

CONSUMPTION RITUALS

Any form of consumption which is done by more than one person and which moves the meaning of consumption from private to public. Consumption rituals are a way of demonstrating identity and even forging communities of use. The use of mobile phones, for example, while at one level facilitates communication, also inevitably displays something about the individual, using them. The particular phone a person owns may communicate something about their identity in terms of their profession or preferences. This can be expressed with the choice of fascias for phones, or otherwise keeping up with phone fashion and innovation. Further, conventions (or rituals) about when it is and is not appropriate to use mobile phones also develop. Advertisers and manufacturers may construct or at least appeal to some of these rituals in an attempt to get people to buy newer, more up-to-date or advanced technology.

See also: **commodity fetishism, identity politics, lifestyle**

Further reading: Douglas and Isherwood 1996

CONTEXTUAL UNIVERSALISM

Contextual universalism is a middle way between, and a potential solution to, the stand off between absolute **relativism** and **universalism**. It refers to the idea that there are many truths relative to time and place and yet that there is only one truth which applies universally. Contextual universalism is a philosophical marriage between the global and the local. It is most likely to be used in discussion of cultural variation and the ethical dilemmas this may pose.

Ulrich Beck argues that we have to accept that *universalisms* exist, that is, there is more than one universal. To argue that there is only one truth (universalism) refuses to acknowledge that there is in fact difference in the world. For relativists to claim that no universals exist is to refuse to try to understand other points of view. Beck also claims that contextual universalism starts from the notion that "*non*-interference is *im*possible" (2000: 83), that is, we can no longer pretend that we live in separate spaces (that is, in the confines of the **nation–state**). Thus for Beck, contextual universalism is not simply philosophical theorizing, but a mode of political and social action in the world of second modernity. "What is up for debate is the *how*, not the whether, of mutual interference and conflicting forms of involvement" (2000: 84).

See also: **asymptotic progression, communicative rationality, constructive postmodernism (or Integralism)**

Further reading: Beck 1998, 2000

CONTINGENCY THEORY

Contingency theory refers to the need for organizations and leaders to be responsive to local and contextual conditions (legislation, unions, employee numbers, size, location etc.). Contingency theory thus puts emphasis on considering these variables in conjunction with such considerations as production costs and economies of scale.

Further reading: Donaldson 1994; Friedkin and Slater 1994

CONTRACTING OUT

See: **offshoring**

CONVERGENCE THESIS

This phrase can have many meanings in various spheres of globalization discourse roughly equivalent to **homogenization**. Probably the most central meaning refers to the theory that **neoliberal** free trade will reduce government intervention and government spending on social security (Ohmae, 1996). This is also called institutional or governmental convergence. Governments change their policies and behavior, not simply because of direct pressure, but because of cultural shifts and the need to be competitive. Convergence is a consequence of the opening of markets, the freeing up of trade and the like but it is also a driver for these things. Thus it is part of the argument that **nation–states** are losing their power to **transnational corporations (TNCs)**.

In the more general context of **homogenization**, the thesis can also be applied to convergence of consumption and cultural habits that are said to be part of globalization (Levitt 1983).

See also: **commodity fetishism, consumerism, consumption rituals, hyperglobalist thesis**

CORE-PERIPHERY MODEL

This theory, developed in the 1950s, attempts to explain the uneven global patterns of economic and social development. It classified the world into areas and nations that are either core or periphery and later added semi–periphery. Classification depends on stage of development and control over resources, especially when interests of an area are in competition with another area. Core areas are distinguished by highly developed political and economic systems while periphery areas the opposite. As such, the periphery is dependent economically (and, perhaps, culturally) on the core. Unsurprisingly, many periphery areas are former colonies. The bimodal core-periphery model is essentially a neo-Marxist dependency theory. Adding the third category, semi–periphery, is typical of **world systems theory**.

See also: **income polarization, Marx/Marxism, realist paradigm**

Further reading: Freidman 1986; Wallerstein 2004

CORPORATISM

While this term has a particular (though contested) meaning in political science, it is used in relation to globalization to describe the power of multinational corporations. Strictly, it means the consultation of the state with representatives from production in order to come to agreement about policies and in turn to use the intermediary to get the policies enforced. It is associated closely with Mussolini and Fascism.

See also: **transnational corporation (TNC)**

COSMOCRACY

Cosmocracy can be understood as a conceptual blend of **democracy** that is **cosmopolitanism** at the global level. A cosmocracy would be a way of doing **global governance**, in the form of a world polity or government. John Keane (2002) describes the four basic features of cosmocracy: it is global, it involves different "zones" of government, it is dynamic and it is unstable. Essentially the identification of a global interdependence and how this might best be managed is what cosmocracy seeks to address. Keane seems to be the primary instigator of this term. Cosmocracy can also be understood as a particular version of **cosmopolitan democracy**.

See also: **civil society**

Further reading: Keane 2003

COSMOPOLIS

Technically, a city inhabited by people from all over the world is a cosmopolis. While this means that such places are multicultural and diverse, questions also arise about how such enterprises can be sustained, especially in places used to being more or less homogenous. Certainly the cosmopolis is not new, but has tended to be more an ideal than a reality.

See also: **cosmopolitan democracy**

COSMOPOLITAN DEMOCRACY

Cosmopolitan democracy refers to a model of political organization in which citizens, regardless of their geographical location, have rights to political participation through representation in global affairs, in parallel with and independently of their own government. Although the term originated in Greek stoic philosophy (*cosmos* = world, *polis* = city, *demos* = people, *cratos* = power), the modern use of the cosmopolitan ideal was first proposed by Kant with the concept of *jus cosmopoliticum* deployed in his project for a *Perpetual Peace* (1795 [1983]). More recently, David Held and Daniele Archibugi (1995) revived this notion, initiating the contemporary discussion of **cosmopolitanism**.

Underpinning the model of cosmopolitan democracy are two prescriptive assumptions concerning moral cosmopolitanism and political democracy, and an empirical assumption regarding world interdependence. According to the prescriptive assumptions, the scope of justice should be universal insofar as no discrimination is justified when considering the ultimate entitlement of every citizen to control his/her own destiny (ethical universalism). Conversely, the second presupposition holds that individuals as equals should be entitled to exercise collective self-determination over public issues that affect them, insofar as only by simultaneously retaining the status of legislators and subjects can citizens remain free (congruence/reflexivity between decision-takers and decision-makers). Finally, when these principles are coupled with the empirical observation of the increasing global interdependence of current international affairs, a fundamental right to autonomy and self-legislation emerges, which requires the creation of an authoritative global institutional framework to permit the implementation of such democratic prerogatives.

In presenting a model in between confederation and federation, cosmopolitan democracy aims to avoid both the indirect representation of the first (and consequently the likely exclusive pursuit of national interests) and the risk of despotism of the second (and consequently the likely pursuit of technocracy and homogenization). Through cosmopolitan citizenship, individuals are allowed to have a direct political voice on several decision-making levels, participating thus in the deliberative process of local, state and world politics.

Cosmopolitan democracy fosters democratic reform of both **UN** institutions and the wide network of **global governance** organizations. With regard to the UN, the following proposals are supported: the creation of a second advisory Peoples' Assembly; the abolition of the veto system together with the enlargement of the security council; the compulsory jurisdiction before the International Court of

Justice; and the establishment of an international humanitarian force. Conversely, regarding global governance, the changes recommended are in the direction of the enhancement of regionalization, the diffusion of authority to different bodies, and the strengthening of democratic procedures within such institutions.

Critics point to two principal and opposite deficiencies of cosmopolitan democracy. On the one hand, the model of global institutionalism is seen as inherently dangerous in terms of cultural and political imperialism of the west as the most powerful international actors, which would sanction their *de facto* influence by means of a legal endorsement. On the other extreme, such a model of world democracy is claimed to be failing in establishing a viable structure through which citizens' consensus can be expressed, in that the coordination of several centers of political authority would lack inclusive and super-ordinate democratic control.

See also: **global governance, human rights, UN**

Further reading: Archibugi 2003; Archibugi and Held 1995; Archibugi *et al.* 1998; Beck 1998; Falk 1995; Habermas 2001; Held 1995; Kant 1983; Linklater 1998

RF

COSMOPOLITANISM

The central theme of cosmopolitanism is that all humans belong to a single community and that this should be valued and developed and draws on the notion of interconnectedness. Cosmopolitanism has a long history and various manifestations. Moral cosmopolitanism (Singer 1993; Nussbaum 1996), for example, argues that we have moral responsibilities to other people regardless of nationhood and economic cosmopolitanism stresses free global trade.

See also: **cosmopolitan democracy, global village, human rights**

COUNTER-CULTURE

This term was first used to describe the emergence in the 1960s of a generation of young people who rejected the materialism of their parent culture in favor of a constellation of alternative positions based upon self-expression, sexual liberation, **direct action**, spirituality, pacifism and environmental awareness. Although counter-cultural allegiance was marked by an identifiable mode of dress and behavior, and expressed itself in various media (notably rock music), it was its profound challenge to the status quo and its effect on nearly every aspect of culture that distinguished it from the subcultures that preceded and succeeded it. Many of those who participated in it believed that it offered a genuine alternative to mainstream society, and that events at the time, such as the protests and general strike in Paris (May 1968), the first Woodstock festival (1969), and the civil rights and anti-Vietnam War marches, represented this alternative's birth.

While the radical social revolution envisioned by the most enthusiastic devotees of the counter-culture went unrealized, the movement nonetheless had a significant effect on Western culture. Thus although **feminism**, gay rights and environmentalism predated the counter-culture, it nevertheless gave a considerable impetus to these movements which continue to impact on contemporary society. It has been argued that in their flexibility and their empowerment of the individual, the information technologies that define **global capitalism** reflect the counter-cultural held values of some of their key developers.

This latter example is convergent with another assessment, namely, that in its assertion of individual choice and pleasure and its rejection of traditional social structures, the counter-culture anticipated some of the more destructive trends of contemporary **capitalism**.

See also: **civil society, counter-narratives**

Further reading: Marwick 1998; Roszak 1969

JH

COUNTER-HEGEMONY

From Gramsci's (1971) notion of **hegemony** which describes domination by a section or society and/or by a particular ideology. Counter-hegemony seeks to challenge the discourses and practices which underpin that domination. Sometimes this takes the form of offering direct alternatives, sometimes the reconfiguration of practices and discourses already present in the dominant culture. A good example of the latter is **fair trade** organizations which work within a consumer culture but factor in ethical treatment of the people who are the means of production. Adbusting, where advertisements (especially billboards) are altered in subversive and artistic ways, is another example.

Further reading: Klein 2001

COUNTER-NARRATIVES

A term from Foucault (1977b [1984]), counter-narratives are ways of analyzing and critiquing dominant discourses by revealing the partiality, inadequacy and provisionality of overarching grand theories to make transparent the relations of power behind specific claims to truth. Counter-narratives of globalization break with assumptions that place globalization at the center of the narrative of social transformation.

Globalization is understood in influential accounts as a process of increasing interconnectedness and **time–space compression**; as the growing recognition of the worldwide human commonality; as the ultimate expression of capitalism, where "the market" alone determines the restructuring of economic political and cultural life; and also as the reorganization of networks and institutions across global space (Larner and Walters 2004b). However much globalization is analyzed and criticized in terms of its influence and impact, by assuming that globalization is a real phenomenon marked by new sets of connections between territories and economies that underlie so many changes in the world, globalization remains the dominant narrative. The assumption that the phenomena we are witnessing can be bound together with a term called globalization can be turned around if we use counter-narratives – accounts that do not emphasize interconnectedness, universality etc. Accounts that stress the complexity, ambiguity and contingency of contemporary political formations exemplify counter-narratives of globalization.

See also: **de-governmentalization, geopolitical rationality, hybridity/ hybridization**

Further reading: Foucault 1977 [1984]; Larner and Walters 2004b; Peck and Yeung 2003; Rose 1999

RM

47

CREOLIZATION

In linguistics, this is a process of language formation that may occur where different languages are in contact (e.g. as a result of trade or colonization). The need for communication results in a language compromise, a reduced sort of language called a pidgin language. Over time, the pidgin develops into a fully developed native language called a creole. The term has been extended to nonlinguistic areas such as cultural practices. In this sense, it means the appropriation of discourses or practices into a new context where they become naturalized. If it is used in contrast to embedding (creolization may be treated as a synonym), the emphasis is on the pragmatic and pared back use of the original practice which only later becomes naturalized.

See also: **colonialism; re-embedding**

Further reading: Appadurai 1990; Hannerz 1992; Todd 1990

CULTURAL AUTONOMY

Just as **nation-states** have sovereignty, cultures may also seek to be recognized, develop in their own ways without undue external pressures, influences or constraints (heteronomy) and gain some sovereignty over salient domains. To do this, cultures have to be understood as having agency, but this, as Tomlinson notes, is problematic, as cultures are not things but practices (2001). Cultural autonomy also extends to nation-states who seek to uphold their culture in the face of colonization by other cultures. Here, however, we are only concerned with actions not outcomes (Tomlinson 2001: 97). Smith (1981: 16) takes a holistic view of the situation, writing "Cultural autonomy implies full control by representatives of the ethnic community over every aspect of its cultural life, notably education, the press, the mass media and the courts." Tomlinson (2001) points to bigger questions such as who these representatives might be, whether these institutions are culture or the trappings of culture and how we can determine whether cultures are developing with heteronomy.

Note that cultural autonomy is very different from the **autonomization of culture**.

See also: **colonialism; cultural imperialism, homogenization**

Further reading: Ghai 2002

CULTURAL CAPITAL

A concept first introduced by the sociologists Pierre Bourdieu and Jean-Claude Passeron (1973), it refers to certain cultural knowledge that individuals possess that can be generated and exchanged like economic capital. Knowing how to conduct oneself in particular social situations such as knowing formal etiquette, for example, is a form of cultural capital. This extends to knowing how to speak (particularly identified as a type of linguistic capital). What exactly constitutes cultural capital will shift from place to place as different cultures and subcultures value different skills and forms of knowledge. Cultural capital itself has three kinds: embodied, objectified and institutionalized. Embodied capital (also known as an individual's **habitus**) relates to an individual's way of thinking and behaving and as such cannot be easily "exchanged." It can be improved by spending time developing the self (self-improvement for example). Objectified cultural capital consists of material things, such as books, works of art and the like. These objects have a certain economic value but this value is dependent on their objectified cultural capital. That is, a rare edition of a book which is much in demand has a much higher objectified cultural capital than a facsimile or new edition. Very often knowing what counts as objectified cultural capital, and how to identify objects with it, requires that one has the right kind of embodied capital. Finally, institutionalized cultural capital is another type of nonmaterial capital that is typically acquired through education or other institutions which bestow "recognition," membership or certification.

These forms of capital are exchangeable in the economic market. For example, a law degree is a form of institutionalized cultural capital (as one has to attend an accredited university) which then can be "exchanged" for economic and social status.

See also: **autonomization of culture, social capital, symbolic capital**

Further reading: Bourdieu 1985, 1989

CULTURAL CONVERGENCE

See: **homogenization**

CULTURAL DEFENCE PLEA

A plea used especially in judicial proceedings in an attempt to excuse or mitigate a crime on the basis of cultural practices. This is a case of law developing to take cultural plurality into account.

See also: **colonialism, cultural autonomy, human rights, multicultural/ism, pluralism**

CULTURAL DUMPING

This term describes the saturation of a market (or **cultural landscape**) with material culture from another place. It is a negative term mainly due to the perceptual threat that this material poses to local culture.

See also: **Americanization, colonialism, cultural imperialism, homogenization**

CULTURAL ECONOMY

Cultural economy describes what is considered a new approach to social action, especially in the fields of work and employment, production and consumption. In contrast to theories and approaches which prioritise economic structures and processes, those working in the field of cultural economy seek a different perspective. Some read Marxism, for example, as arguing that economic factors in some way pre-exist cultural concerns. That is, that economic decisions and structures influence culture. This is not so much under dispute in cultural economy, but it is certainly revised. Rather than seeing culture merely as an additional factor (a surplus of some kind), cultural economy recognises that even if a field is determined by economic concerns, this takes place in a cultural context and has cultural effects.

Those working in the field look at any number of spaces and practices, often depending on what their home discipline is. Work on subjects traditionally regarded as creative (e.g. advertising, design and media) are popular, however even the most 'economic' of spaces have cultural dimensions (banks and financial institutions for example). Thus cultural economy does not designate an object of study but rather foregrounds a particular way of looking at practices, spaces and structure, that is, one that seeks to articulate the interplay and mutual flows between the economic and the cultural. Neither the economic nor the cultural is primary; both are always present. Further, economic events and decisions will have effects on the cultural and vice versa.

Cultural economy as a field of study attempts to distinguish itself from Lash and Urry's 'culturalization thesis' which argues that the economic sphere is now, more than ever, culturalized (1994). This is in turn linked to their concept of **disorganized capitalism**, especially their emphasis on the production of signs as typical of this. **Lifestyle**, for example, is a key in the marketing of commodities and is an obvious way in which symbolic value, or **exchange value**, can be radically different from use value. Lash and Urry's argument is read as somehow privileging cultural industries, that is, the economic effects of the production of cultural products. du Gay in particular argues that the culturalization thesis presupposes what it attempts to prove (2003). It is possible to separate two distinct elements of Lash and Urry's work. In *Economies of Signs and Space* (1994), these two elements can be understood as two claims. The first is essentially a claim about theoretical approaches and perspectives similar to that of cultural economy, that is, that to understand post-Fordist economies, culture needs to be taken into account. Many working in cultural economy may not confine this to present times. The second is a descriptive claim. That is,

> ...economic and symbolic processes are more than ever interlaced and interarticulated; that is, the economy is increasingly culturally inflected and that culture is more and more economically inflected. Thus the boundaries between the two become more and more blurred and the economy and culture no longer function in regard to one another as system and environment (1994: 64)

Whether or not this claim is true is a question for empirical investigation. However du Gay (2003) also critiques the conclusion because of its epochal or totalising nature.

Finally, 'cultural economy' has also been used to refer to the economic profile of creative (or cultural) industries. Others use the term 'aesthetic economy' in this way.

See also: **consumerism, cultural capital, Global Commodity Chain (GCC), knowledge society, Marx/Marxism, network society, post-Fordism**

Further reading: du Gay and Pryke 2002

CULTURAL ENTREPRENEURS

Someone who treats culture as a commodity and a business in the manner of an entrepreneur, that is, with consideration of the market, seeking to be somehow novel or innovative and to make money (e.g. those who arrange for musicians and art festivals to occur and tour). Cultural entrepreneurs include governments or representative bodies of cultures such as the British Council (which sells British culture, education and language to the world). Though sometimes such relationships are said to be based on exchange, the flows of people and information generated by cultural entrepreneurs are sometimes one-way. This form of cultural export is also a form of soft power.

See also: **colonialism, hard/soft power, hegemony, homogenization**

CULTURAL FATE

Cultural fate comes about when traditional social roles are no longer adhered to. One of the key features of **modernity** (in Giddens' terms) is that traditional social roles no longer exist. Because of this absence of set roles, people are compelled to make choices. Our cultural fate is that we *have* to make choices that then impact on who we are as individuals; we are *required* to constantly "self develop." Obviously, whenever choices have to be made, **risk** is present. Cultural fate can be understood as being connected to Sartre's existentialism: Sartre held that we are "condemned to freedom" and existential *angst*. In that vein, Tomlinson writes, "Freedom is an ambiguous gift, but one we cannot refuse" (2001: 140).

Cultural fate is connected to the move to modernity and is a challenge not only to individuals but also to societies (whether they be nations, communities or any kind of group). Tomlinson argues that

> As global cultures fall into the conditions of modernity through the spread of the institutions of modernity, they all face the same problem of the failure of a collective will to generate shared narratives of meaning and orientation.
>
> (2001: 165)

Castoriadis, however, sees things differently. Whereas some (such as Berman (1983) and Giddens (1990)) see modernity as fundamentally different from traditional societies, Castoriadis does not agree that there is such a fundamental difference between the traditional and the modern societies. Castoriadis focuses on human agency. For Castoriadis, cultural *fate* is more properly spoken about as cultural *decision*. Castoriadis stresses that people have to want to "act responsibly in order to take on their own fate" (Tomlinson 2001: 165); it does not happen of itself.

See also: **expert systems, liquid modernity, modernity, postmodernity/ postmodernism, reflexivity, structuration theory**

Further reading: Berger 1974; Berman 1983; Castoriadis 1997; Tomlinson 2001

CULTURAL HERITAGE

Cultural heritage refers to things that are of historical cultural importance to a particular group. It can include tangible things such as buildings, sacred sites or areas and even plants and animals but also include, intangible things such as customs and practices, ritual, language and world views. Cultural heritage becomes an issue in globalization because of the way in which these artifacts are under threat, either by forced removal or loss of **cultural capital.** A secondary, but no less important issue, is how to preserve such heritage. While some objects can be put in museums, the object itself, out of context, cannot always signify what it originally did. The challenge is to find and access resources to implement ways of sustaining cultural traditions in an appropriate, respectful way.

See also: **Americanization, cultural imperialism, cultural tourism, homogenization, simulacrum**

CULTURAL IMPERIALISM

The way in which some cultures exert their power over others such that practices of more powerful nations and cultures are forcefully exported to new areas. This practice now extends not just to music and literature, but to patterns of **consumerism**, objects of consumption, political and economic systems. It is not a new phenomena, though formerly analysis tended to focus on language and religion. Cultural imperialism can be accomplished through formal laws, threats, overt social pressure of (perhaps) an occupying culture or through soft power. Probably the most effective forms of cultural imperialism are those which are invisible, in which discourse and society shift in such a way that practices become untenable or unpopular. The term is connected to debates around global English and the widening influence of US culture. It is also used in support of arguments that claim globalization is not a new phenomenon, but rather a continuation of colonizing and imperialist practices.

See also: **Americanization, colonialism, cultural integration, Ideological State Apparatus**

Further reading: Said 1978; Tomlinson 2001

CULTURAL INTEGRATION

While often used with respect to corporations (especially when mergers are taking place or new geographical areas are being worked in and managed), this term generally refers to one of the possible outcomes of two different cultures meeting, whether because of merging or moving. While cultural integration usually results in a harmonious resolution of differences, the term may be used to mean assimilation. In this case, the owners of the culture with lower prestige will have a force exerted on them such that they adopt and internalize the values of the new/higher prestige culture. Whether integration is a process between equals or a more assimilative one, will depend on the particular groups involved. What is of concern, however, is "integration" into a culture which one has not asked for. In such cases, one is dealing with colonization.

See also: **colonialism, cultural imperialism, homogenization, hybrid/ hybridization**

CULTURAL LANDSCAPE

In geography, this means the way in which landscapes have been altered by people throughout history. The cultural landscape is contrasted with the natural landscape. Generally, it seems to be used to talk about visible "everyday" phenomena which are linked to culture. It might be used as a way of talking about the changing nature of television, shopping and recreation areas or architectural styles insofar as these are part of our day-to-day lives (and thus of landscape) and are not naturally occurring phenomena thus, cultural.

Further reading: Gupta and Ferguson 1992; Jameson 1991

CULTURAL STORAGE

Cultural storage is another way of talking about tradition but with emphasis on the multifarious ways culture is encoded and passed on (traditionally). Cultural storage isn't always a tangible thing, like a sacred text or relic, but involves also language, the way the **cultural landscape** is shaped and apprehended, the body, behavior, social groupings, gender and kinship relations, how the outsider is conceived, relationship with the land and so on.

Some instances of culture may be physical and can be stored in a very literal way in museums and other institutions. Questions abound in relation to this. Firstly, is it ethical or appropriate to store artifacts in this way, and is it then possible to refer to them with the tag "culture" when so decontextualized. Secondly, how are they to be presented? In terms of geography, chronology or use? Will the taxonomies of storage and exhibition actually capture (or even approximate) the cultural categories which the artifacts originally inhabited? It is also crucial that any storage or use respects the values of the originating people.

The "storage" of intangible culture is even more problematic as to be stored in any meaningful way, a human agent has to be involved. A language, for example, might be written down by a linguist, but if there are no speakers of the language, such linguistic work is really only historical documentation. Thus storage of intangible culture requires maintenance of practices. This in turn may require protection of land, adjustments to laws and an active respect for difference.

See also: **aura (of cultural phenomenon), cultural heritage, cultural imperialism, heritage tourism, human rights, language rights, simulacrum**

Further reading: Shils 1981

CULTURAL SYNCHRONIZATION

This is another term for the **homogenization** of culture that some argue globalization promotes. A secondary use, as it is not related to globalization, appears in pedagogical works describing the importance of fit between the culture of teacher and student.

Further reading: Hamelink 1983

CULTURAL TOURISM

A form of tourism where the object of the tourism is the culture of the people being visited (Van Den Berghe's *tourees* (1994)). For example, tourists may visit "ethnic" villages to see how the host population lives. This may in turn lead to displays of staged authenticity, where hosts perform their culture for the tourists (e.g. dance, traditional crafts). In some cases this may lead to the revival and **commodification** of obsolescent traditional activities. Cultural tourism is an important element in the quest for authenticity

See also: **aura (of cultural phenomenon), heritage tourism**

SL

CULTURALISM

Dahl notes that "It is striking how central 'culture', as a point of reference and orientation, has become during the last decades" (1999: 179). Here, culture means something like traditional values and traditions rather than the "high culture" of art and music. Dahl notes the continental "new right" mobilizing a discourse of "culture" with an implicit reference to "civilization." Both are "used in their classical German conservative sense. Culture stands for spiritual growth, civilization for materialism, atomism, individualism and economism and ... hyper-intellectualism" (1999: 179). "Culture" in this sense, then, stands in for something like tradition. It appears to be regionally (if not nationally) rooted and more or less homogenous. The call to this kind of world and the discourse used to call for it, can be called "culturalism."

See also: **multicultural/ism, nationalism**

Further reading: Beck 1992; Dahl 1999

CULTURE INDUSTRY

This is a term put forward by Theodor Adorno and Max Horkheimer (2002 [1947]), two members of the highly influential Frankfurt School of Social Research. Their thesis was that in the context of industrial capitalism, culture could not be understood as the creation of artisans or artistic geniuses. Rather, it had become a commodity produced by an industrial process. While the work of craftsmen and artists retained a certain autonomy, being produced "for itself," the products of the culture industry reflect the general logic of profit, reproducibility, and standardization that characterizes industrial production. Culture had been reduced to something to be bought and sold, and in portraying an ideal vision of the consumerist lifestyle, serve to generate profit for other sectors.

Cultural production in this context is marked by a superficial novelty or difference that conceals an essential repetition. Cultural products must be different enough to stimulate consumption, but not so different that they challenge this activity. Hence the culture industry's preference for the formulaic (soap operas, genre films, interchangeable pop acts etc.). This process results in the decline of autonomous "folk" and "high" art, both are plundered as sources of desirable novelty and so are strip-mined of their unique qualities. The culture industry is an integral component in a wider system of exploitation, because it creates and maintains an ideological framework. It programs its audience to think that the only values are those of capitalism, and siphons off its frustrations and resentments at life under this system. Often criticized for being too deterministic, debates about the role of Western media networks in consolidating a global **hegemony** have given this thesis a new lease of life.

See also: **global media, lifestyle enclaves, postmodernity/postmodernism, simulacrum**

Further reading: Adorno 1991; Cook 1996

JH

CULTURE OF CIVILITY

Originally coined by sociologists Becker and Horowitz in 1970 in relation to the prevailing social norms in San Francisco, California where "deviants" were given more room for expression, and proponents of law and order were less likely to enforce some rules than elsewhere in the US. Each group gives up something but they all achieve stability and social harmony. The "mainstream" is also guided somewhat in their attitudes by civic leaders who articulate and enact a liberal environment.

The phrase seems to have acquired another meaning, especially in relation to business and institutional behavior where "civil" means polite. Thus, a concept of "civility" is appealed to as a putatively common value to which all should adhere as it would make working life happier, less stressful and altogether more pleasant. Thus while Becker and Horowitz's culture of civility means that some people can flout cultural and legal norms, the more recent usage is an implicit imperative not to.

See also: **civil inattention, civil society**

Further reading: Becker and Horowitz 1970

CYBERACTIVISM

Cyberactivism describes the convergence of political protest and digital technology. It may be divided into two trends. The first is that of activists engaged in ongoing political struggles who employ technology as means of more effective intervention, the second relates to those concerned with the politics of information technology in itself.

The first group uses these technologies as a vehicle for disseminating information on political issues, and as means of organizing **direct action** and of carrying out "virtual" direct action. This latter use is exemplified in various strategies of electronic disruption, such as web defaces (when a group vandalizes the site of their opponents) and "virtual sit-ins," which involve hundreds of users simultaneously employing the same piece of software to request information from a target site, so bringing the site down.

The second group argues that unless actively challenged, corporations and states will artificially delimit the potential of these technologies in the interests of maximizing profit and control. An issue vocalized by the "free" or "open" source movements where software is developed (using the networking potential of the **internet**) as a collaborative project whose resources are in principle open to further development by any user that wishes to contribute so long as they make their contribution similarly open to other users. This is known as "copyleft" and is preserved through the use of licenses. These cyberactivists argue that the internet is by design open and free, and that it dissolves the distinction between user and producer, and they strive to preserve and extend these freedoms.

See also: **antiglobalization, civil society**

Further reading: Jordan and Taylor 2004; Terranova 2000

JH

DEBT RELIEF

In the context of globalization, debt relief usually refers to measures to ease the burden of repaying loans to banks, other countries or financial institutions (such as the **World Bank**) for countries that are struggling economically. It has been an enduring topic for campaigners in the area of development. The Make Poverty History campaign was primarily oriented towards such debt relief.

See also: **IMF**

Further reading: Boote and Thugge 1997; Payer 1991; Woodward 1998

DECISIONISM

This is the political theorist Carl Schmitt's (1976) notion that a central feature of politics is the importance and necessity of operating in a polarized world where there are two sides to an issue: "ours" and "theirs." In that sense, it shares something of the **realist paradigm** though does not see the enemies as other states only; "they" can also exist internally. In the end, however, decisionism, and the view of political action it forwards, is about power. While Schmitt has been unfashionable in the past, his ideas seem to be enjoying renewed interest, especially in the fields of international relations and international law.

Further reading: Mouffe 1999; Roach 2005

DECOLONIZATION

This is the process by which former colonies become independent. It may be through war with the colonial power (as was the case with the US) or through a gradual giving over of powers (as with

Australia). Since the end of World War I especially, many former colonies have become independent. Article 22 of the Covenant of the League of Nations sought to advance and continue this process. The General Assembly of the UN has also been behind the move for decolonization. Resolution 1514 of the General Assembly was adopted in 1960, *Declaration on the Granting of Independence to Colonial Countries and Peoples*. There has since been a Resolution (55/146) which declared the first decade of the twenty-first century to be the *Second International Decade for the Eradication of Colonialism*. While in principle this is good policy, to push for independence without considering other local issues is potentially more traumatic than beneficial, depending on existing infrastructures for example. If a country has been governed by a colonial power for some time, withdrawing completely may leave that nation without the time to develop administrative resources, governing skills and indeed present it with problems impossible to solve at such an early stage of self-governance.

It should be noted that some countries have chosen to retain their colonial status, for example Puerto Rico, Gibraltar and the Falkland Islands. What it means to be a colony now differs markedly from when such countries were viewed as second-rate members of the empire useful for raw materials and performing the role of markets for colonial powers and their products.

See also: **citizenship, colonialism, nation–state, nationalism, world systems theory**

Further reading: Bleich 2005; McIntyre 1998; Strang 1990

DECOMMODITIZATION

This term refers to changing any product in a way which seeks to keep competition at bay, by adding value to it, usually through the application of new or complex knowledge and procedures. In this sense, it is not unlike niche marketing. The term is commonly used in relation to software, agricultural and other primary products. In relation to software, for example, decommoditization would involve adding increasingly useful features to programs which competitors did not or could not offer.

Decommoditization should not be confused with commodification.

Further reading: Appadurai 1986; Kaplinsky and Fitter 2004

DE-GOVERNMENTALIZATION

De-governmentalization is a **counter-narrative** of **neoliberalism** and is associated with the work of **governmentality** scholars. As the conventional account of the rise of neoliberalism is directly linked to the globalization of capital, de-governmentalization challenges the explanatory power of globalization. The conventional account understands neoliberalism as a policy framework and marked by a shift from Keynesian welfarism (see **welfare state**) toward a political agenda favoring free markets and often directly linked to the globalization of capital. The assumption tends to be that "neo-liberalism is a policy reform program initiated and rationalized through a relatively coherent theoretical and ideological framework" (Larner 2000: 7). But many accounts argue that neoliberalism as policy is an inadequate explanation for these transformations. Instead, they use the concept of de-governmentalization to understand the rise of neoliberalism as a shift in types of governance from the Welfare State to Advanced Liberalism. State-orientated governance is marked by heavy direct involvement of state bureaucracies and institutions to achieve governance. The shift to post-welfare state governance is marked by a new understanding of national community where firms are to be entrepreneurial, enterprising and innovative, but so too are citizens. In opposition to the conventional account of a coherent program of reform, the shift came about, according to Rose (1999), because critiques of the welfare state from both sides of the political spectrum got linked to the political technologies associated with marketization and it was this that provided the basis for advanced liberalism. Some limitations of the de-governmentalization thesis are that it fails to define the object which is to take the place of the state in political sociology, it deprives liberal government of any historical specificity, it fails to comment on relations between "real" social groups, and that human agency is ignored (Curtis 1995).

See also: **active citizen, counter-narrative**

Further reading: Barry *et al.* 1996; Burchell *et al.* 1991; Curtis 1995; Rose 1996a, 1999

RM

DEMOCRACY

At the beginning of the twenty-first century, scholars count some 120 democracies (of different "quality") in the world, and the rhetoric of "democracy" has become a default option for legitimizing political claims. At the same time, hardly any concept of political thought is as contested as that of democracy. Various political movements, not least liberal, conservative and socialist ones, have appealed to democracy, noted democratic deficits or criticized "excesses" of democracy. With the advent of 'globalization' on the public agenda, things have become even more complex: in the last decade, almost every conceivable way of linking "the global" with "democracy" has been discussed.

1. Democracy as a political regime

Historians of systems of political order have had an easier task. Instead of working with definitions and normative conceptions of democracy, they turned to the history of democratic institutions and practices. Of course, the example of Ancient Greece is central here. Athenians used the term "democracy" since the late fifth century BC to refer to their political community, where the people (*demos*) themselves ruled (*kratein*) the polis. Indeed, Athenian democracy was characterized by an extremely high degree of political participation, although, as often noted, women and slaves were excluded from political life. Historians estimate attendance at the sovereign Assembly (*ekklesia*) at about 6,000 citizens. And only the Assembly made laws. Even jurisdiction was directly carried out by the *demos*. There were no stable bureaucratic structures, and no class of professional civil servants. Officials were selected by lot rather than by election, and period in office was strictly limited.

Athenian democracy lasted for about 200 years, and with its end the term "democracy" came to be mostly negatively connoted, namely as the unstable, irrational rule of the populace. However, historians have identified many other examples of democratic practices and institutions which partly influenced the models and conceptions of modern democracy. The codification of law in the Roman Republic, for instance, is seen as precursor of modern ways of protecting citizens against oppression and arbitrary acts by the rulers. In the Italian city states of the Renaissance, forms of citizens' deliberation, participation (e.g. election, consent) and control were practiced. The English Revolutionaries of the seventeenth century conceived of a commonwealth of free citizens, i.e. an *empire of laws, and not of men*, as James Harrington put it. For the entry of democracy into political modernity, though, the most crucial invention was that of representation. In large-scale territorial states, democracy had to rely on representative assemblies. Here, the model of the French

Revolution turned out to be decisive in conceiving of the parliament as both a miniature model of society, and as representative of the unitary subject of political authority, i.e. the nation.

However, democracy was not conquered once and for all; on the contrary it has been and still is an ongoing experience and experiment. Democracy has been confronted with various problems, conflicts and even paradoxes, accompanied by violence and injustice, and it was always a site of conflicting claims and imaginations. Thus, the history of democracy, as well as its institutions, differs to a large degree in various countries, and its evolution cannot be separated from the realm of political ideas, from theoretical reflection and institutional creativity.

2. Democracy as a political idea

The advent of democracy presupposes a major leap in Man's conception of himself and of the world: to recognize that social relations are open to change, i.e. to invent politics as a realm of collective autonomy, beyond religious or traditionalist claims. The revolutionaries of 1789 expressed such self-understanding with a radical pathos: the French nation constitutes itself in an act of sovereign will.

This affirmation of political autonomy brings a whole range of fundamental questions of political order, i.e. of justice, into the domain of human deliberation. One influential answer to such normative concerns goes back to Aristotelian political thought. To distinguish good from bad political regimes, Aristotle proposed the basic criterion of whether the rulers rule in the interest of all, or rather in their own interest. Such an idea still echoes in Abraham Lincoln's famous formula, defining democracy as *government of the people, by the people, for the people.* It implies that every individual is represented in the political community on an equal basis. Democratic government is only legitimate insofar as it is based on the people, and it always remains accountable to the people, i.e. to every single citizen. However, who is "we the people" (*demos*), and who counts as a citizen, and who does not?

The French philosopher Claude Lefort has defined modern democracy with the famous formula that *the place of the King is empty.* While democratic authority always refers to the *demos* as its subject, the *demos* cannot be touched or located. Everyone can speak in the name of the *demos*, but nobody can monopolize such reference. Is "popular sovereignty," this sacred conception of modern democratic constitutions, only a myth? Have "we the people" never really spoken? Such questions miss the point. While the *demos* is not simply given, democracy is constituted by reference to the absent *demos*, by leaving the "place" of the *demos* open, and, consequently, by providing a space for contesting democratic claims. Modern democracy is fundamentally "unfounded." It is an adventure that remains open to the future.

3. Democracy and globalization discourse

Only recently, intellectuals and **social movements** have extended the prophetic pathos of democracy to the global scale. This should not obscure the fact, though, that it was *local* struggles for autonomy (e.g. in former colonies) or for the reappropriation of power from corrupted regimes that has marked recent decades and are ongoing in every corner of the globe. In Western public discourse, such colonial struggles often passed without getting much attention. Globalization, on the other hand, soon caught the public's imagination, and various ways are discussed for "transferring" democracy to a higher, i.e. the global, level.

No other slogan characterizes this new democratic claim as accurately as the one of protesters at the G8 summit 2001 in the Italian city of Genoa: "you are G8, we are eight billion." The "we" articulated here repeats the universalistic claim of the French national assembly of 1789: to represent the *demos* and its will. The history of democracy in France revealed the contradiction of the claim for unity with the actual diversity of the country: often violent **homogenization** and oppression of minorities were symptoms of democratic movements. The plurality of human life makes such unity impossible; just like the finitude of nature and its resources, it rather reveals the "limits of growth," i.e. of unilateral expansion and political domination. Each of the democratic **nation–states** during its heroic times had projected the eventual expansion of a singular just political order on the global scale: the "world state" was the logical corollary of the nation-state, projected in the future. The condition of the contemporary world finally confronts such utopia with the realities of a finite planet: there will be no uniform *demos*, no universal political community, no unitary global leadership.

While the notion of "global democracy," thus, seems practically impossible, the various challenges for political order in a globalized world are real, and they trigger new types of experiences, conflicts and institutional developments. From this perspective, the slogan of the Genoa protesters takes on a different meaning: it challenges the legitimacy of a new **global elite**, it demands a say in the functional organizations of the world economy (like the **WTO**), it places the question of justice over and above economic or technical pressures. The state, political scientists note, is no longer at the center of social processes, and consequently it is no longer the only address for political claims. In the context of globalization, democratic practices transcend the state, actors and forums proliferate, local and global claims are made at the same time. The heroism of democracy, i.e. the unilateral affirmation of autonomy, thus, seems to be replaced by a renewed concern with interdependency and coexistence of human as well as nonhuman ("natural") others.

See also: **global managerial class/global elite, global sub-politics, human rights, knowledge society, liberal democracy, nation–state, nation–state (decline of), network society**

Further reading: Albrow 1996; Dahl 2000; Latour and Porter 2004

FO

DEPENDENCY THEORY

Dependency theory is a contemporary take on patterns of trade that prevailed in colonial times, when colonies were clearly understood to be providers of raw goods and consumers of commodities. The theory derives from research by Raul Prebisch (Director of the United Nations Economic Commission for Latin America) in the 1950s, that found a relation between the increasing wealth of rich countries and the increasing poverty of poorer countries. It is historically rooted in patterns of economic development and external forces are involved. Dos Santos (1971) describes it as follows.

> ... an historical condition which shapes a certain structure of the world economy such that it favors some countries to the detriment of others and limits the development possibilities of the subordinate economics ... a situation in which the economy of a certain group of countries is conditioned by the development and expansion of another economy, to which their own is subjected (226).

This is in contrast to classical and liberal economics which sees economic development for some as good for all; often called the "trickle down" theory. The notion that the market always works to distribute goods fairly does not apply in dependency theory. The theory was

65

popular in the 1960s and 1970s, mainly as an opponent of development theory (that is, the possibility of development of these states). Now, **world systems theory** puts forward a similar model.

Frank (1988) sees dependency theory as linked to **capitalism**, but it has also been argued that it is connected to other forms of dominant power relations (mostly ideological and economic). It should be noted that development theory seeks to explain underdevelopment and thus has a very different perspective from **Marxism**. Underdevelopment is not undevelopment. The former refers to processes which are occurring but which only benefit the dominant powers. The problem is not just economic development, but the kind of economic and social development that needs to happen.

Dependency theory does rely on a concept of what is good for the nation, including not only economic indicators favored by liberal economics (Gross Domestic Product for example) but also other indicators of progress (health, life expectancy and so on). This may mean opting out of certain economic policies prevalent in the dominant countries. For example, a nation may decide that despite the economy of importing food that it is more important to be able to fulfil national needs at the domestic level. This would mean adopting at the very least a policy of national subsistence production.

Cultural issues are also linked to dependency theory, usually referred to as flows, **cultural imperialism** or **cultural dumping**.

See also: **core–periphery model, IMF, World Bank, world systems theory**

Further reading: Dos Santos 1971; Frank 1988; Schiller 1971; Seers 1981

DEVELOPMENTAL STATE

Sometimes also called a "state monopoly capitalism" (Castells and Hall 1993: 113). Castells writes,

A state is developmental when it establishes as its principle of legitimacy its ability to promote and sustain development, understanding by development the combination of steady high rates of economic growth and structural change in the economic system, both domestically and in its relationship to the international economy.

(Castells 1996: 182)

Examples of the developmental state include the Asian "tiger" economies which positioned themselves to be globally competitive and to increase economic growth by encouraging **Foreign Direct Investment (FDI)** and the development of production capabilities in key areas (electronic goods for example). In the face of the open borders of the rest of the world, however, it is not always possible to continue to implement the necessary policies for continued growth of this kind. Further, because economic development is prioritized before all else, democratic and **human rights** reform may cease or recede. Attaining a level of economic development does allow one a voice in the global world, however, especially if one has developed in an industry crucial to the interests of the powerful.

See also: **network society**

Further reading: Bello 2005; Castells and Hall 1993; Doner 1992; Douglass 1994; Onis 1991; Woo-Cumings 1999

DIASPORA

While diaspora is a contested term, it generally refers to people who have left their place of origin and yet maintain identification with this place in some way. Diaspora literally means dispersion and originally referred chiefly to the exodus of the Jews from their homeland. Now the term is used in relation to any number of cultural and/or ethnic groups dispersed around the world from their original place. It does not depend on ethnicity, however. The movement from the homeland may be forced or voluntary. Thus diasporas may come about because of war and natural disaster on the one hand (forced migration) or economic and opportunistic migration on the other.

What does seem to be necessary for the term diaspora to be used is a continuing identification with the place of origin. This can be understood as an **imagined community** in Anderson's (1983) terms. This may be expressed in the formation of communities in new nations (or across national boundaries) and specifically through such actions as the maintenance of language, cultural practices, endogenous marriage, religious practices, modes of dress and so on. Further, cultural products such as films, television programs and books (diasporic media) help to sustain diasporic communities. Indeed, these media are produced and exported with diasporic communities in mind.

Given the present sophistication of communication technology, contact with the homeland is increasingly possible. "Global communication technology makes it easier both to sustain links at a distance and to sustain [200] and affirm cultural identity within the global cultural space" (Albrow 1996: 199–200). However, it should be remembered that access to such technology may well not be possible to those forced to migrate because of war, political persecution or natural disaster.

Castles (2002) notes that there seems to be an increase in diaspora at the moment which may be due to technological factors (travel, for example) but also for social and cultural reasons which have not yet been fully explored. Certainly members of diasporic communities will have hybrid identities, if only because they retain an identity connection to the homeland without residing there. However, as Tsagarousianou notes, "diasporas should better be seen as depending not so much on displacement but on connectivity, or on the complex nexus of linkages that contemporary transnational dynamics make possible and sustain" (2004: 52).

Safran's understanding of diaspora includes a belief on the behalf of the migrant that there will never be full acceptance in the host culture and that returning to the homeland remains a real (if perhaps quiescent) desire (1991: 83–84). Perhaps the most significant feature of diasporic communities in the terms of globalization is that they live transnational lives at least in terms of identity. While diasporas are far from uniform, they do provide a focus for assessing both the challenges and opportunities that changes in the world bring.

See also: **clash of civilizations, migration, multicultural/ism, nation-state, nation-state (decline of), territorialization (de- & re-), transnational, world cities/global cities**

Further reading: Appadurai 1990, 1996; Clifford 1992; Cohen 1997; Fazal and Tsagarousianou 2002

DIGITAL DIVIDE

Term used to distinguish between those who have access to digital technology (e.g. the **internet**) and those who do not. The term was popularized in the 1990s and related not only to the internet but any technology (telephones, computers etc.) and especially state-of-the-art technologies. The concept is an important one in response to claims that the internet is global, democratic and somehow working as a catalyst in a move to a technological utopia. This divide need not be geographic, it can quite easily be based upon class, earning capacity and access to education.

Further reading: Davison and Cotton 2003; Norris 2001; Warschauer 2004

DIGITAL NOMADS

A term coined by Makimoto and Manners (1997) to describe those who are able to hold down jobs without being located in one place, exactly because of advances in technology and the associated collapse of time and space identified by Giddens (1990). Some digital nomads comprise the **global elite** because the jobs that can be performed in this way come at a high cost (both educational and financial). Being a digital nomad may be a **lifestyle** choice that sees travel and relocation as desirable, though some individuals may be required to work more or less as nomads because of the dispersed locations of the corporations that employ them. Telecommuting and hot desking are a marginal part of this phenomena

See also: **global managerial class/global elite, time–space compression**

DIRECT ACTION

A theory developed primarily in relation to labor issues by William Mellor in his book *Direct Action* (1920). The "direct" aspect involves not using intermediaries to try and exert pressure on corporations, management and even government. Mellor saw direct action as available to both workers and owners, for example strikes for the former and lock-outs for the latter. The action should involve some kind of economic power, for example, workers on strike are using the resource of their labor (which their employers need) to assert demands or voice protest. Direct action may involve civil disobedience.

Non-violent direct action (NVDA) was endorsed by Gandhi, working for independence in India, and Martin Luther King for the civil rights movement in the USA.

In globalization, direct action most often refers to the activities of those grouped loosely together as "antiglobalizers."

Note that some groups take "Direct Action" as a name in homage to the general idea, but they will have a more specific ideological program.

See also: **antiglobalization**

Further reading: Carter 2004; Mellor 1920; Starr 2005

DISCONNECTED CONTIGUITY

A term coined by Albrow (1996) to describe the relationships between people who inhabit the same space (they exist contiguously, or, next to each other), but do not have traditional relationships with each other and are therefore disconnected from each other. This concept fits well into Giddens' modern world landscape (as opposed to traditional life).

See also: **civil inattention, modernity, risk, trust**

DISCREPANT COSMOPOLITANISM

A term coined by the anthropologist James Clifford to capture the paradox of modern living in which people are moving and migratory (modernity as a "travelling culture") yet at the same time linked to the local in various (often contradictory) ways. It is perhaps best described as a kind of constant alienation or uneasiness brought about by modern conditions of living and the imperative of individualization. This concept draws attention to that fact that while **cosmopolitanism** is usually seen as the preserve of the voluntarily mobile, there are other populations who are forced by circumstance, power or other people to move as well. Further, local environments can change so much that even staying in the same place is in effect to be moved into a foreign place. It is worth remembering that the "travelling culture" refers to mobility of individuals as well as things, ideas and cultural practices. That is, one is destined to "travel" and juggle the demands of the modern world even if one never actually moves.

See also: **cosmopolitan democracy, digital nomads, offshoring, service work**

Further reading: Clifford 1997; Robbins 1992

DISORGANIZED CAPITALISM

Disorganized capitalism stands in contrast to the organized **capitalism** of the twentieth century. This new realization of capitalism is linked both to **reflexive modernization** and to the **network society**.

Disorganized capitalism is a phrase attributable to Lash and Urry (1987) and can be seen as a virtual synonym for **global capitalism**. The "disorganized" is significant because Weber and **Marx** held that capitalism tends to increase organization. In globalization, instead of **nation-states** being the main agents of trade and financial flows at a global level, other actors are now involved (**TNCs,** and banks for example). One of the results of this is, arguably, an increasing disparity between those gaining and those losing in terms of economics. Capitalism is "disorganized" in the sense that the nation-state cannot regulate the global flows of commodities and finance. Nation-states are simply players in the global scene; they don't absolutely control corporations, the financial sector or human resources. As a result, some nations are ill-equipped to provide protection from any downturn in economic performance, and thus their populations are liable to economic depressions, unemployment and in some cases, famine. Institutions of global financial governance (the **WTO**, the **World Bank** and the **IMF**) are also not adequately equipped to deal with such problems in an effective or timely manner.

Lash and Urry (1987) argue that the period of disorganized capitalism is centered on the production of signs rather than things. Thus **lifestyle** choices especially with respect to consumption are important. The intense effort that firms put into marketing their goods, brand management and brand loyalty are all typical of this move from things to signs. Lash notes that "An increasing proportion of our social interactions and communicative interchanges are going on external to institutions." (1994b: 209) in a manner not dissimilar to the concept of **global sub-politics**.

Disorganized capitalism is essentially what the geographer David Harvey calls **post-Fordism**, but is related not only to the production of goods and the organization of such industry, but also to how people consume and indeed live in a post-traditional society.

See also: **capitalism, cultural economy, lifestyle, network society, reflexive modernization/modernity, simulacrum**

Further reading: Beck 2000; Lash 1994b; Offe 1985

DISTANT PROXIMITIES

A phrase coined by political theorist James Rosenau and explored in the book of the same name (2003). Rosenau essentially asks what globalization means now, post-Cold War, and indeed post-September 11. The concept of distant proximities takes into account both the macro and the micro level. It captures the dynamic of, for example, the **TNC** and the (arguably declining) **nation–state** at the macro level as well as the important influence of **NGO**s, **civil society** and individuals at the micro levels. He considers "globalization as a concept" insufficient to "organize understanding of world affairs" (2003: 3). He argues that

> the best way to grasp world affairs today requires viewing them as an endless series of distant proximities in which the forces pressing for greater globalization and those inducing greater localization interactively play themselves out. To do otherwise, to focus only on globalizing dynamics, or only on localizing dynamics, is to risk overlooking what makes events unfold as they do.
>
> (2003: 4)

The concept of distant proximities captures both the integrative and fragmentive aspects of living in a world where we are connected to people, places and events which may be physically distant. Indeed it is fragmentation that Rosenau wants to put at the center of discussion and debate. "Fragmentation" is "intended to suggest the pervasive interaction between fragmenting and integrating dynamics unfolding at every level of community" (2003: 11) The idea of distant proximities is thus related to the concept of the collapse of time and space, the **global village** and **transnational** practices.

See also: **complexity theory, glocal/glocalization, homogenization, migration, re-embedding, risk, time-space compression**

Further reading: Benjamin 2001; Friedman 2000; Robertson 1995; Schierup 1998

DIVERGENCE/CONVERGENCE

See: **homogenization, heterogeneity**

DIVIDED SELF

The *Divided Self* is the name of a book by the psychiatrist Ronald David Laing (1960) which seeks to understand mental illness in the context of existential philosophy. Laing opens the book,

> The term schizoid refers to an individual the totality of whose experience is split in two main ways: in the first place, there is a rent in his relation with his world and, in the second, there is a disruption of his relation with himself.

The phrase sometimes occurs in globalization studies to describe the situation of people who feel alienated from themselves and their environment because of processes associated with globalization. It is a relevant term in globalization studies because it focuses on how people experience the processes of globalization at a local level.

See also: **globalization from below**

DOWNSIZING

This is a strategy used in business to enact the belief that the more efficient and productive a workforce or corporation is, the better. It usually involves reducing the workforce of a corporation or selling a part of a corporation. It is possible to downsize too much and lose corporate expertise and culture (this is sometimes called "corporate anorexia"). It is a strategy that often involves filling gaps in expertise by hiring employees on a fixed contract, and is not confined to the private sector. It can also be seen as a kind of risk management.

See also: **neoliberalism, offshoring, risk**

Further reading: Danaher 1997

73

ECONOMIC LIBERALIZATION

Economic liberalization is a term used to refer to a comprehensive program of economic policies designed to deregulate national economies. Economic liberalization marks a move away from high levels of government involvement and regulation of the economy, considerable state ownership of infrastructure and trading activities, and high tariff protection of internally manufactured goods through import substitution towards low levels of government involvement in, and regulation of the economy. Strategies to liberalize economies have included: reducing the fiscal deficit, broadening of the tax base, deflation policies, labor market deregulation, increasing efficiency in the economy and corporatization, then selling off of government assets. Economic liberalization is a means to bring about global markets as it pulls down institutional barriers to free trade. In some quarters economic liberalization is seen as a necessary and positive economic reform that enables **nation–states** and their economies to step up to the demands and challenges of global markets by rendering internal economies and workforces more flexible. Others regard economic liberalization as a deliberate strategy to reduce the role of the state in society, and is an ideology used to push for reforms to drastically cut public spending on social welfare, health and education and a more general move to **privatization**.

See also: **global labor markets, protectionism (economic)**

Further reading: Kelsey 1995; Wolf 2004

RM

ECOTOURISM

Coined by Hector Ceballos-Lascuráin in 1983, the term ecotourism is a combination of the words ecology and tourism (also referred to as responsible tourism or sustainable tourism). It is a type of tourism where people visit sites of ecological or environmental interest, often to take part in conservation work or observe nature and/or wildlife, frequently with a loosely defined educational agenda. The term also incorporates the principle of responsibility towards the environment, and ensures that the trip makes only minimal impact on the places and people visited. This can include actions such as tourists being careful with the amount of water they use in areas where it is scarce, and disposing of their rubbish responsibly. As a form of sustainable tourism, ecotourism should also involve contributing to the local community and economy, e.g. patronizing **fair trade** organizations, staying in small locally owned hotels and ensuring that the people working in the tourism industry are properly treated and remunerated. This contributes to the sustainability of the tourism business. Having contact with host populations and respecting their cultures and way of life are also important features of ecotourism. Ecotourists are encouraged to remember that their holiday destination is someone else's home. Ecotourism operators often have names including terms such as "green" or "planet," thus emphasizing the idea of global responsibility, following the motto: "leave only footprints and take only memories." Ecotourism is the fastest growing sector of the tourism market.

Further reading: The International Ecotourism Society, United Nations Environment Programme, Weaver 2001

SL

EMBEDDED JOURNALISTS

Embedded journalist was the term given to journalists in the second Gulf War of 2003 who signed a contract with US and British military. In exchange for partial journalistic freedom, access was given to military events and the use of accommodation and transport. They were also promised protection from enemy gunfire and given unprecedented access to combat. In effect, embedded journalists experienced the war side by side with the soldiers and were free to report, in theory, events as they unfolded.

Such a relationship had advantages and disadvantages. On one level, reporters' closeness to the military meant that they could empathize with the particular unit they were assigned to. However, this very closeness attracted the criticism that journalistic objectivity was sacrificed and that reports lacked context. Television viewers saw a highly stylized state of war where the coalition forces directed the action and only the allied perspective was considered in any detail. A perceived consequence of reliance on embeds for news was a lack of critical analysis.

This is not to say that the media was entirely happy with their lot. Many reporters felt it necessary to inform their audience that they were only relaying what the military was allowing them to.

Those reporters not embedded, referred to as "unilaterals," were denied the special treatments afforded to the embeds. They had the freedom of movement unavailable to their embedded colleagues and were often met with the open hostility by the military.

See also: **CNN effect**

Further reading: Tumber and Palmer 2004

JJ

EMBEDDING

See: **Re-embedding**

EMBODIMENT

Strictly, this is the philosophical theory that the body is part of the self, that is, an emphasis on the experience of being human as profoundly physical. In this sense it is related to phenomenology which takes phenomena, intuitive experience as its starting point. It is best understood by considering it in contrast to dualist theories, such as Descartes mind/body division, which sees the thinking mind as separate from the physical body. This has implications for various disciplines. Lakoff and Johnson (1999), for example, working in the field of linguistics, argue that the physical experience of the world affects language and thought in structured ways. The educational theorist Grumet writes, "It is not 'I think therefore I am'; rather it is because I am embodied and situated that I think in particular ways" (1990: 336).

In the field of globalization studies, embodiment is most likely to be related to tourism and, to a lesser extent, culture. The concepts of bodily display and corporeal travel rely on a foregrounding of the physical body in the tourist experience.

Also in relation to globalization, and indeed generally, embodiment is also used in a nontechnical sense to refer to an example of an abstract notion. For example, one might say that global institutions such as the **IMF** and the **World Bank** are embodiments of globalization.

See also: **bodily display**

Further reading: Csordas 1990; Fern Haber and Weiss 1999; Merleau-Ponty 1974; Urry 1990

EMPIRE

Talk of empire related to globalization is not usually about the empires of the colonial period. While such use of empire is certainly linked to debates about **cultural imperialism** and indeed capitalist exploitation, this kind of empire is related to the rise and prominence of the **nation-state**. Despite some arguments to the contrary, proponents of this usage of empire maintain that the nation-state is alive and well. The question is rather how much power do they have, and who holds the residue.

This concept of empire comes specifically from the book of the same name by Hardt and Negri (2000). For Hardt and Negri, empire is a new, global social, political and economic order. It is one with no center of control. And while they accept the power of the United States, for example, they also point to global institutions, nations and transnational entities as having power in this new system. It is not a system that is about to arise, they consider empire to be descriptive. This does not mean that there are not implications for, or calls to, future action. One of the groups with power is the multitude. As such, multitude can be seen as a reworking of the notion of "working class" which is considered by some to be outdated. The connection can be drawn at least on the basis that *Empire* is considered a post-Marxist text.

Despite contemporary capitalism seeming impervious to anti-systemic challenge, empire is seen as being vulnerable at all points to a variety of forms of resistance. As such empire is seen as offering major potentials for revolutionary change and liberation. Hardt and Negri see communication, both face to face and facilitated by technology, as essential to the multitude and challenging power.

See also: **colonialism, communicative rationality, Marx/Marxism, Transnational Corporation (TNC)**

Further reading: Johnson 2004

ENCLAVE

In political geography, an enclave is simply a territory completely surrounded by another. Globalization studies also refer to language enclaves and **lifestyle enclaves**. A language enclave (also sometimes called a "language island") exists where a group of people speaking one language are completely surrounded by those with another language. Note this is not quite the same as intermingled languages (a case of multilingual communities).

The phrase "lifestyle enclave" (Bellah *et al.* 1985) is also used to refer to "the way sociality may be configured in such a way which is neither total, functional not local and yet serves as a vital reference point for its adherents" (Albrow 1996: 156). In this case, the group (the lifestyle enclave) is not territorially defined but rather character- ized by the particular beliefs or practices central to their life and identity. Thus, as Albrow points out, this often refers to religious groups. At the same time, in some cases such lifestyle enclaves can be spatially defined in the sense above (e.g. communes, religious institutions such as monasteries).

See also: **pluralism**

ENCLAVED COMMODITIES

A concept from Appadurai referring to the way in which commod- ities may have restricted value, that is, they only carry value of a monetary or social kind in limited contexts. "[W]hereas enclaving seeks to protect certain things from commoditization, diversion fre- quently is aimed at drawing protected things into the zone of com- moditization" (Appadurai 1986: 25–26). Featherstone (1995) points out the problems of some enclaved commodities especially in respect of high culture, "From one perspective, artistic and intellectual goods are enclaved commodities whose capacity to move around in the social space is limited by their ascribed sacred qualities" (23). For high culture to remain "high" and exclusive, these commodities cannot be allowed to circulate generally or purely on the basis of economic worth: then the objects become commodities only and lose their "scared" and symbolic qualities.

Featherstone (ibid.) also points out the problems associated with overproduction. The example of fake luxury goods (such as designer handbags) makes the point nicely. An authentic Chanel handbag has a certain symbolic and economic value. A copy threatens these sacred (and exclusive) commodities.

See also: **autonomization of culture, aura (of cultural phenomenon), commodity candidacy, commodity chain, lifestyle, simulacrum**

END OF HISTORY

The "end of history" is an often misunderstood concept coming directly from two of Francis Fukuyama's works, "The End of History" (1989) and *The End of History and the Last Man* (1992). That we are living at the "end of history" is often taken literally to mean that history is finished in the sense that (historic) events will stop happening. Fukuyama's argument was rather that we have arrived "at the end point of mankind's ideological evolution and universalization of Western liberal democracy as the final form of human government" (1989). Essentially Fukuyama argues that **democracy** is here to stay as the dominant political order, and will in the long-term only become more prevalent. Further, he sees that trade liberalization has provided "unprecedented levels of material prosperity" globally. Fukuyama argues for a teleological view of history, one that culminates in democracy.

This is rather a different view to that of **Marxism** in that the end of history there is the presence of a communist state. But Marx (and Hegel) had a concept of the "end of history" meaning, as Fukuyama glosses it, "that there would be no further progress in the development of underlying principles and institutions, because all of the really big questions had been settled" (1992: xii).

Tomlinson sees Fukuyama's claims as amounting "to an acceptance of the eternal condition of modernity" (1999: 44). Albrow puts it thus, "modernity cannot imagine the future except as its own continuation, or else chaos" (1996: 9). This is not a view that all share.

See also: **clash of civilizations, modernity**

Further reading: Baudrillard 1994a; Gray 1998

EPISTEMIC COMMUNITIES

Epistemic communities consist of people who share the same views about knowledge and how it is possible to know things (epistemology). The term was usually applied to networks of scientists, and to faith in scientific method generally (the latter especially in the work of **Marx**), but it has been used in many disciplines, from international relations to sociology, and can be generally understood as a mindset, though this does not capture the details of particular epistemic communities. Some epistemic communities, exactly because of their expertise and knowledge, have a certain power in the realm of, for example, international politics and national policy decisions. The epistemic community of neoliberal economics, for example, has a great deal of influence in many Western governments. Epistemic communities are distinguished from other groups, like interest groups, by the fact they share a knowledge base, a set of causal and principled beliefs and a common enterprise.

In the context of globalization, the expertise that epistemic communities provide is required because of the **risk** and uncertainty associated with globalization.

The term appears to owe at least some of its currency to the work of Peter M. Haas (1992) in the field of international relations (IR). It is worth examining some of the features of epistemic communities in this field as it is closely linked to global politics and policy.

Haas argues that epistemic communities help states to identify their interests by "framing the issues of collective debate, proposing specific policies, and identifying salient points of negotiation" (1992: 2). An epistemic community is particularly defined in IR as "a network of professionals with recognized expertise and competence in a particular domain and an authoritative claim to policy-relevant knowledge within that domain or issue-area" (1992: 3).

While the theory assumes that states are uncertainty minimisers, it is not clear that epistemic communities will always have access to policy-setting agendas. The influence of **experts** on state decision-making depends very much on particular political realities. It also depends on whether the epistemic community is somehow sited within the state **bureaucracy** or outside it. It is worth remembering that an epistemic community in this sense has to have a form of expertise which is both validated and valued by the wider community in which it is placed. That is to say, an epistemic community is not powerful simply because it is an epistemic community.

Foucault's notion of the episteme, from which the concept of epistemic community was developed, is arguably more like Thomas Kuhn's paradigm than an epistemic community. Foucault argues that each period of history has a particular episteme which defines it; when it changes it does so relatively suddenly, in the manner of Kuhn's paradigm shift or an axial shift. Foucault's episteme also has the advantage of drawing attention to that fact that some epistemes and their related discourses will be generally acceptable, that is, hegemonic, and others will be marginalized. In the *History of Sexuality*

Foucault writes, "discourse can be both an instrument and an effect of power, but also a hindrance, a stumbling-block, a point of resistance and a starting point for an opposing strategy" (1990: 110)

See also: **axial period, experts/expert systems, risk**

Further reading: Foucault 1974, 1975; Knorr Cetina 1999; Ruggie 1999

EPISTEMIC VIOLENCE

The feminist theorist Gayatri Chakravorty Spivak uses this phrase to describe the way in which in a period of (post) **colonialism**, the **subaltern** is silenced both by the colonizers and the indigenous power groups (1988). The concept in full is usually the "epistemic violence of imperialism." Naturally this silence does not have to be literal. Spivak's point is that the historical effects of colonialism remove any position from which the subaltern can be heard. While epistemic violence is particularly salient to the postcolonial setting, it, or something like it, is comparable to the silencing of some voices as a result of any hegemonic ideology.

See also: **colonialism, cultural imperialism**

ESSENTIALISM

A philosophical school of thought that sees things and people as having a defining, underlying and unchanging core of features, that is, an essence. It is most often used to refer to conceptions of what people and individuals are.

See also: **postmodernism**

ETHNIC DIVERSITY

See: **colonialism, cultural imperialism, ethnocide, homogenization**

ETHNIC TOURISM

See: **cultural tourism**

ETHNOCENTRISM

This term is usually applied as a critique of analytical work which privileges the author's culture over any other. Often this is a reaction to cultural difference. Ethnocentrism can occur at the national, ethnic or even other subgroup level. Essentially, it is the recognition of difference (us vs. them) with a prioritizing of the self's group. Tomlinson sees the ethnocentrism of modernity as reflexive, "dependent on the cultural 'other' to sustain myths of cultural superiority" (1999: 74).

Tomlinson identifies a "naiv ethnocentrism" characteristic of people who have little contact with an outside world of different cultures (1999).

See also: **cosmopolitanism, cultural imperialism**

Further reading: Said 1978

ETHNOCIDE

Analogous to genocide, ethnocide refers to actions which seek to destroy an ethnicity. While genocide is a recognized crime against humanity (since 1948, with the promulgation of the Convention on the Prevention and Punishment of the Crime of Genocide) and generally refers to physically killing members of a race, ethnocide can be perpetrated in less obviously violent ways. Language discrimination, **cultural imperialism**, and **homogenization** generally can all be understood as allowing the extinction of cultures to take place. Ethnocide is also referred to as cultural genocide or culturecide.

See also: **ethnolinguistic**

ETHNOLINGUISTIC

The term ethnolinguistic incorporates the concepts of ethnicity, culture and language, and, as such, has a wide variety of applications as a branch of anthropology or the sociology of language. It is argued that the dimensions of ethnicity, culture and language form essential aspects of both individual and group identity. For some (e.g. Joshua Fishman), language is viewed as the defining characteristic of group identity, as members can choose to use it (or not). Studying the relative vitality (demography, status and institutional support) of ethnolinguistic groups can be a useful way of assessing the social structure of multiethnic and multicultural communities and of predicting future group behavior. For example, groups perceiving their language and culture to be under threat may take steps to protect them, as in Québec. With the advent of the internet, it has become easier for diasporic groups to maintain close links with their communities of origin.

See also: **diaspora, global English**

Further reading: Landry and Allard 1994

SL

EUROPEAN UNION (EU)

The European Union is an organization established in 1993 following the ratification of the Maastricht Treaty (1992), comprising 25 member states with a total population of 461.5 million. Historically, European integration traces back to efforts of reconstruction after 1945, when political leaders looked for ways to overcome the stalemate of hostile nationalisms (above all: reconcile France and Germany), guarantee stability and prosperity in Europe and also to regain political power. In 1957, the signing of the Treaty of Rome established those structures which characterize the EU's institutions until today, namely a common Court of Justice, an Assembly (since 1987: the European Parliament), and a Commission and Council of Ministers. In subsequent decades, European integration was mainly marked by the gradual evolution towards a common market: integrating or replacing the policies of individual member states, "harmonizing" legislation, extending action to new areas of competence. At the same time, a series of *enlargements* expanded membership: the United Kingdom, Ireland and Denmark joined in 1973, Greece in 1981, Spain and Portugal in 1986. With the end of the Cold War, Europe's political landscape changed dramatically again: in 1995, three neutral countries joined the EU (Sweden, Austria, Finland), and in 2004, eight former Soviet bloc states along with Malta and Cyprus followed. Such widening was paralleled by deepening, i.e. a process of profound institutional reform leading to increasingly "**state**-like" features of the EU. The EU's common market ensures the free circulation of goods, persons, services and capital, as well as a common commercial policy. Twelve countries are also members of the European Economic and Monetary Union and share a single currency, the Euro. In a number of other policy areas, ranging from agriculture to education, police cooperation or social policy, the EU has additional expertise and is coordinating or supplementing the actions of the member states; it thus administrates a budget of more than 100 billion Euros. Since the 1990s, the EU is also developing a Common Foreign and Security Policy. However, many of the EU's policies as well as its institutional framework are in a state of ongoing change and renegotiation.

Many **civil society** actors criticize the EU as a facilitator of globalization, while others see in it a possible response to global challenges. Such contesting views give evidence of widespread disorientation and insecurity due to the massive changes brought about by European integration. While policy-making has been ever more Europeanized, the workings and meaning of EU politics are opaque to the majority of the population, causing people to question their legitimacy (a "legitimacy deficit"). At the same time, transferring the model of national **democracy** to the European level is strongly contested, not only for the problem of size, but also for repeating the vices of **nationalism** at a higher level. Thus, while the expectations in the EU as providing stability and meeting economic challenges are rising, at the same time the contingency of the political construction of Europe comes to the fore, and while free competition accelerates social change, the fabric of **trust**, tolerance and social solidarity that **liberal democracy** is built upon seems increasingly fragile.

See also: **Europeanization, legitimation crisis**

Further reading: McCormick 2002

FO

EUROPEANIZATION

Europeanization has become a popular term in public discourse since the 1990s when the "integration process" in Europe gained new momentum and the foundations and finality of the "European project" were increasingly an issue in public debates. It should be noted that all these terms, at one level, see "Europe" and "European" as unproblematic concepts.

A variety of phenomena and processes have been described as "Europeanization," among which are: (a) the successive enlargement of the **European Union's (EU)** boundaries; (b) the continuous agglomeration of organizational and legal structures of vertical (hierarchical) authority at a European level; (c) a process of modernization and **homogenization**; (d) the exporting of forms of governance that are typical of the European Union; and (e) effects on domestic political systems brought about by something "European" (usually something institutional or legal).

In the social sciences, the bulk of the literature on Europeanization understood the term in the last way. For instance, Goetz and Hix (2000: 27) define it as "a process of change in national institutional and policy practices that can be attributed to European integration." Such research focus has become pertinent due to the growing relative importance of legislation and structures of governance at the EU level. Since the Single European Act (1987), the scope of the EU has grown considerably, and its output of decisions has increased. Thus, the *Acquis communautaire* (the legislation in force at a given moment and which new members have to adopt) now extends to some 60,000 pages, and about half of the legislation passed by member states' parliaments is considered to be implementation of legal acts decided in "Brussels" (where the headquarters of the EU is).

In terms of debates around globalization, the above trends have been rather critically discussed. In the course of Europeanization (most clearly identifiable in the formation of the EU and what followed), it is argued, the legislative branch became increasingly dominated by the executive, since governments are able to bypass the domestic political arena by implementing legislation at the European level. As a result, the quality of **democracy** in the member states is eroded, while at the EU level no adequate mechanisms for democratic control and participation exist. This so-called "democratic deficit" is not characteristic only of the EU, but is a problem for all organizations of **global governance** which make important decisions without direct democratic legitimacy or even behind closed doors (the most well-known for such secretive practices being the **WTO**). In those cases, there are no official institutional arenas where popular discontent and demands can be articulated and transformed within a regular political process. Consequently, the gap between elites and institutions on the one hand and citizens and their expectations on the other hand widens: the former are no longer perceived as agents of the self-government of "We, the people," but as representing alien forces and pressures. At the same time, the growing complexity of contemporary societies is calling for more specialization and expert knowledge in order to guarantee efficient governance. Clearly, institutional creativity is needed to once again reconcile those opposing requirements, the capability for efficient political action on the one hand, and democratic representation, participation and control on the other.

See also: **democracy, European Union, modernity**

Further reading: Goetz and Hix 2000; Vink 2002

FO

EXCHANGE VALUE

From **Marx** and part of a trio of values that a commodity can have: value, use value and exchange value. The exchange value is roughly the price of an object, that is, what needs to be given for it. This does not necessarily relate to any practical value (use value) or the labor value it represents (value). In an age of **lifestyle** products and branding, the exchange value of some consumer goods is much higher than its use value or value. At the same time, **fair trade** enterprises attempt to achieve an exchange value (price) appropriate to the work that has produced the commodity.

"Exchange value" may also be used for currency and their relative worth to other currencies, where exchange value is the same as exchange rate.

See also: **commodification, cultural capital, surplus value**

Further reading: Beasley-Murray 2000

EXPERTS/EXPERT SYSTEMS

Expert systems, a notion from Giddens and related work, are decision-making systems of particular kinds. Definitions of such systems vary, but they usually "include technology, but also any form of expert knowledge that substitutes for indigenous local arts or capacities" (1994b: 95). It is important to know that Giddens often uses "expert systems" to mean the experts who use such systems, whether they be concrete systems (like a weather prediction program) or theoretical systems (like neoliberal economics).

While these expert systems can be questioned, according to Giddens there is no way of opting out of them (1990: 84). Thus **trust** is intimately bound up with **risk** as we count on experts (however unreliable) to negotiate decisions about future and thus risk. So, for example, because we don't know how to predict the weather ourselves we trust weather reports on television. In addition, this expert system can only be accessed by us through the expert weather forecasters, however, even they do not control the prediction system; no one person controls the expert system.

See also: **abstract systems, modernity, re-embedding, risk**

Further reading: Dijkstra *et al.* 1998; Dreyfus and Dreyfus 1985

EXPORT PROCESSING ZONE (EPZ)

Variously known as export oriented zone, special economic zone, free trade zone.

These areas (zones) are subject to different laws than the rest of the country in which they are situated. This is exactly to encourage **Foreign Direct Investment** (**FDI**). The goods manufactured in these zones are primarily intended for export which in economic development terms is supposed to improve a country's international economic standing and also trickle down such that the country as a whole benefits. Indeed, there is usually a requirement to export the goods manufactured. At the same time, there are special export tariffs and taxes (usually none) which are agreed upon. The different laws will usually include tax incentives, providing factories, and relaxing environmental and workers' rights regulations for foreign investors. They are usually sited in developing countries.

Much controversy has erupted over workers' rights in such zones. Further, the proliferation of such zones means that foreign investors can take advantage of incentives (which are usually time capped) and then move elsewhere, or simply reform as a "new" company.

See also: **free trade, income polarization**

Further reading: Kariuki and Smith 2004

EXTRA-LEGAL ECONOMY

Term coined by Hernando de Soto (2000), Peruvian economist and president of the think tank Institute for Liberty and Democracy

87

(ILD). De Soto argues that at least one of the reasons **capitalism** works in the West is a formalized property ownership system in which assets can be used to guarantee loans and thus access capital. Conversely, in countries where capitalism is not "working," people participate in an extra-legal economy. Often this may be known as a black or gray market depending on the degree of illegality involved. Such an economy is not formally recognized, just as their property rights are not formally recognized. Thus people in an extra-legal economy cannot use their employment and assets to gain access to further credit. In addition, because they are not registered with a formal state infrastructure, they are not paying taxes, and are difficult to trace.

See also: **capitalism, formal/informal economies, world systems theory**

Further reading: De Soto 1989

FAIR TRADE/FREE TRADE

This term has a long history meaning anything from legal trade to its exact opposite, that is, smuggling (in the eighteenth century). In the nineteenth century it came to mean bilateral free trade. Thus fair trade between or among nations occurred when one's goods were accepted without tariff or restriction and that one received others' goods in the same way. This is now normally referred to as free trade. A number of treaties and agreements can be seen as underpinning the principles of free trade; the UN declaration of human rights, various International Labor Organization (ILO) agreements on labor and working conditions as well as environmental treaties. The more contemporary, and usual meaning of fair trade is about ethical trade, from an economic, development and environmental point of view.

In relation to free trade, if a government passes legislation which restricts the type of products which are allowed into the market and which seeks to protect the environment or a certain species of animal, for example, this needs to be done in accordance with rules of international trade. There are a number of international law principles of free trade, one of the most central being that of the "most favored nation."

Perhaps the most famous of such cases was when the US passed legislation to protect a certain kind of turtle often killed in the process of shrimp fishing; it is commonly known as the "shrimp–turtle" case. As a result, the US refused to accept shrimp or shrimp products that were not obtained by methods considered safe for the turtles.

The case was brought before the **WTO**'s Dispute Settlement Board (and under appeal to the Appellate Body). In 1998 the protective measure was found to be unjustified because "this measure has been applied by the United States in a manner which constitutes arbitrary and unjustifiable discrimination between Members of the WTO … " (www.wto.org). The Appellate Body was adamant that they had not decided "that the protection and preservation of the environment is of no significance to the Members of the WTO" nor "that the sovereign nations that are Members of the WTO cannot adopt effective measures to protect endangered species, such as sea turtles" again, nor that "sovereign states should not act together bilaterally, plurilaterally or multilaterally, either within the WTO or in other international fora, to protect endangered species or to otherwise protect the environment" (185).

Fair trade, as it is more usually used, ethical trade, is said not to impact on international and national trading laws. Rather, it usually supplements them. Thus questions of what nations can allow into their markets are deferred to the decision of the consumer. Advocates for fair trade argue that given labeling conventions, consumers are free to choose fair trade products, thus such products are not given an advantage over other comparable products. The consumer, they argue, is then guaranteed quality as well as supporting reasonable working conditions, local development, fair prices for producers and environmental protection. Perhaps the best known examples of fair trade are coffee and tea. However, many other goods are being produced and marketed in this way, often in conjunction with development agencies such as OXFAM who help develop fair production and also serve as distributors of products. Especially in the case of OXFAM, goods are not limited to coffee and chocolate, but extend to crafts, paper products, toys, glassware and cloth.

Fair-trade as one word is a trademark of Fair-trade Labeling Organizations International, which seeks to promote fair trade.

See also: **human rights, NGO, protectionism (economic)**

Further reading: Barratt Brown 1993; Bovard 1991; Littrell and Dickson 1999

FALSE CONSCIOUSNESS

False consciousness means an inability (or unwillingness) to see things as they really are. It is most associated with Marxist theory particularly with false consciousness in respect of political and economic realties.

See also: **communities of fate, hegemony, ideology, Marx/Marxism**

Further reading: Rosen 1996

FALSE NEEDS

Generally related to **consumerism** and contrasted with **basic needs**. False needs are often thought essential because of the ideologies of consumerism and the indoctrinating power of commodities. The distinction is found in the work of Herbert Marcuse (1972) and Douglas Kellner (1983), but is implicit in any critique of unthinking consumption. While Marcuse argues that there is a small set of basic physiological needs that will always qualify as needs, Kellner wants to make finer distinctions and judge commodities on the basis of them being "beneficial, life enhancing and useful" (1983: 71).

See also: **basic needs, consumption rituals, false consciousness, lifestyle**

Further reading: Baudrillard 1975; Kellner 1984; Lefebvre 1971; Turner 1984

FAMILY WAGE (DECLINE OF)

This term represents the concept that an employee at the head of a household is paid more (in order to support their dependents) than an employee who lives alone or is dependent on another person. The concept of a family wage originated in an attempt to lessen the effect of changes created by the industrial revolution on families whose members were leaving the home for their employment. Family wage has always been a site for political struggle for the left, the right and **feminism**. Agitation in favor of a "family wage" has declined since the mid twentieth century, and the more usual term for progressive organizers today is "living wage." Its decline is linked to the influence of second wave feminism and the weakening of worker organizations and massive influx of women into paid employment associated with the rise of **neoliberalism** and globalization.

See also: **economic liberalization, feminization of the workforce, wage earner welfare states**

Further reading: Barrett and Mackintosh 1982; Kingfisher 2002; Lewis 2001

RM

FEMINISM

It is important to remember that feminism is not a singular way of thinking or of acting and should not be treated as a monolithic movement or theory, nor can it be separated from other social movements (Waterman 2002). Here, feminism is considered only in respect of globalization. Vargas writes, "Different feminisms are contributing their multiple experiences and relations to this process [of globalization and its negotiation]" (2003: 908). In some ways, it is difficult to distinguish the effects of globalization on feminism because of the changing nature of women's lives at roughly the same time as one might date the start of globalization. In addition, the vastly different experiences of women and attitudes towards equality between men and women make it difficult to provide a global definition of feminism. The 1995 UN Beijing Conference on Women was an important turning point in establishing a better understanding of the global position of women. Women from the Global South worked hard to encourage Western feminists to embrace not just the problems, but the voices of women in these countries.

Feminism can be seen as one of the driving forces in what some call antiglobalizing forces because improving women's rights are often the underlying factor in securing further human rights and workers' rights as well as improving civil participation and access to local and international fora. The growing importance of **human rights** at a local and global level coincides with feminist goals and has been increasingly used as a tool of articulation in naming oppression (Walby 2002).

Walby discusses the struggle of feminism with the turn to human rights in the context of feminism's ongoing challenge to "theorize differences between women while not reifying them and simultaneously addressing commonalities" (2002: 535). In the international arena significant pieces of legislation have acknowledged the common experiences of women. In 2001 mass rape and sexual enslavement, a horrific mode of human rights abuse, was recognized as a "war crime" and a crime against humanity. That this finally occurred was

91

due to the efforts of women's movements, their advocacy and tireless efforts. Walby also reminds us that human rights in a global community are not only the traditionally Western civil and political rights, but also increasingly economic and social. This is so even in the West, where wage gaps, gendered labor, domestic violence and general discrimination against women persists.

The importance of human rights as a discursive mode and legal imperative is arguably due to global institutions, notably the United Nations. This is one of the formal sides of globalization. At the same time, globalization has also "facilitated new spaces, institutions and rhetoric" (Walby 2002) in human rights and institutions but also at local and informal levels. Thus women have access to "traditional" forms of power, such as the opportunity to stand for election or hold positions of power in the corporate sector, but also that feminist networks are able to form, communicate and coordinate action in innovative and flexible ways. Part of this is certainly tied to technological advancement, however the question of access to global print media is not even or assured (Youngs 2001).

Further, women are still seen primarily as doing emotional, caring and private domestic work, notwithstanding their contribution to the public economy. Indeed, Ralston Saul (2005) asks what happened to the labor women contribute to the market; he concludes that it has been "inflated away" (148).

While some argue that feminism is in abeyance, Walby argues that it has simply reframed itself in terms of an "inclusionary rather than anti-system discourse" (2002: 546). Indeed, some terms of globalization, especially social and cultural aspects, are well placed to describe changes in feminist organization. Networks, flows, glocalization and hybridity suggest the context sensitive way feminists now (and perhaps always) have worked. Rather than being a single **epistemic community**, Walby argues, "the basis of claims for justice remains varied" (2002: 547) exactly because even though feminists take advantage of aspects of globalization they are well aware that (for women especially) the world is not yet a utopian **global village**.

See also: **antiglobalization, feminization of the workforce, heterogeneity, hybridity, network society, NGO**

Further reading: Braidotti 1994; Davies 1993; Feree and Hess 1995; Mies 1986; Peters and Wolper 1995; United Nations, Women Watch, United Nations Development Fund for Women

TB

FEMINIZATION OF THE WORKFORCE

Feminization of the workforce refers to the dramatic increase of women's participation in various areas of paid employment. Feminization of specific occupations is also linked to their proletarianization – "as the work becomes less skilled, it is cheaper for employers to employ women" (Abercrombie *et al.* 1994: 164). Feminization of the workforce also links to globalization, as the changing employment characteristics means that many more women are in the workforce, but are mostly employed in low-skilled, low-paid, insecure positions. There is a global pattern of the poorly paid international labor markets being made up of many more women (Kingfisher 2002).

See also: **global labor market**

Further reading: Fuentes and Ehrenreich 1981

RM

FETISHISM THEORY

See: **commodity fetishism, Marx/Marxism**

FINANCIALIZATION

Denotes the shift in power from manufacturing capital to finance capital which occurred since the 1970s. Historically it is linked to the break-down of the post-war regulation of money (e.g. the **Bretton Woods** system of fixed exchange rates). On a macroeconomic level the basis for financialization was laid by the deregulation of credit money and the liberalization of exchange rates which, in turn, underpinned the high interest rates that led to increasing public deficits in the 1980s as well as the general volatility of global financial markets with their recurring crises (e.g. Mexico 1994, East-Asia 1997, Russia 1998, Brazil 1998, Argentina 2001).

Financialization was also driven by changes in corporate governance (i.e. how companies behave and are regulated), at the same time as it crucially shaped corporate strategies. The global emergence of differentiated financial instruments (credit money, derivatives, the role of stock markets) led to the reorientation of corporate strategies to shareholder value. Competition is increasingly influenced by the requirements of global capital markets. Corporate strategies are geared towards high short-term profit requirements of shareholders and thus constitute a significant break with traditional stakeholder interests of long-term growth under product market competition. Financialization engenders continuous restructuring pressures, to **downsize** workforces in order to reduce labor costs, as well as concentration in product markets via mergers and acquisitions.

An important suggestion to limit the volatility of global financial markets (currently the daily turnover of the foreign exchange market is more than $1,500 billion) is via the so-called **Tobin tax**, a levy on financial transactions which would mainly affect short-term speculative transactions.

See also: **global governance, liberalization, post-Fordism**

Further reading: Duménil and Levy 2001; Froud *et al.* 2002; Helleiner 1995

NH

FOREIGN DIRECT INVESTMENT (FDI)

Foreign Direct Investment (FDI) is investment of productive capital in foreign operations, that is, money that actually goes towards an industry of some kind (not portfolio investment in foreign stock markets, which simply buys shares in companies or currencies) resulting in a controlling interest in those enterprises. The main source of FDI is multinational corporations (MNC); any theory of FDI is therefore closely linked to that of MNCs.

Initially, within neoclassical mainstream economics, the central question focussed on why FDI occurs in the first place. Under perfect competition FDI is a more expensive form of corporate expansion than exports or licensing, so what are the advantages of investing abroad? Hymer (1976) argued that MNCs are in fact not perfect competitors: MNCs would take into account higher costs of adapting to a foreign market in exchange for advantages stemming from the location and superior managerial techniques. Other factors identified in the debate relate to technology, the reduction of transaction costs and the nature of oligopolistic competition. Such arguments were synthesized by Dunning (1991) who became a vocal proponent of an "eclectic approach" to FDI, which is drawing on a range of different disciplines in order to theorize the determinants of FDI.

Another consideration relates to the effects of FDI, in particular on developing countries. Whereas FDI can contribute to an increase in the GDP and investment, it can also increase the import dependency, and subsequently the debt, of the recipient economy. The eclectic approach distinguishes between ownership- and country-specific factors in order to explain the variation of FDI across countries.

See also: **neoliberalism, Transnational Corporation (TNC)**

Further reading: Cantwell 1991; Dunning 1991; Hymer 1976; UNCTAD 2004

NH

FORMAL/INFORMAL ECONOMIES

The concept of a formal economy (or sector) refers to the employment of waged labor within a framework of rules and regulations, usually devised and implemented by the state, on working hours, minimum wages, health and safety at work, or the social security obligations of employers and employees. Jobs in the formal sector are relatively secure and in return for regular wages/salaries, individuals contribute to the public good via taxes on their earnings that are used to provide public services, such as health or education. This is the kind of employment that is generally associated with the mega–cities (and economies) in the developed market economies. The concept of a formal economy is generally widely understood and generally accepted. The notion of an informal economy (or sector), on the other hand, is still contested, but most commentators cite the International Labor Organization as "both the midwife and the principal international institutional home for the concept of the informal sector" (Bangasser 2000). There is general agreement that an informal economy incorporates legal and illegal activities and is a very significant part of the labor force in the mega-cities in the developing world. The formal and informal sectors are perceived as functioning independently of each other to a substantial degree, largely because firms in the primary sector have some market power which insulates them somewhat from competition, whereas those in the secondary sector face fierce competition. The concept of formal and informal economies is important to studies of globalization as it allows the analysis of transformations in the global labor market. For instance, understanding that there are formal and informal economies allows researchers to examine the increasing interdependence of formal and informal economies within and across nations; where women have entered the labor market (mostly into informal employment); the links between legal and illegal immigration and the formal and informal economy; and also how people survive economically, when formal sectors have been severely eroded.

See also: **feminization of the workforce, global labor market**

Further reading: Constable 1997; Hondagneu–Sotelo 2001

RM

FRAGMENTATION (SOCIAL)

Social fragmentation is used to denote transformations in the social fabric associated with technological, economic and societal changes and suggests that the world as we know it is breaking up. Social fragmentation is a contested concept within globalization studies. Some commentators believe that social fragmentation is the opposite of globalization (e.g. Clark 1997), while others see it as a contra-diction of globalization (e.g. Jones 2001). The concept of social fragmentation is also used more positively as an attempt to break up the fixedness and inevitability of the concept of the "social" in accounts of **neoliberalism**. This perspective is outlined by Rose, in "The death of the social? Re-figuring the territory of govern-ment" (1996a) where he talks of the refiguring of the territory of government away from the "social" as an entity toward the population and individual.

See also: **counter-narratives, de–governmentalization, territorialization (de & re)**

Further reading: Clark 1997; Jones 2001; Rose 1996a

RM

FRAGMENTED STATE

A term from political geography referring to a state which comprises discontinuous parts. May also be used to refer to the general decline of the **nation–state** in the sense of a nation being politically or cultu-rally fragmented.

96

FREE TRADE

See: **fair trade/free trade**

FUNDAMENTALISM

While the term fundamentalism has negative connotations, because of its association with various "terrorist" groups, fundamentalism can mean anything from a literal interpretation of (usually) scared texts, to an emphasis on tradition and also a privileged place for a particular form of knowledge (that it, and only it, is correct). Because fundamentalism works as a synomym for dogmatism and tradition, it is a label that could be applied to any number of ways of thinking. It tends to be used as a pejorative term, however.

Robins notes that the turn to fundamentalism in globalization is hardly surprising given the **postmodern** world of **reflexive modernity** in which we live. The changes of globalization may result in a turn "or return, to what are seen as traditional and more fundamental loyalties" (Robins 2003: 244). These changes need not be religious but also "national, regional, ethnic and territorial" (Robins 2003: 244). Giddens too points out that the appearance of fundamentalism is not "mysterious" (1994a: 100) as "it is nothing more or less than 'tradition in its traditional sense' though today embattled rather than in the ascendant" (1994a: 100). Yet such identity and community building is explicable *especially* in the face of such upheaval. Indeed Giddens sees fundamentalism as "in genuine dialogue with modernity" (1994a: 190).

The emergence of fundamentalism suggests a need to identify and respond to problems rather than to identify and defeat enemies. As Robins points out, "What we must recognize is the aspiration to create a space within global culture" (2003: 244) especially as places often claim to be tolerant, multicultural and cosmopolitan and are in practice not. The placelessness typical of global spaces hardly celebrates or accommodates difference. While identity is said to be fluid, reflexive and negotiable, some identities are easier to express than others. Giddens urges, "fundamentalisms need to be listened to by those whom they do not persuade" (1994a: 190).

See also: **clash of civilizations, nationalism, placeless geography**

Further reading: Almond 2003; Juergensmeyer 2003; Marty 1995; Robins 1997; Tariq 2003

FUTURIST/FUTUROLOGY/FUTURE STUDIES

A futurist can be a member of the twentieth century art movement called futurism. In globalization, however, a futurist is most likely to be someone in the philosophic or academic field of future studies. While predicting the future is the role of various practitioners including clairvoyants and astrologists, futurists are more experts than soothsayers.

While not strictly scientific, futurists will extrapolate into the future from observation of the present and recent past. Topics that futurologists deal with range from environmental issues (Toffler 1970) to status of the English language (Graddol 1997, 2006).

However, these practitioners are unlikely to call themselves futur-ologists but rather may opt for "consultant" (in particular fields), "think tank" (groups of experts, often following a clear ideological line) or even simply "expert." Such practitioners may hail from the private sector, especially in the fields of finance and economics. This is not to say that they are infallible, indeed futurists are concerned with **risk** and will often be allied (explicitly or otherwise) with one **expert system** or way of projecting future possibilities.

The influence of professional futurists on government policy and planning cannot be underestimated (and requires that their creden-tials and experience be scrutinized). One text (Bell and Strieber 2000) forecasting cataclysmic global warming was part of the basis of the Hollywood film *The Day After Tomorrow* (2004). This intersection of popular culture is symptomatic of the **hybridity** of contemporary culture. Unsurprisingly, there are also works which predict the demise of *global capitalism* (Gray 1998, Ralston Saul 2005).

Further, as experts are concerned with increasingly narrow domains, using them may make it more difficult to manage for the future in a holistic manner. One of the most fundamental conflicts in this respect is between economics and the environment. While an economic theory may base itself on axioms of unlimited natural resources, this is simply not physically possible. Further, economic "costings" routinely fail to take account of human and environmental costs. The deregulated airline industry has made low-cost flights available for the short- and long-haul market, consequently increasing the number of people using airplanes for travel. However, the cost to the environment in terms of carbon emissions is not accounted for in any conventional economic model.

At the same time, looking into the future is essential for risk management. Projections about future socioeconomic profiles based on longitudinal demographic data are necessary if public infra-structure is to keep up with changing societies. Censuses, for example, provide valuable data which can be used to plan for new hospitals, schools, transport and the like.

See also: **communities of fate, cultural fate**

Further reading: Gray 1998; Homer-Dixon 2001; Loye 1978; Ralston Saul 2005

G7/G8

The G7 is a group of nations, started in 1975, when the heads of state of six developed nations (hence G6) started meeting (at summits) to address political and economic concerns. With the addition of Canada in 1976, the familiar G7 was born. The G7 nations were France, US, Britain, Germany, Japan, Italy and Canada. Russia joined fully in 1998, turning G7 into G8, though was consulted post-summit from 1991. The summits deal primarily with international trade and political relations with developing countries. They also deal with such issues of terrorism, energy use, arms control and human rights abuses. The summits are held annually, though representatives of heads of state ("sherpas") meet throughout the year to discuss and negotiate ongoing issues and progress. While the summits are seen as important for heads of state to communicate and negotiate about these issues as well as build personal relationships, the summits have recently come into the spotlight as a target for protest and demonstration from **civil society**. By many, G8 is seen as embodying the spirit of globalization and global governance. Because of this, and because of the summits' focus on economic issues, there are often protests of a vibrant or violent nature.

See also: **antiglobalization, community participation, global governance, human rights**

Further reading: G8 Information Center

GATT

See: **WTO**

GDI (GENDER DEVELOPMENT INDEX)

A statistical measure originating from the **United Nations** (particularly the UN Development Program – UNDP) to compare life expectancy, literacy, income and education of women and men. It is the same as the Human Development Index (HDI) in what it measures, but it adds a comparative parameter of gender. It is part of a vocabulary from the field of development and thus often central to discussions about relative north–south development.

See also: **core–periphery model**

GEM (GENDER EMPOWERMENT MEASURE)

Another measure used by those working in development which, like the **GDI**, has a built-in gender comparison. The GEM, however, deals with economic and political spheres of activity and is thus more interested in women's involvement in these areas of life, not just with their standard of living. Economic figures are gathered about women in administration, management, professional, and technical work. Political involvement is measured in terms of seats in government.

See also: **feminism, feminization of the workforce, global labor market, human rights**

Further reading: United Nations Development Program

GEMEINSCHAFT

The term Gemeinschaft is usually related to the work of the German philosopher and sociologist Ferdinand Tönnies (1855–1936) who gave it a central place in his book *Gemeinschaft and Gesellschaft* (2001 [1887]) which was widely read in the first half of the twentieth century. In English, the two concepts are translated as community (Gemeinschaft) and society or association (Gesellschaft). For Tönnies, the former is defined by close emotional ties through face-to-face interactions, common values and attachment to place. Individuals in Gemeinschaft are embedded in a strong social network of friends and relatives, and their actions are rather intrinsically motivated than

100

influenced by external constraints. Gesellschaft, in contrast, is characterized by **heterogeneity** and diverse belief systems. Social relations are governed by external constraints, they tend to be more superficial, impersonal and anonymous, while individual action is based on the rational pursuit of self-interest.

The attempt to define and explain the transition from traditional to modern societies was central to early sociological theory. Ferdinand Tönnies, like many of his contemporaries, criticized the alienating effects of **modernization** such as mass society, individualization or urban rootlessness. At the same time, such images of a "cold" civilization elicited desires for warmth, authenticity and belonging which came to be a particularly strong cultural current in Germany after World War I. In 1924, the philosopher Helmuth Plessner (1892–1925) wrote a fierce critique of such constructions of community spreading in youth culture and political movements, while he gave an anthropological account of the virtues of mediated social relations and etiquette.

Contemporary sociology has discarded concepts like *Gemeinschaft/ Gesellschaft* as dualistic and overly simplistic. On the other hand, said traits might also be used to explain the ongoing appeal of those terms in public discourse. Words like "community" transport concrete images and at the same time appeal to emotions. Everyone can relate memories of his or her childhood with *Gemeinschaft*, and, on the other hand, terms like society or "the system" are catch-all words for negative experiences and feelings of unease. As it seems, the critique of civilization (pessimism) represents a powerful current, just as its dialectical counterpart: naive belief in progress (optimism). The example of Germany after World War I shows how, in times of rapid social change and the erosion of traditional institutions, such basic emotional orientations can play a decisive role in political life.

See also: **civil society, imagined communities**

Further reading: Freud (1989 [1930])

FO

GENEALOGIES (OF GLOBALIZATION)

Genealogies of globalization refers to a particular post-structuralist, post-Foucauldian (that is, after the influence of Foucault's work) way of answering "how" and "when" questions about globalization. Genealogies of globalization are accounts of globalization that do not seek its origins in a particular set of circumstances, or distant antecedents. Rather genealogies of globalization seek to give an account of globalization at the level of forms of knowledge and practice. As Larner and Walters put it "at what point does the global emerge as a way of knowing and acting on and in the world?" (2004a). Genealogies of globalization focus on questions about: how did it become possible to think in terms of the global? What techniques were required? How are these ideas and techniques transferred in and between organizations? Embodied in what forms of expertise? Answering these questions requires different kinds of studies than would be required for a "point of origin" account of globalization. For instance examining how technical advances in statistical mapping allowed particular kinds of indicators to be developed that made it possible to think of a space beyond the nation-state (Ó Tuathail and Dalby 1998). This recognizes that globalization does not exist as a phenomenon or entity waiting to be charted, analyzed, understood and then reacted to. Seeing globalization in a genealogical light recognizes that globalization does not exist "in a strong sense until governments, international agencies, corporate actors, scholars and activists began to name globalization, and develop ways to measure its extents and effects" (Larner and Walters 2004a). Genealogies of globalization would implicate scholars and key theorists in the "territorialization" of globalization, as their works, including this collection, help constitute what globalization is rather than just reflect the "effects" of globalization.

See also: **counter–narratives, geopolitical rationality, individuation, territorialization (de & re)**

Further reading: Larner and Walters 2004a

RM

GENOA

The seventeenth **G8** gathering took place in Genoa (July 2001). It is often mentioned because a protestor was shot and there were allegations of widespread police violence.

See also: **antiglobalization**

GEOPOLITICAL RATIONALITY

Geopolitics is the recognition that geography, land and physical position have a bearing on the global power structure. The concept of geopolitical rationality is even more analytical. It is used to refer to globalization as a way to sensitize us to the ways in which political space is read, written and practiced: how ways of imagining the world work to both facilitate some political possibilities and actions and exclude and silence others. It emerged from a discipline called critical geopolitics. As Simon Dalby (2000) explains, through the 1990s a number of geographers used the term critical geopolitics to encompass a diverse range of academic challenges to the conventional ways in which political space was written, read and practiced (Ó Tuathail and Dalby 1998). These writings all challenge common sense and "modern" assumptions that national identities and the states that govern populations are the necessary starting point for both policy discussion and scholarly analysis (Lewis and Wigen 1997).

The value of the term geopolitical rationality lies in its ability to phrase arguments which assert that globalization is not just "out there" as a natural phenomenon that we must respond to, but that it is a particular way of imagining the world that in turn facilitates particular kinds of political possibilities and action (such as the free flow of global capital and the just wars in the cause of global democracy). Using the term geopolitical rationality highlights the oversimplification inherent in specific forms of geopolitical reasoning and draws our attention to the subtleties and local circumstances of the effects of and resistance to these geopolitical rationalities. Using this term relativizes globalization and encourages us to stop taking globalization at face value. Rather than being the contemporary condition that determines and envelops us, or the epoch in which we live, we would see it as what we might call a "particular-universal" (Larner and Walters 2004b). Geopolitical rationality allows one way to question the existence and the details of "globalization." It emphasizes the power relations that are part of "globalization" generally, that is, the interests and motivations which lie behind the increased attention to "globalization."

See also: **counter-narratives, genealogies (of globalization), rationalities of risk, territorialization (de & re)**

Further reading: Larner and Walters 2004b; Ó Tuathail and Dalby 1998

RM

GLOBAL CAPITALISM

Global capitalism is the idea that the contemporary period is witnessing the emergence of a single integrated global economic system based on a capitalist logic which is subsuming all other national and regional economies. Capital (both productive and financial) is said to becoming increasingly liberated from the constraints of national territorial boundaries. As such, **nation–states** are said to have lost their place as the primary and sole legitimate agents of governance of the world economy and have to continuously adjust to the conditions and dictates of global capitalist market forces. It is now multinational corporations (who many see as spearheading the expansion and integration of global markets) that are the key players within the emerging global economic order. Their ability to move their operations gives them immense bargaining power and it is thus they and not states that exercise the "decisive influence over the organization, location and distribution of economic power and resources in the contemporary global economy" (Held and McGrew 2002: 53–54). What also makes the current period distinctive is the unparalleled scale and magnitude of economic integration with the economic fates of different national and regional areas now more intimately interconnected than at any other point in history.

However, this perspective is strongly disputed by a number of analysts. The idea that capital has become "footloose" severely underestimates the continued power that nation–states (and regional associations of states, such as the **EU**) wield over the corporations within the territories under their jurisdiction. Furthermore, many argue that the existence of an international capitalist economy is nothing new and such a system in one form or another has been around since early modern times and perhaps even longer with many pointing to the *belle époque* (1890–1914) as the period when international trade was at its height and the world markets most integrated. Indeed Abu-Lughod (1991) traces global capitalism, or something akin to it in any case, back to the thirteenth century. Arrighi (1994) also argues that the present cycle of world **hegemony** is one similar to, and yet different from, previous periods of national dominance over the world.

See also: **capitalism, nation–state (decline of), Transnational Corporation (TNC)**

Further reading: Gray 1999; Hirst and Thompson 1996; Scholte 1997

HB

GLOBAL CITIES

See: **world cities/global cities**

GLOBAL COMMODITY CHAIN (GCC)

Global commodity chain analysis focuses on the sets of inputs and outputs at different stages in the production of a commodity (mainly physical goods but also services) as well as the specific relation between enterprises, states and consumers in this process. Gereffi, one of the key proponents of this approach, identifies four dimensions of global commodity chains: the input–output structure, the geographical coverage, the governance structure, and the institutional framework.

The commodity chain concept is also referred to more narrowly as "supply chain" or "value chain" in business studies, focussing primarily on the input–output aspect in the production process.

GCC analysis has concerned itself very much with the governance structure and institutional framework dimensions, as these are central in determining access to a GCC as well as its forms of hierarchy and cooperation. An important distinction in this respect is drawn between producer- and buyer-driven commodity chains. The former require high investment of capital and technology, thereby creating high-entry barriers, so that large manufacturers (e.g. in the automobile and aircraft industries) assume a leading role vis-à-vis their suppliers. Buyer-driven chains are characterized by easier access to production (e.g. in textiles, agricultural products) leaving the leadership to those agents which are concerned with design, marketing, branding and retailing.

There is a hierarchy within commodity chains meaning that segments with higher value-added production are located further up in the chain. Enterprises and industries can enter processes of learning and industrial upgrading, so that they move further up on the chain. Commodity chain analysis explores the uneven patterns and dynamics of up- and downgrading of industries with respect to their position on this chain at a global level.

See also: **commodity chain, commodification, world systems theory**

Further reading: Gereffi and Korzeniewicz 1994; Kaplinksy and Morris 2001; Raikes *et al.* 2000

NH

GLOBAL ELITE

See: **global managerial class/global elite**

GLOBAL ENGLISH

Global English refers to both a collection of varieties of English (often called Global Englishes or International Englishes) and a phenomenon (the global spread of English). While the term "global English" may suggest a new variety of English which is used globally, such a variety does not yet exist.

The growing widespread usage of the English language creates a variety of debates, most importantly those about language rights (e.g. minority language maintenance, official languages, language education) and cultural loss. Because of the growing number of speakers of English as a first or additional language, many perceive the status of English as hegemonic (or the language of linguistic imperialism) because, as the argument goes, as more people learn/speak English, the less other languages are learned/spoken. Debates about the **hegemony** of English often take place as though English itself were the enemy. It is important to remember that the current status of the English language arises from the politics, economic status, etc. of those who use English rather than the language itself. Language policy, education and attitudes have to be monitored to stop other languages being marginalized, but, more importantly, to stop *speakers* of languages other than English from being marginalized.

Whether there is a variety that has emerged as "standard global English" is a complex issue without a clear answer because it relies on the perceived status of a particular variety and the purpose for which it is used. While it is safe to say that certain varieties of English are preferred for certain purposes (see Evans 2005), though not due to their inherent superiority but to the value assigned to them by people. Because there are so many varieties of English spoken in the world (see Crystal 1997) it is impossible to say that only *one* of those is the "standard" global variety.

In addition, there is popular belief that the growing use of English in conjunction with the widespread availability of various kinds of media have the effect of **homogenization** of the English language. Current linguistic research provides very little support for this popular view (Bauer and Trudgill 1998).

See also: **cultural imperialism**

Further reading: Crystal 1988, 1997; Graddol 1997; Kachru 1992; McArthur 1992, 2001; Milroy and Milroy 1999

GLOBAL FLUIDS

This is one of John Urry's (2000) metaphors of global space, the other two being networks and regions. The concept of global fluids helps describe the way people, objects, images, risks and practices move around the world. Once deterritorialized, they shift and inter-act in other space, especially in liminal spaces like the internet, air-ports and international hotels. Their interaction and movement is also complex and chaotic; there is no end point to their movement, and no set "speed." In that sense, global fluids circulate rather than travel. Global fluids tend towards heterogeneous results, as opposed to regions and networks which are more likely to homogenize.

See also: **chaos theory, complexity theory, homogenization, network society, territorialization (de- & re-)**

Further reading: Castells 1996, 2000a, 2000b, 2000c, 2000d; Urry 2002a

GLOBAL GOVERNANCE

Global governance is a descriptive term with two main strands. The first refers to the actual institutions of global governance (e.g. the **UN, WTO** and the like). The second refers to how organization and events occur in the absence of institutions directly responsible for them. Thus global governance is in many ways a field rather than an object of study; one in which describing and accounting for how decisions are made is a fundamental step if one wants to suggest ways in which decisions should be made. Thus global governance includes a number of actors from **nation–states** to citizens and community groups (**civil society**), working within discourses of rights and indeed globalization (Weiss and Gordenker 1996). Institutions involved in global governance include the UN, WTO, **WHO,** and **IMF.**

The importance of civil society both practically and rhetorically also needs to be stressed when talking about global governance. In political rhetoric, it is civil society that is often asked to take up a task or responsibility, however this is almost certainly doomed in practical terms because of the nature of civil society. At the same time, to include "civil society" in political rhetoric often supplies the democratic deficit of other global insitutions and indeed domestic governments.

See also: **global sub-politics, Global Union Federations (GUF)**

Further reading: Diehl 2001; Kennedy *et al.* 2002; Weiss and Gordenker 1996

GLOBAL HEALTH POLICY

Global health policy is an attempt to re-scale public health strategies from the national to the global scale because national public health strategies are no longer seen as effective against the specific health risks associated with global movements of people and illnesses. The **World Health Organization (WHO)** has led the way in developing and promoting a global health policy although its role is increasingly contested and transformed. A crucial moment in the emergence of global health policy was the *Alma-Ata Declaration* in 1978. Delegates attending the Conference on Primary Health Care declared that the health status of hundreds of millions of people in the world was deemed to be unacceptable, that the attainment of health required the action of social and economic sectors as well as the health sector, and that primary health care, by focusing on curing, played a leading role in meeting that objective. This set in motion substantial developments in the field of health promotion, including the move to incorporate preventative health care. "The aim was to achieve a greater balance between curative and preventive services, and training of health professionals to appreciate the social and environmental causes of ill-health" (Crombie *et al.* 2003). The recently ratified *Health For All in the 21st Century* sets global priorities and targets for 2020. The targets aim to make it possible for people throughout the world to reach the highest possible level of health. Global health policy is read in a much more critical light by social theorists, who interpret its focus on **risk** as a means to comprehend and manage health as indicative of either the double **reflexivity** associated with the move to a globalized world (Giddens 1991; Beck 1992) or as a rationality of advanced liberal governance (Dean 1999b).

See also: **choice (discourse of), rationalities of risk, WHO**

Further reading: Beaglehole 2003; Petersen 1997

RM

GLOBAL LABOR MARKET

The concept of the global labor market captures a significant trans-formation in the scale and boundaries of labor markets (the arena where those who are in need of labor and those who can supply the labor come together) from geographic locality and nation-state to a global context. The global labor market presumes and fosters work-ers' global **mobility**. Not only that, mobility is now a key char-acteristic of work. Although for time immemorial people have moved to work, now, more than ever people migrate for employment without settling for their entire lives. This migratory labor has a huge impact upon domestic economies as it is unpredictable and far reaching. The global labor market is seen to pose significant risks and opportunities both for national labor markets and individuals. The global labor market also poses risks and benefits for domestic econo-mies. The freer movement of people with highly sought after skills can allow local economies to participate more effectively in the global market, as their workers have the required skills, yet it can also lead to long-term skill shortages and increase costs of gaining and retaining highly skilled workers. Also, many migrants bring education and skills obtained at no cost to the host nation while those departing use their publicly funded training elsewhere. As labor becomes increasingly glo-balized, it also becomes harder to maintain effective labor regulation and prevent the escalation of economic exploitation. At a personal level, workers can experience increased exploitation with no recourse, they also lose the benefits associated with long-term settlement and employ-ment such as state pensions and health care. Workers can also experience dramatic cultural and personal losses as ties with family, friends and associates who live far away become harder and harder to maintain.

See also: **digital nomads, knowledge society, migration, work rich/ work poor**

Further reading: Mehmet *et al.* 1999

RM

GLOBAL MANAGERIAL CLASS/GLOBAL ELITE

The global managerial class might also be called "global elite" or "transnational managerial elite" (Hannerz 1996). These people are mobile, often employed in business and finance, but inhabiting globalized spaces. They are part of the **global fluids** that Urry identifies and are thus influential. Hannerz (1996: 129) suggests, they "stand a better chance than others to extend their habitats ... into other locations." Unlike the super rich, however, they are less likely to interact or inhabit local spaces, clustering rather in "personal micro-networks" (Beaverstock and Boardwell 2000) situated by and large in spaces abstracted from the local (e.g. international hotels). Scholte sees the global elite as more or less isolated from the rest of society. He also points to the heterogeneous nature of the global elite. Specifically, he identifies three groups, the official (government or quasi government), the corporate and the intellectual elites. "The three sectors regularly intersect, for instance, at WEF events, **WTO** meetings, AEA conventions, and conferences of national bankers associations" (2005: 28). In addition, casual contact in globalized spaces is continual. "Both deliberately and subtly, these continual interactions have provided a strong social basis for neoliberal discourse" (Scholte 2005: 28).

Global managerial individuals are "knowledge rich" and serviced by the "knowledge poor." Castells (1989) is particularly concerned about the growing gap between these two groups, in terms of affluence and opportunity.

See also: **cultural capital, digital nomads, experts/expert systems, global labor market, knowledge society, symbolic analyst, Transnational Capitalist Class (TCC)**

Further reading: Butler and Savage 1995; Daniels 1991; van der Pijl 1998; Sklair 2002; Slaughter 2000; Strange 1994

GLOBAL MEDIA

The first true global media were the news agencies. It is through these agencies that much of the world's international news is collected. These agencies have the advantage of economy of scale. Individual newspapers, and broadcasters, cannot afford to have reporters all around the world, or even across a single country.

The first agencies were in Europe and the US and were, and still are, tied into international finance and banking. After WWII the British Reuters and US Associated Press made an agreement to carve up and share out world news. Reuters at the turn of the millennium had around 400 client networks around the world to which it will supply satellite feeds of about 25 minutes. These will be sent out scheduled for local news production. A more wealthy network might use only a little of this. But a poor African one may use most of it. AP and Reuters, therefore, have a huge say in the news agenda of the world. Such has been the monopoly of control over global news that there has been much complaint by Third World organizations

One of the most obvious aspects of global media is the pre-dominance of American movies around the planet. Wherever you go in the world people know of Mickey Mouse, Star Wars and Rambo. Movies, after news agencies, were the next big global shift in the media. Many countries set up their own movie industries in order to provide a challenge to Hollywood. But none had the might of the Hollywood conglomerates such as Viacom, Time Warner, Disney, and News Corporation. Each of these produces and distributes its films and owns most cinemas, video rental stores, and movie channels around the world. This economy of scale has been difficult to rival and only a few countries have been able to maintain a film industry that is independent of Hollywood. Those that have copy its formats and styles.

Television is also a global media, whose formats have their origins in the West, although audiences tend to prefer local or regional programming. While Hollywood may be the leading exporter of television programming around the world, people prefer "culturally proximate" programming. Sinclair, Jacka and Cunningham (1996) give the example of Mexico's Televisa and Brasil's Globo, who dominate in Latin American television production. Some writers such as Ang (1994) argue that this fact challenges the idea that we now live in a world dominated by the Western media (1994: 325).

But Sinclair et al. (1996) also concede that "the US generic models, in establishing themselves as 'international best practice', also invite domestic imitation" (p. 13). Butcher (2003), referring to the arrival of STAR TV in Asia, says that we should be mindful not only of content "but the adoption of western broadcasting structures (commercialization, management hierarchies, broadcasting schedules, etc.)" (16). Broadcasting markets are only exploited where there are associated advertising possibilities. The need to attract advertising in a privatized market has a huge effect on programming even in the case of competing state–controlled television. Ray and Jacka (1996) have noted in the case of ZeeTV in India that many programs, due to the needs of advertisers, were simply Western imitations. Advertising is crucial in media globalization.

Like movies and news agencies the advertising business is another case of increased conglomeratization and internationalization and concentration of ownership. The last few decades have seen waves of buyouts as companies seek to consolidate, with the trends towards privatization around the world, which is opening up massive new markets particularly in Asia. The big, increasingly worldwide, manufacturing corporations such as Procter and Gamble, Coke, and Colgate-Palmolive want global deals to ensure a global brand. Such has been the consolidation that about a quarter of the world's advertising now lies in the hands of three US and UK advertising groups: Omnicom and Interpublic, based in New York, and WPP, based in London.

See also: **CNN effect, cultural imperialism, Transnational Corporation (TNC)**

Further reading: Sinclair *et al.* 1996

DM

GLOBAL POLITICS

Global politics means politics conducted at a global rather than national or regional level. Although not totally superseding existing forms of international politics, global politics is understood to be qualitatively different, not least because it is encompassing rather than composite. According to Held and McGrew (2003), global politics is part and parcel of globalization, that is, the widening, intensifying, speeding up, and growing impact of worldwide interconnectedness and can be understood through a series of key transformations in the constitution of contemporary political life. These transformations include an "internationalization of the state" where there is a growing political coordination amongst governments, intergovernmental and transnational agencies to realize common goals through making or implementing global rules and embodied in organizations like the **WTO** and **UN**. Also a "trans-nationalization of political activity" that refers to an explosion of citizen democracy in the proliferation of associations, **social movements**, advocacy networks and citizens groups that are mobilizing, organizing and exercising across national boundaries. There is also a transformation in the scope and content of international law towards restricting the political power of individual states that, under the Westphalian system, had autonomy and authority within their political boundaries. There is much debate about the extent and future of global politics. The emergence of global politics is seen to bring very diverse interests into relation with each other. This marks a growth in political **pluralism** as well as the development of a common language and values (such as **democracy**, rights etc.) in which conflicts are articulated (Shaw 1994). While global politics can thus in some ways be seen as an intensification of already existing international and transnational connections between states, the existence of global political bodies and the changing way in which states relate to other states through these bodies rather than on an individual level is novel.

See also: **global sub–politics, time–space compression, UN, WTO**

Further reading: Hardt and Negri 2000; Held and McGrew 2003; Shaw 1994

RM

GLOBAL SOCIAL POLICY

Global social policy is social policy that unfolds at a global rather than a national level. Global social policy approaches issues of social redistribution, social regulation, social provision and empowerment from an international rather than national perspective. Global social policy can be understood as a necessary response to the negative and damaging effects of globalized capitalism on the ability of individual **nation-states** to look after and provide human necessities for their populations (such as health care, food, and basic infrastructure). Global social policy is coming to the fore because national social policy agendas are less able to control for global economic and political factors which have a huge impact on nation-states' ability to provide standards of wellbeing. Global social policy is embodied in organizations like the **WHO**, which aims to set global standards of health care and welfare rights.

See also: **global health policy, global labor market**

Further reading: Deacon *et al.* 1997; Mishra 1999

RM

GLOBAL SUB-POLITICS

Beck (1994) describes global sub-politics as a force which shapes society
"*from below*" (23). It is linked to the individualization which characterizes
reflexive modernity and our **cultural fate**. Beck distinguishes
politics from sub-politics in two ways. First, in sub-politics "agents
outside the political or corporatist system are allowed to appear on
the stage of social design" (22). This includes coalitions of people but
also experts of various kinds. Second, "not only social and collective agents
but individuals as well compete with the latter and each other for the
emerging shaping power of the political" (22). Indeed, sub-politics
means that we have to look for political action (broadly construed) not
just in institutions of government, governance and law, but everywhere.
This occurs not just at a local and national level but also at a global
level. The recognition that is granted to **NGOs** in courts of law and
global institutions such as the **UN** is also symptomatic and con-
stitutive of this new way of being politically active.

See also: **antiglobalization, NGO, re-embedding**

GLOBAL UNION FEDERATIONS (GUFs)

Global Union Federations represent the interests of national industrial
or occupational trade unions at international level (to be distinguished from the International Confederation of Free Trade Unions,
ICFTU, which represents national trade union centers and con-
federations). The first International Trade Secretariat (ITS) to emerge
in the context of increasing trade union cooperation in the second
half of the nineteenth century was that of the typographers and
printers, formed in 1889. The twentieth century has seen numerous
mergers between the craft and occupation-based ITSs, resulting in
today's ten industry-based organizations: Education International
(EI), International Federation of Building and Wood Workers
(IFBWW), International Federation of Chemical, Energy, Mine and
General Workers' Union (ICEM), International Federation of Journalists (IFJ), International Metalworkers' Federation (IMF), International Textile, Garment and Leather Workers' Federation (ITGLWF),
International Transport Workers' Federation (ITF), International
Union of Food, Agricultural, Hotel, Restaurant, Catering, Tobacco
and Allied Workers' Association (IUF), Public Services International
(PSI), and Union Network International (UNI). Historically, the

main purpose of ITSs was to support international solidarity actions as well as the exchange of information on employment and bargaining issues. During the last decades ITSs have grown from bureaucratic peak organizations into resource and coordination centers and have taken on a more active campaigning role, in particular vis-à-vis multinational corporations. This development was reflected in the 2002 relaunch of ITSs as "Global Unions" (http://www.global-unions.org), a general term that comprises the ICFTU as well as the Trade Union Advisory Committee (TUAC), the international trade unions' advisory committee to the OECD.

See also: **global labor market, International Framework Agreements (IFA), Marx/Marxism, World Works Council**

Further reading: Carew *et al.* 2000; Fairbrother and Hammer 2005; Harrod and O'Brien 2002

NH

GLOBAL VILLAGE

This term was popularized by Marshall McLuhan in the 1960s, who claimed that the advent of electronic media would result in the emergence of a "global village." By this he meant that instantaneous communication would effectively eliminate distance; as information was transmitted across geographic boundaries at an unprecedented pace, the world would effectively shrink. McLuhan believed that the global village would result in a change in the nature of individuality. He argued that print (the predominant media prior to the twentieth century) had produced the rational individual, an isolated subject possessed of a single point of view. In contrast to the linear rational individual, the electronic media would result in the resurgence of a tribal identity, a shifting collective, where the boundary between self and other was permeable. Thus the global village would be peopled not by individuals but by collectives or tribes.

At the time McLuhan's prophecy was seen in terms of a coming era of global peace: a world linked by media and travel would become a single polity. However, he stressed that like a village, the global media space was one in which rumors proliferated; the immediacy of media would result in flashpoints, sudden conflicts that resulted from too-easy-to-access information.

Stripped of its speculative dimension, McLuhan's phrase has passed into common parlance and many feel that the **internet** has brought the vision of a global village to fruition.

See also: **time-space compresssion**

Further reading: McLuhan and Fiore 1967, 1968

JH

GLOBALISM

Beck defines globalism as "the view that the world market eliminates or supplants political action – that is, the ideology of rule by the world market, the ideology of neoliberalism" (2000: 9). Beck argues that globalism sees everything as economically determined and determinable. Any political, social or cultural matters are subsumed under economic (and particularly neoliberal economic) paradigms.

See also: **neoliberalism**

GLOBALITY

Beck writes that globality *"means that we have been living for a long time in a world society"* (2000: 10, emphasis in original). The concept of globality is linked to the notion of a world society, that is, at least a consciousness of living in a single world. Globality is a position which sees "world society as an irrevocable fact" and one which is characterized as being: multidimensional, polycentric, contingent and political (Beck 2000: 87–88). Beck claims that this construct is one opposed to a view which can understand the world in terms of **nation–states** (that is, an international view) and that globality and the world society require reflexivity. Indeed, the world society is one that does not have states as we are used to knowing them (Beck 2000: 103); globality means "world society *without a world state* and *without world government*" (2000: 117). The non-state society means that there are political players other than states, institutions and even corporations. These new political players are typically transnational and are very often understood as **NGO**s.

See also: **disorganized capitalism, global sub-politics, global village, reflexive modernization/modernity**

116

GLOBALIZATION FROM BELOW

The terms, both slogan and organizing principle, suggest that the phenomenon of globalization is a bidirectional process. In contrast to the imposition of a neoliberal economic and political order imposed by **global elites**, globalization from below captures the overlapping politics of contention and resistance amongst marginalized communities, social and labor movements, environmentalists and many others: global power begets global resistance.

This "movement of movements" has been most often presented as anti-institutional protest, with the default representation one of anarchic youths demonstrating outside meetings of the World Trade Organization. This serves as a proxy for the chief criticism that the movement only knows what it is against, not what it is for. Indeed, the central challenge of the "**antiglobalization**" movement has been the development of unified political strategies or even feelings of solidarity that link groups across ethnic, cultural and other divides.

The criticism is somewhat out of date, however, with striking new global political formations and networks developing to address the issue of creating alternatives to the global orthodoxy. Most successful to date have been the World Social Forums, and the emerging regional Social Forums, at which a panoply of grass-roots activists have not only begun to coordinate their thinking but actually embody global alternatives for decision-making.

See also: **anarchism**

Further reading: Barlow and Clarke 2001; Brecher *et al.* 2000; Notes from Nowhere 2003

RC

GLOCAL/GLOCALIZATION

This term has a range of meanings, all of which revolve around the apparent paradox of the relation between global markets and processes, and local needs and nodes. As a contraction of "global" and "local," the "glocal" refers to the increasing entanglement of these two spheres. On one level glocal can be used to designate the manner in which global products adapt or tailor themselves for local markets and sensitivities. It can also describe global or potentially global services that operate at a local level, for instant international websites that coordinate meetings (for instance dating) at a local level, and thus provide a "glocal" service. Attempts to integrate the decision-making procedures of global governance and the particularities of individual territories are also described in terms of "glocalization." Other examples of glocal processes could include the resurgence of the range of ethnic and religious identities in direct response to the process of globalization. These identities, which have their origin in a locality and history, are often shared by **diasporas** linked by telecommunications.

The glocal then, would seem another instance of the way in which globalization seems to involve an interplay between micro (individual, localities) and the macro (global forces and players) that often bypasses the meso (states and other forms of collective representation).

See also: **homogenization, hybridity**

JH

GOVERNMENTALITY

It is important to understand that "governmentality" (coined by Foucault 1991 [1982]) is often used to simultaneously denote a specific *way* of governing and a historically specific *form* of governing associated with liberalism. Governmentality as a *way* of governance is marked by the preeminence of the "art-of-government," and is achieved through concentrating "upon the problematic of government in general." This way of governance asks questions about "how to govern oneself, how to be governed, how to govern others, by whom the people will accept being governed [and] how to become the best possible governor." This approach to government "has as its primary target the population and as its essential mechanism the apparatus of security" (Foucault 1991 [1982]). This constant reflection about government, Foucault argues, is characteristic of early Modern Europe, the emergence of liberalism, and the **nation–state**'s rise to preeminence. liberalism's central tenets, that attempts to over-govern will be counter-productive and that a space apart from government is vital to ensure effective rule, constitutes self-governing (entrepreneurial) subjects through a rationality of government based on a concern with the problem of governing i.e. the historical period we habitually associate with liberalism and the rise of the sovereign nation-state exemplifies governmentality. Liberal government then, is no longer restricted to the state. It is achieved through forging "alignments" between the authorities and the "personal projects of those organizations, groups and individuals who are the subjects of government" (Rose 1999) utilizing them in the "programs and rationalities of government, particularly those of the government of the state" (Dean 1999a). This account of liberal rule removes the state from its central position. Instead, it is just "simply one element – whose function is historically specific and contextually variable – in multiple circuits of power, connecting a diversity of authorities and forces, within a whole variety of complex assemblages" (Rose 1999). Larner and Walters (2004a, 2004b) argue that this approach to governance is able to recast globalization as a "governmental rationality" as it allows particular kinds of questions to be asked such as: what is globalization? When is globalization? Where is globalization? What are the politics of globalization? The purpose is not to offer another, truer or more complete definition of globalization, or a typology of competing theories terms, rather, this approach attempts to de-substantiate globalization, in other words, it encourages us to stop taking globalization at face value and avoid being engulfed by it.

See also: **counter-narratives, de-governmentalization, genealogies (of globalization), geopolitical rationality, individuation**

Further reading: Burchell *et al.* 1991; Foucault 1991 [1982]; Larner and Walters 2004a; 2004b

RM

HABITUS

Habitus is a theoretical concept from the sociologist Pierre Bourdieu (1977). Habitus is a shorthand for thinking about the habits, cultural rules and ideological conditions that influence the way people behave and think. It is necessary to draw theoretical attention to these influences because they are normally unnoticed. The habitus may also be referred to as the "life world" of the person, their existential environment. The form of the habitus may mean that some options are virtually unavailable, but habitus is not a synonym for determinism. Habitus is perhaps similar to some understandings of culture; we draw on our habitus to continually create our habitus, thus it is recursive. Like culture, habitus can be individual and collective, that is individuals have a habitus and groups also can have a habitus.

Because of free will, we can behave in all sorts of unpredictable ways, nevertheless, all things being equal people deal with the world and act in it by relying on conscious or unconsious knowledge, culture and scripts. Because of the unconsious aspect of the habitus, it is difficult to be fully reflexive about it.

Hyperglobalists argue that globalization is creating a new global habitus. Whether this is constant in all locales is an empirical question. However, claims made about the collapse of space and time, which are core to many understandings of globalization, are fundamentally altering the world and human positions in it.

See also: **glocal/glocalization, hyperglobalist thesis, hyperreality, modernity, reflexivity, structuration theory, time-space compression**

Further reading: Bourdieu 1979; Bourdieu and Passeron 1977; Norris and Jones 2005

HARD/SOFT POWER

Refers to a **state's** power over other states due to superior military and financial resources. This was a central asset in the Cold War, where the arms race was essentially about both military and economic assets. Hard power is about coercion, threats and sanctions. Soft power, on the other hand, is about persuasion, diplomacy and culture. The importance of soft power is reflected in the attention given by **nation-states** to the promotion and export of their culture, products and language. This is not purely for economic benefit from trade of these articles, but also to increase one's prestige in the global cultural market place. In the case of language in particular, if one's native language is esteemed this will be an asset in all dealings with other states.

See also: **core-periphery model, global English**

Further reading: Hoffmann 2004; Mattern 2004

HEGEMONY

This term comes from Ancient Greece, but more usually refers to Gramsci's work (1971) which relates more to power and the dominant ideology than to states as such. The term is used with reference to **nation–states** and their politics, however sometimes this is more generalized than political. Thus to talk about American hegemony can invoke anything from consumer items, cultural practices, politics or economics.

The ideology of the dominant group in a society is said to be hegemonic. According to Gramsci, the dominant group somehow secures the consent and complicity of other groups in terms of their favored ideology. This "spontaneous consent" (Gramsci 1971: 12) may be achieved through acts of force and coercion, but less visibly simply through a sustained insistence on the ideology as common sense. Hegemony is loosely analogous to mainstream culture and practices. Thus if something is considered beyond the pale or "not done," it is not part of the dominant ideology.

To overturn the hegemony, or rather take it over, one can conduct either a "war of maneuver" or a "war of position." The former is shorter in time duration and usually the strategy with a strong central state and a weak hegemony. This is often the case when the hege-mony has been secured through force and threat. Thus military dic-tatorships (of the non–beneficent kind) are potential targets for such wars of maneuver. The war of position is a much longer ordeal. It is used when the hegemony is generally accepted, though the state might not be so strong. The strength of the state has to be seen in the context of the hegemony. In the dictatorship, the state dictates the hegemony and enforces it with force. In the "weak" state, the hegemony is more diffuse in the sense that it is accepted as "common sense."

Hegemony is generally used in a negative way, however there is nothing, in Gramsci at least, which would suggest that it is inherently negative. It is theoretically possible to have "good" hegemony in the sense that the power exercised is beneficial.

Hegemony is used not only in an ideological sense but also in descriptive terms in relation to international relations. Thus it is possible to speak of "world hegemony" as a shorthand for the nation or alliance which holds power internationally. Taylor notes that "World hegemony is seen as a property of the whole system and not just of the hegemon itself" (1996: 25). Many see the current period as a time of US hegemony, however such domin-ance of a nation is not new. Arrighi (1994), for example, points to previous examples in former times. This suggests, at the very least, that the dominance of a nation (here the USA) is not unprece-dented.

See also: **counter-narratives, global governance, ideological state apparatus, Marx/Marxism**

Further reading: Herman and Chomsky 1988; Mouffe 1979; Taylor 1996

HERITAGE TOURISM

Linked to the **postmodern** quest for authenticity (MacCannell 1999), heritage tourism focuses on historical and cultural sites as tourist destinations where the way of life of a particular historical period or group is displayed. At some sites hosts also dress in the costumes of the day and may reenact the way of life of the historical period in question, or put on cultural performances for the tourists.

See also: **bodily display, cultural capital, cultural imperialism, culture industry, simulacrum**

SL

HETEROGENEITY

The opposite of homogeneity, however, "heterogeneity" is not the only term used in opposition to homogeneity in the globalization literature. Rather, melange, bricolage, **hybridity**, and **glocalization** are more likely to occur. The varied picture of the globe that these terms suggest, physically and culturally, is also referred to as the global mosaic. It is vital to remember that claims about the homogenizing or diversification of the world in any area (economic, demographic, cultural and so on) have to be made on the basis of material claims. Such substantive arguments will always be confined to certain fields, geographic or otherwise. The pushes and pulls between homogeneity and heterogeneity, theoretically and actually, are central to globalization debates. They have to be understood as tendencies rather than absolutes. It should also be remembered that generally theorists (especially **skeptics**) consider **homogenization** negative and heterogeneity positive.

See also: **postmodernity/postmodernism**

HIGH MODERNITY

Anthony Giddens divides **modernity** into early and late periods. The late period is known as "Radicalized modernity" (1990: 150) or "high modernity" (1990: 176) and is associated with globalization. While some argue that we are presently in a period of **postmodernity**, Giddens argues that we are still in a period of modernity, although a period of late modernity. He contrasts modern societies with traditional societies. Essentially, traditional societies have rules and conventions that constrain behavior, practice and thinking. Giddens argues that traditional societies don't question why things are done in particular ways. In the characteristics of Giddens' modern societies, we find the issues and themes normally associated with globalization.

Modern societies think about why certain practices are the way they are, why we behave the way we do and so on. Thinking in this way is described as being reflexive. Essentially, **reflexivity** involves observing our own behavior and asking questions about it. Reflexivity is one of the key characteristics that distinguishes modern societies from traditional ones. When people start being reflexive, changes also occur in institutions and customs. This reflexivity is directed towards the features of modernity and thus is still part of the project of modernity rather than a break with it.

See also: **liquid modernity, reflexive modernization/modernity, structuration theory**

Further reading: Giddens 1991

HOMOGENIZATION

This is a central term in globalization studies. At a basic level, it means things becoming the same. This can be anything from politics, cultural practices, language, consumer products, ideologies, media and entertainment. Such convergence is made possible in an unprecedented way (or so hyperglobalists would argue) because of technology (such as the **internet** and telecommunications) and travel. Homogenization is most obvious in the spread of **capitalism** and neoliberal politics. Given that many of the truly global institutions (**IMF, World Bank, WTO**) are concerned with business and finance and the political infrastructure considered necessary to these activities, this is hardly surprising. It is largely against these geopolitical forces that antiglobalizers work.

Questions of which practices are dominant and where they come from are of concern to many. Tomlinson (1991), for example, writes about what others would consider globalization in terms of **cultural imperialism**. Thus central to homogenization are issues of power. Relative might is theorized in geopolitical as well as class terms, often specifically in terms of core and periphery states and groups.

Others argue that the global landscape is not so much one of homogenization but of **hybridization**. The contact with others means that practices and products are dis-embedded from their original context and **re-embedded** into new locales; thus called **glocalization**.

It is important to note that homogenization is only one of many aspects of globalization. Robertson (1992), for example, argues that globalization is driven by two forces: the "universalization of particularlism" and the "particularlization of universalism."

See also: **Americanization, antiglobalization, Coca-colonization, convergence thesis, global media, hard/soft power, heterogeneity, hyperglobalist thesis, McDonaldization, time-space compression, world systems theory**

Further reading: Goldblatt and Perraton 1999; Hamelink 1983; Hannerz 1992; Howes 1996; Morley and Robins 1995; Schiller 1971; Sorkin 1992

HUMAN CAPITAL

Human capital is the knowledge, skills, abilities and capacities possessed by people. A concept popularized by Nobel prize winning economist Gary Becker (1994), he claims that, just as organizations make investments in physical production-related resources like plants or equipment, expenditures in such areas as training and education are investments in human capital which contribute to rises in productivity and earnings. Human capital can be accumulated in many ways, including education of workforce, on-the-job training, on-the-job experience, investments in health, outreach and extension programs, life experience, migration, and searching for information about goods, services, employment opportunities etc. The concept of human capital is relevant to the discourse of globalization through the growing influence of Interactive and Communication Technologies (ICTs) usually in the form of computers, the **internet** World Wide Web etc. The widespread dissemination of ICTs means that an ability to work with them is becoming an increasing necessity. The role that ICTs play – as tradeable commodities and as enabling global trade – means the ability for individuals to both use and program ICTs has become very important in today's economy. The need to make sure that citizens have "the knowledge" if a given economy is going to survive and prosper on the global market means that raising a nation's human capital has become a key policy focus in many countries. The **knowledge society** not only requires a facility to use ICTs but also to adapt to new developments. Lifelong learning is essential. This has led to political controversy over whether national educational systems or employers should foot the bill.

See also: **digital nomads, knowledge society, policy programs, social capital, symbolic capital**

Further reading: Beck 1992; Becker 1994; Castells 1996; Giddens 1994; Putnam 2000

RM

HUMAN RIGHTS

While human rights has always been something of concern to philosophers and political theorists, since WWII, they have achieved a global significance. This is largely due to the establishment of the **UN** and its Universal Declaration of Human Rights (1948) as well as other resolutions, treaties and covenants to do with a range of civil, political, social and economic rights (collectively, the International Bill of Human Rights). Here, we deal mainly with legal human rights, as opposed to those grounded in religion, natural law and philosophy.

There are two main issues to consider with human rights, universality and enforceability. While some **nation-states** have Bills of Rights, especially if they were established post-war, these generally reflect concerns of the founding constitutionalists, as in the case of the United States Constitution (1789) and the French Declaration of the Rights of Man and of the Citizen (1793). The South African Constitution, for example, makes very explicit its concern for human rights by establishing institutions for their monitoring and enforcement. Despite, and perhaps because of, the UN's Universal declaration, cultural variation means that these rights are not always appropriate to certain religious, cultural and civil concerns.

Also related to the universal declaration is the question of enforceability. If rights are enshrined in national legislation and constitutions, the relevant judiciary will usually be charged with and be competent to assess rights, enforce them, and provide appropriate remedies in the case of breaches. The US Supreme Court, for example, can render legislation unconstitutional on the basis of rights contained in amendments to the Constitution.

Regionally, enforcement might also be possible. The European Convention on Human rights is justiciable by the European Court of Human Rights in Strasbourg. However accessing this court is difficult and taxing on the time and financial resources of the complainant. Further, in this case it is only possible to bring an action if one is a "victim" under the Declaration. It was only in 1998 that the UK incorporated the Declaration into domestic law with the Human Rights Act (1998; coming into force in 1999), even though they had been a signatory since 1951. Further, some rights are not absolute, and can be either derogated from or reserved, that is, suspended. In addition, nation-states are awarded a "margin of appreciability" by the courts which means they have discretion as to the limitation of some rights insofar as this is in support of a legitimate aim and whatever limiting measure is proportionate to this aim.

At a global level, there is sometimes effectively nothing that can be done to enforce a nation's obligations under human rights instruments. While various bodies may monitor human rights, there is no Universal Court of Human Rights to assess alleged breaches and mete out punishments. This role often falls to other nation-states wherein lie political and legal difficulties.

It is a well established principle of international law that nation-states are sovereign entities and as such, other nations cannot intervene in their affairs. Not withstanding definitions of and precedents for enforcing crimes against humanity and breaches of human rights, there is no systematic enforcement of these. That does not mean that states never intervene. However, it is arguable that such intervention is only driven by national concerns (regional or global security of the nation or its interests) or, less commonly, by media and public pressure.

There have been suggestions about how to remedy this situation, most obvious being the creation of a UN standing army, rather than the UN having to ask member states for troops when the need arises (which is usually well after serious atrocities). Annan, in 2001, had this to say about the difficulties:

> Member States have not been willing to consider the idea of a standing UN force for several reasons. First is the question of budget. How do you pay for it? Second, where do you locate it?

And which legal regime covers it and a whole range of issues (www.un.org).

There is also a resistance from the big powers in that they do not want to give the UN or the Secretary-General military capacity but the resistance doesn't only come from here. Some of smaller states do not want to have a standing army which can be used against them on the basis that they are either abusing their people, say humanitarian reasons, or they are not doing what they ought to do. (http://www.un.org/apps/sg/offthecuff.asp?nid = 158)

Thus while there are some effective actions against breaches of human rights at a national and regional level, the global enforcement of global human rights is far from a reality. The rhetoric of human rights, however, is a global phenomenon, even though it may be masking less pleasant strategic objectives.

See also: **basic needs, language rights, universal human rights**

Further reading: Alston and Robinson 2005; Donnelly 2003; Ignatieff 2002; McCorquodale and Faribrother 1999; Moseley and Norman 2002; O'Flaherty 1996; Steiner and Alston 1996

HYBRIDITY/HYBRIDIZATION

Hybridity is a concept that emerged from postcolonial literary studies, particularly the work of Homi Bhabha (1994). In relation to globalization, hybridity is associated with Jan Nederveen Pieterse (1995), and is a concept used to collapse the global/local binary, and capture the variety of outcomes from the same global processes. For example, while arguments are made about the homogenization of the world because the same products are available everywhere, different people make use of products in different ways. White rap music is a genre that is present all over the world, local versions can be understood as changing the "original" into a new hybrid.

According to Nederveen Pieterse, there are no "global" or "local" but only "hybrid" phenomena that are always already mixed. Globalization becomes a process of accelerated mixture, with a concomitant production of new forms. So, the Western "cultural, economic, and political forms that are said to be homogenizing the world – here the neoliberalising conceptualization of the person and the market – are themselves hybrids, which then interact with 'local'

127

national cultures, also hybrid in form" (Kingfisher 2002: 52). Nederveen Pieterse points out that hybridity entails power relations. There are a "a continuum of hybridities: on the one hand, an assimilationist hybridity that leans toward the center, adopts the canon and mimics the hegemony, and at the other end, a destabilizing hybridity that blurs the canon, reverses the current, subverts the center" (Nederveen Pieterse 1995: 56–57). The problem with the concept of hybridity is that it assumes an initial purity or at least a state prior to hybridization. This assumption invokes the very binary that the concept seeks to get beyond. Roland Robertson's **"glocalization"** is another concept that seeks to collapse the global/local boundary (1995).

See also: **counter-narratives, homogenization, re-embedding**

Further reading: Kingfisher 2002; Nederveen Pieterse 1995; Robertson 1995

RM

HYPERGLOBALIST THESIS

Held *et al.* (1999: 10) distinguish between hyperglobalists, **skeptics** and transformationalists based on their respective theorizing of globalization. Hyperglobalists believe that we are presently in an unprecedented global era (that is a new phase entirely rather than just a continuation of processes that have always operated), where global economics, governance and civil society are in their ascendance at the expense of the **nation–state**. A new world order fuelled and driven by the logic of **capitalism** (particularly consumption) and technology is upon us.

See also: **colonialism, traditionalist**

Further reading: Albrow 1996; Ohmae 1995

HYPERMASCULINITY

Ashis Nandy (1988) identified hypermasculinity as a cultural pathology in **colonialism**. Hypermasculinity celebrates and values stereotypically male characteristics of physical strength. However, Nandy identifies two kinds of masculinity opposed to each other emerging in the Victorian period. The first is typified by violence, the second by self-control. While both are about strength, the former is asso-ciated with colonized classes, the latter with colonizing classes. At the same time, feminized qualities, such as nurturing, caring and consumption, are stigmatized.

The concept of hypermasculinity has been applied to the world economy and thus is present in work on globalization. Here, hyper-masculinity is associated with economic power. The feminized in such a scenario are marginal populations, who are dependent on those claiming or performing hypermasculinity (i.e. on the basis of nation, race, or region).

See also: **colonialism, cultural imperialism, feminism, subaltern**

Further reading: Ling 2000

HYPERREALITY

The concept of hyperreality is most closely associated with the French cultural theorist Jean Baudrillard (1995). It articulates the status of collective "reality" under informational capitalism. The basic idea is that the image, sign, or representation of reality, has reached a critical threshold where it supercedes the "real" or represented. This means the end of authenticity; it also means that authenticity is end-lessly sought. Thus media representations have a greater reality or are of more consequence than the events they portray, while manufactured or artificial objects take the place of natural ones. Baudrillard sees this as a result of **capitalism**, which reduces all objects to their **exchange value** (initially their monetary value). As this exchange has become increasingly informational, the relation between object and value becomes reversed; rather than the object being the source of exchange value, it is now determined by this value.

Moreover, because capitalism seeks to commodify new aspects of our **lifeworld**, it converts more of this world into exchangeable signs. Our world is literally remade in the sign's image. Spaces such as Dis-neyland and shopping malls are often cited as examples of the hyperreal environments that this process produces. At its most extreme the hyperreal suggests a *Matrix*-like world (the film contains direct refer-ences to Baudrillard) of total simulation. But hyperreality is not simply a triumph of simulation, as if there were only an infinite regress of images, but rather a condition in which representations and simulations determine real events. This results in a situation in which events occur precisely so that they can be represented, and in an age of simulation the production and control of images is of paramount importance.

Baudrillard (1995) famously argued that the first (1991) Gulf War would not (before), was not (during), and did not (afterwards) take place. He didn't argue that it didn't really happen but was referring to the war that television viewers were being shown. He argued that the war viewers believed was happening, was not the war that was really happening. While the war was real in an immediately visceral and embodied way for the people involved directly in it, it was also "real" to those who watched it on the news (especially real-time news coverage). The "reality" of the war was no longer unified; there was no singular "truth" or "reality" (or "origin"). The fact that these realities can coexist quite happily is why postmodernists use the term hyperreality. Hyperreality is in part, then, a crisis of signification.

See also: **postmodernity/postmodernism, pseudo events, simulacrum**

Further reading: Belk 1996; Eco 1985; Goldstein-Gidoni 2005; Kellner 1989; Norris 1992

IDENTITY POLITICS

Identity politics is a concern of marginalized groups within society who seek to create a community based on cultural, social or ethnic features. The term came to prominence with black activists in the USA in the 1960s. Examples of other groups that may be said to participate in identity politics include indigenous people, homosexuals and lesbians, and people of color. Central to identity politics is the notion of marginalization and seeking to rectify this through an appeal to a distinctive (and often inalienable) identity, that is, something that differentiates the group from the "mainstream."

In the context of globalization there are two things to consider. The first is the politicization of groups within and perhaps against the **nation–state**, in as much as the state is the agent of oppression. Thus some argue that such identity affiliations are more salient than, for example, citizenship. Such connections between groups and individuals has in part been made possible by technological innovations, especially the **internet**.

The second is that some groups are, in the context of globalization, reassessing their identity and their politics. **Feminism** is perhaps the best example of this. However, the idea that globalization is the only force that leads to such reassessment is far from certain. Any identity can shift; globalization and the related changes are merely an example of the kind of social, political and economic change that any community has to take into account. Further, the processes of identity politics have been mobilized to identities which are chosen rather than given, and thus more akin to ideologies.

Especially in recent times, there is a populist notion that identity is absolutely fluid and something that individuals can completely construct for themselves. This is part of the transition from **modern** to **postmodern** times (or traditional to modern, in Giddens' terms). There are limits to this, however, as there is no guarantee that the "constructed" identity will be perceived as it is intended.

In terms of globalization studies, the area in which identity (as opposed to identity politics) is often discussed is not so much political as consumerist. The notion of a **lifestyle** is central to such discussion.

See also: **antiglobalization, feminism, fundamentalism**

Further reading: Nicholson and Seidman 1995; Thomas *et al.* 2004; Whisman 1996

IDENTITY THINKING

This phrase has three meanings. The first was coined by Alfred Korzybski (1958), the founder of General Semantics, and is essentially a way of describing referential meaning, that is, that words describe or create equivalences (identity) between things. Korzybski wanted to draw attention to this in language, note that it is problematic and then move beyond thinking simply in terms of equivalences.

Secondly, the philosopher Theodor W. Adorno used the phrase to contrast with his own dialectical thinking. "Dialectics seeks to say what something is, while identarian thinking says what something comes under, what it exemplifies or represents, and what, accordingly, it is not itself" (1973: 149). For Adorno, the latter is a way of exercising power and domination, as identity thinking is not concerned with understanding something or someone, but with controlling it.

Thirdly, identity thinking is used by some writers to simply mean thinking about identity.

IDEOLOGICAL STATE APPARATUS

A term from the Marxist Louis Althusser (1977), in contrast to the *repressive* state apparatus. The Ideological State Apparatus (ISA) are those institutions not technically part of the **state** but which nevertheless communicate and inculcate the values of the state, particularly capitalist modes and relationships of production. Education is now the major ISA, though previously the church was a powerful agent. Other institutions in the ISA include family units and the media, though all such institutions have at least some autonomy as they are not under the direct control of the state (at least in a functioning democracy).

The repressive state apparatus comprises state agents which work to assure order and compliance with the state in a direct way.

See also: **hegemony, Marx/Marxism, nation state**

Further reading: Laclau and Mouffe 1985

IFA (INTERNATIONAL FRAMEWORK AGREEMENTS)

Agreements between **Global Union Federations** and MNCs on fundamental human and labor rights, usually revolving around the eight core conventions defined in the 1998 ILO Declaration on Fundamental Principles and Rights at Work. IFAs encourage the global application of core labor rights not only by MNCs but also their suppliers, involve trade unions in the implementation and monitoring and give them a right to bring complaints.

See also: **human rights**

Further reading: Hammer 2005; Wills 2002

NH

IGO (INTERGOVERNMENTAL ORGANIZATION)

See: **EU, nation-state, NGO**

IMAGINATIVE HEDONISM

Coined by Colin Campbell (1997, 2003), imaginative hedonism is the continuous creation of desires we can't satisfy. It is intimately linked with *consumerism* and the conditioning of consumers to want what they can't have. The term in full is often "modern autonomous imaginative hedonism." According to Campbell, this kind of ethos developed in the nineteenth century, it was a Romantic ethic replacing Puritanical self-denial.

IMAGINED COMMUNITIES

In his book *Imagined Communities* (1983), Benedict Anderson attempted to address what appeared to be a major gap in both "liberal" and "Marxist" social theory of the time, namely to explain the pervasive force of **nationalism** in **modernity** and its spread in every corner of the globe. By defining nationalism as an "imagined community," i.e. a cultural product, Anderson inaugurated a wide range of studies on the cultural and symbolic aspects of nationalism. His point, though, was not to deconstruct nations as "just" invented. On the contrary, he emphasized that authenticity was not a meaningful criteria to apply to human communities, because when relationships are not face-to-face, people must imagine and create the collective social bond. Consequently, Anderson argued, scholars ought to focus on the ways, forms and media of such imaginations and of their (re-)production.

In his study, Anderson emphasized the reciprocal relations of **capitalism** and the printing press which over time lead to the emergence of standardized national and administrative languages, and thus lay the ground for mass communication and national consciousness. In the course of this development, newspapers, museums and other "media" facilitated articulating and representing a collective national symbolic space and experience. Focussing on very recent examples of nationalism in South-East Asia, Anderson also demonstrated how censuses or maps imprinted on people's imaginations and implemented nationalism in everyday practices of administration. The formation of new **nation-states** in South America, for their part, are connected with the specific administrative "careers" of creole elites in the course of which the consciousness of representing a distinct national community emerged.

See also: **Creolizations, Gemeinschaft, Marx/Marxism, nation-state**

Further reading: Pecora 2001

FO

IMF (INTERNATIONAL MONETARY FUND)

In terms of globalization, the IMF and other global financial institutions, such as the **WTO** and the **World Bank**, offer the clearest example of indisputable globalization. These organizations, all created post-WWII, do have global reach and influence. That they are also concerned with trade and economics probably means that even globalization **skeptics** concede that the global landscape has altered at least in relation to these fields.

The IMF is one of the institutional outcomes of the post-WWII conference at Bretton Woods. The IMF's purpose was to stop national and global financial crises by monitoring and remedying macroeconomic performance. In short, the goal was to ensure economic stability post-war and post-Depression. It sought to control and ease international currency conversion to help international trade. It monitors balance of payments and foreign exchange rates. By convention, the president of the IMF is European.

When first established, it was a "lender of last resort," giving emergency loans to countries short of cash. The English economist Maynard Keynes wanted the IMF to be an International Clearing Union that would automatically provide money to economies with balance of payments problems. There would be no conditions on these loans and they were essentially to stabilize economies (maintain employment levels and standard of living etc.). Keynes saw the IMF as an agent of fairness, that those in front financially should help out those behind, to keep a relative stability. This is not the form the IMF eventually took. Instead, loans were to be given according to quotas, calculated in Special Drawing Rights (SDRs). SDRs are calculated according to how much capital a national already has, which seems to work exactly against the goals that Keynes, at least, had in mind.

Loans are granted at less than commercial interest rates, and technically are to be short-term and repaid within 5 years. The early stages of the IMF did not clearly contemplate the absolute **free trade** that it appears to lobby for now. The complete removal of tariffs and barriers was also not quite so clear – though there was a general feeling that these should be gradually removed. Keynes felt that the unfettered movement of capital around the world would lead to massive inequalities and instability.

Now, the IMF has a number of programs for poverty relief including the Poverty Reduction and Growth Facility (PRGF). The low interest lending facility for poor countries was not established until 1999. Eligibility for such programs is based on the IMF's assessment of per capita income. In making such decisions, the IMF may draw on World Bank expertise thus the two institutions are linked. In conjunction with the World Bank the IMF also has a Heavily Indebted Poor Countries Initiative (HIPC).

The IMF is perhaps most infamous for its Structural Adjustment Program (SAPs) and other conditionalities. Essentially, the IMF provides conditional loans to countries that are deemed eligible, usually because of balance of payments shortfalls. Critiques of these programs have come from many quarters, not least from the Chief Economist at the World Bank, Joseph Stiglitz. The conditions on loans usually require cuts in public service spending, such as welfare and health, and **privatization** of certain industries, such as water and electricity. The effects of water privatization especially have been catastrophic to some areas, with the cost of water becoming prohibitive. There have also been allegations of favoritism in the determination of the consortia that are awarded these tenders.

See also: **antiglobalization, capitalism, civil society, global capitalism**

Further reading: Killick 1995; Peet and Born 2003; Stiglitz 2002; Vines and Gilbert 2004; Vreeland 2003

IMPERIALISM

See: **colonialism, cultural imperialism**

INCOME POLARIZATION

Income polarization is associated with increased income disparity between groups of people. This increase in disparity is caused by one of the most salient features of labor markets in the context of globalization which is the increasing divide between highly skilled, well-paid and unskilled, low-paid work. We find this divide both within labor markets in developed countries, and between the labor markets of north and south. Nationally, it is often associated with the rise of neoliberal policies that stress market freedoms, reduced control on wages – which has the effect of pushing up high incomes and pushing down the level of low incomes. Within the national labor markets of countries like Australia and Canada, significant transformations in the way people work are taking place. These changes are often described in terms of the movement towards greater flexibility. However, flexibility means different things for different parts of the workforce. At the top end, highly paid information workers are expected to continue to upgrade their skills and credentials in many areas, to become "entrepreneurs" of their own careers by moving from firm to firm, and to work long hours. Flexibility for low-skilled workers, on the other hand, means employment in part time or casualized positions, unpredictable hours, minimal job security and few benefits. The divisions within global labor markets are not dissimilar to the ones we find within some national arenas. Richer countries continue to provide highly valued services such as management, legal, financial, accounting, design and advertising. Firms have sought out less-developed countries such as those in South-East Asia for the cheap production of consumer goods such as running shoes, computer chips, and automobile components. Often, to minimize costs, goods are made and assembled in a series of countries, a process which has given rise to the expression the "global assembly line." Less-developed states, eager for foreign investment, often create special zones (**Export Processing Zones** or Special Economic Zones) in which goods manufactured for export are not subject to tariffs, and there are fewer taxes, and relaxed labor and environmental standards. Income polarization is linked to the **knowledge economy**: increasing skills polarization may lead to increased social exclusion and widening income gaps. The knowledge-driven economy creates fewer, high-skill jobs, which tends to reinforce income polarization. The concept of income polarization tends to focus on collating the disparity between individuals' incomes. There is a problem with this, as most people do not live alone. The limits of income polarization studies are linked to the concept of work rich/work poor.

See also: **core–periphery model, foreign direct investiment, global labor market, knowledge society, work rich/work poor**

Further reading: Pusey 2003

RM

INCORPORATION THEORY

A term emanating from the neo-Marxist Frankfurt school referring to the way the working classes are incorporated into the capitalist and

consumer culture. Because these classes desire the articles of consumer culture (see **false needs**), the argument runs, they accept the
structures which support the production of such articles.

See also: **Marx/Marxism**

Further reading: Horkheimer and Adorno 2002; Marcuse 1972; Tomlinson 1991

INDEX OF SOCIAL PROGRESS

The International Index of Social Progress (ISP) and the Weighted
Index of Social Progress (WISP) were developed by Richard Estes.
ISP is one of the many measures of social and economic development.
For the specific elements taken into account and the development of the
measures, see Estes (1988).

INDIGENIZATION

At least three quite divergent meanings of this term can be found in
scholarly and more popular writings. The sense of *indigenous* as
referring to "the original peoples" is common to the first two, and
indicates an ethno–cultural usage. The third places an emphasis on
"the local" and is a spatial description.

First, the term is used in indigenous studies to describe the
process by which indigenous peoples have gone about reclaiming
their culture and status. That is, those groups who were the original
inhabitants of "New World" territories invaded by European imperi-
alists, who are now setting about regrouping and asserting their rights
and identity. The term indigenization is then used to describe specific
acts of reclamation or reform, such as the creation of a school curri-
culum informed by indigenous knowledge and values.

A second meaning is emerging in cultural studies and elsewhere, to
describe processes by which the descendants of *settler* peoples have
begun to identify with the territories which they now call home and
with those territories' original inhabitants. This is often presented as
an antidote to the guilt or alienation that settler societies feel as the
dispossessors of the original inhabitants. Indigenization, for example
in the context of the Australian reconciliation process, implies that
settler peoples are reaching a better understanding of history and a
closer relationship with their landscape and environment as they

come to "belong." Many indigenous peoples see such acts as an appropriation and a further injustice.

The final meaning appears most frequently in economics and political science literatures to describe a process very like import–substitution. That is, industries or nations, particularly in developing countries, will seek to end their reliance on external sources of goods and services by identifying and promoting local businesses and providers.

See also: **human rights, identity politics, indigenous culture, nation–state**

Further reading: Greer 2004

RC

INDIGENOUS CULTURE

In the context of globalization, the search for a standard meaning for "indigenous" culture is elusive. At a first level of approximation, it is used to describe the cultures of those peoples whose territories were invaded by imperial powers who established settler colonies which now comprise the dominant population groups. Yet within and across these "First Nations" or Aboriginal peoples, there are very diverse cultural practices and ways of being "indigenous."

In international institutions there has been some attempt to set the parameters of "indigenous" as above – the original peoples of lands colonized by Europeans – and then to leave further definition to the peoples themselves as an ethical response to centuries of imposed categorization and misrepresentation. This has created difficulty in the case of Asia and Africa, where imperialism was extremely disruptive but where the governing majorities are not the descendants of European settlers but African and Asian peoples. "Indigenous" peoples in this context include, for example, the Bushmen of southern Africa and the Adivasis or "tribal peoples" of India. Such groups find themselves trapped in by developing states for whom traditional indigenous modes of life are impediments to development and where their traditional lands are continually encroached upon for further development. One explanation for the growing solidarity of these groups with those already accepted as "indigenous" is the possibility that the historical dimension of dispossession may be key to understanding indigenous culture.

There is a growing literature, however, in anthropology particularly, that is examining indigenous knowledge, often as part of broader categorizations such as Traditional (Environmental) Knowledge.

Though this debate has not reached a consensus, in these discussions there is a uniformity of emphasis on active and respectful engagements with environment, family and community.

See also: **colonialism, cultural tourism, human rights, imagined communities, indigenization**

Further reading: Addison Posey 2000

RC

INDIVIDUATION

Individuation is about the power of naming. Naming globalization as a practice of individuation shifts concern away from the substance of globalization to a concern with empirically tracing power/knowledge networks that examine how globalization emerged as a way of imagining the world. Individuation draws attention to the ways that naming these myriad of phenomena "globalization" simultaneously makes globalization visible and renders other ways of seeing these phenomena invisible. Individuation draws attention to the epistemological and intellectual systems that make globalization visible and focuses attention on the conditions of truth and practice "under which the phenomenon of globalization acquire its positivity" (Larner and Walters 2004a: 3). A case in point is that many of the elements now studied as globalization were previously known otherwise – as the "new international division of labor," the "restructuring of the welfare state," "transnational interdependence" etc.

See also: **counter-narratives, genealogies (of globalization)**

Further reading: Larner and Walters 2004b

RM

INDUSTRIALIZATION

This is the process by which a society changes economically and socially because of a shift from agriculture to industrial technology. Where people live, the kind of work they do and the way in which time is managed all change with the advent of industrially mechanized modes of production. Here, we will not be concerned with what is commonly known as the industrial revolution of the West, but rather with the significance of industrialization in the global context.

While developed countries industrialized in the eighteenth and nineteenth century, some developing nations are still within that process of change, often labeled newly industrialized countries (NICS). This has dramatic effects on population density, as people move to cities and industrial centers, and thus on living conditions generally, including the structure of families or other traditional support units. Those who lag even further behind the NICS are the least developed countries.

As the West becomes predominantly knowledge based, developing countries take up much more of the global production of articles, including textiles, automotive products and electronic devices. This is largely because of cheaper labor costs and the enthusiasm of developing countries for foreign investment. This has led in some places to **export processing zones**.

The relative development of a nation's industry is also central to whether they can meet other obligations, most obviously those related to employee rights, open markets and environmental targets. In the early stages of industrialization, reliance on fossil fuels is great and it is not reasonable to expect fledging industries to be able to match the technology in industry that the West has (even though it is not always deployed even there). Similarly, in the early stages of developing an industry (and early stages can last for decades) it is not always realistic that new nations can compete on a level playing field, without the need for some protection of their own products in home markets. As it has often been pointed out, the West protected their own industries in such a way and, further, had the captive colonies as markets and suppliers of cheap raw materials.

See also: **global labor market, human rights, modernity, nationalization, offshoring, privatization**

Further reading: Kaplinsky 1998; Thomas 1995; Weiss 2002

INFORMAL ECONOMIES

See: **Formal/informal economies**

INFORMATION AGE

Refers to the period since mid twentieth century when information became much more available due to technological innovations such as the **internet**, digital storage, transmission and broadcasting and wireless technology.

See also: **post-information age**

INFOTAINMENT

A genre mixing information and entertainment, most usually information of the kind considered appropriate for journalists. In one way it is a hybrid genre, however aspects of infotainment are visible even in hard news programs, which might end with a public interest story (soft news) or utilize personality presenters and technical gadgetry to deliver "proper" stories (hard news).

It can be argued that infotainment results in delivering viewers to advertisers rather than providing information.

See also: **global media, mass media conglomerates**

Further reading: Anderson 2004; Lewis 1991

INGO (INTERNATIONAL NON-GOVERNMENTAL ORGANIZATION)

See: **NGO**

INHUMAN HYBRIDS

A term used by British sociologist John Urry (2000) to describe the increasingly complex assemblages of humans and technological systems. These networks are not simply technological, since they serve to transmit human flows, but neither are they purely human, since all the activities carried out within them are a result of these networks. Thus they are irreducibly hybrid.

See also: **experts/expert systems, internet**

Further reading: Latour 1999

JH

INSTITUTIONAL REFLEXIVITY

See: **reflexive modernization/modernity**

INTERNATIONAL FINANCIAL INSTITUTIONS

See: **IMF, World Bank, WTO**

INTERNATIONALIZATION

Internationalization can be used as a term to describe processes (at a theoretical level) and also to suggest how relations between states and institutions should proceed (a more prescriptive level). Internationalization stands in contrast to strict economic globalization, to **nationalism** and to **cosmopolitanism.**

Internationalization as a process foregrounds the connections of nations and other institutions. Essentially, in terms of globalization, **skeptics** argue that the changes that are occurring in the world can be accounted for in terms of internationalization. They argue that what the processes that hyperglobalists hold as typifying globalization are in fact merely new forms of internationalization.

Internationalism also advocates mutual cooperation between nations as equals, recognizing and respecting differences, for mutual benefit. Initially, the term was deployed by socialists and continues to remain largely in the political left. Antiglobalists, for example, seek an internationalism which is not simply economic **free trade** – their interpretation of globalization. The economic integration and freedom that narrow globalization represents does not take into account cultural and social difference, nor does it treat nations as cultural and social entities, merely as economic ones. In terms of globalization, internationalists are committed to **heterogeneity** rather than **homogenization.** However, they see difference as being an asset, and argue that nations can work with each other without being dominated by interests not their own.

See also: **antiglobilization, hyperglobalist thesis, individuation**

INTERNET

As is well known, the internet was originally developed by the US Defense Department's Advanced Research Projects Agency in their attempts to design a computerized communication system that would remain intact after the outbreak of a nuclear war. This was achieved through a crucial innovation: decentralization. Information was to be divided into myriad "packets" which would find their own path across a network to their given destination, where they would be reassembled. This meant that the system could carry large amounts of data without bottlenecks and that it would continually reroute around absent nodes, making it difficult to paralyze the network. This process of "packet switching" and the protocols that coordinate are the key principles behind the internet. The underlying architecture of the internet is thus decentralized and the wide-reaching effects of the medium arise directly from this open architecture.

The internet has repeatedly developed in unpredictable ways. This tendency was apparent almost from the outset, when ARPANET (effectively the first node in what is now the internet) was installed, linking up a number of American universities. As more and more computers were added to the network it became a burgeoning email service. The 1980s saw the introduction of bulletin boards, forums where users could post messages and exchange information on a given topic. In the early 1990s Tim Berners Lee invented hypertext (although the idea was not new), the protocol that allowed the creation of Web pages and means of interlinking and indexing them. It was hypertext, and the Web browser (graphical software that allowed the user to read and interface with hypertexual pages) that took the internet out of the hands of institutions and allowed it to become the medium that it is today – a naturalized element of the Western workplace and home. This "World Wide Web" is what most people understand as the internet, and since its emergence in the mid 1990s it has grown at an unprecedented pace, spawning a system that we can neither control nor conceptualize.

The latter difficulty is reflected in the fates of a range of ideologies and models that have attempted to determine the internet. In its early days the internet was sometimes associated with a kind of informatics **anarchism**, a "hacker ethic" drawn from the **counter–culture** that was a formative influence on a generation of programmers. This ideology (neatly summarized in the statement "information wants to be free") captured the enthusiasm that the internet initially inspired, as democratic forum in which every user was potentially a creator. By the end of the 1990s this vision was supplanted by the powerful commercial interests, whose appetites had been stimulated by the first wave of net multi-millionaires – individuals who with apparently little more than a "neat" idea had amassed vast fortunes. This trend culminated in the "dot-com boom," which resulted within a few years in a "bust," and the internet as commercial space largely in the hands of a few big players.

However, the internet's open architecture has proved problematic even for established industries, as the experience of the music, film and software industries demonstrate. Given the inevitability of media convergence (the collapse of separate media into a single digital medium), the ability to maintain ownership of content has become a prime objective. However, all attempts to centralize or regulate the internet carry the risk of sacrificing the very principle that make it such a unique medium, and so its likely that it will remain an unpredictable technology for the foreseeable future.

As a global real-time information system, the internet is an integral component of globalization, and it accelerates many of the trends of a **network society.** Its decentralization provides a platform for marginalized groups to disseminate their views, and to challenge the orthodoxy of conventional media. Nevertheless, it should be borne in mind that a large percentage of the world's population does not have access to this resource, resulting in a very real digital divide.

See also: **global media, global village, knowledge society, time-space compression**

JH

INTERPELLATION

See: **Ideological State Apparatus**

KIN COUNTRY RALLYING

Part of Huntington's **clash of civilizations** paradigm, though first used by Greenaway (1992: 19). Huntington argues that **nation-states** are not the only holders of power, but that other entities, defined in terms of their civilization, also have input. Such cultures are not bound by nation–state borders. If cultures are similar, nation-states may act in the international stage more from cultural identification than from other pragmatic concerns. Each civilization, Huntington argues, has a "core state" which directs some of the actions of

144

its kin, "because member states perceive it as a cultural kin. A civilization is an extended family and, like older members of a family, core states provide their relatives with both support and discipline" (Huntington 1996: 156). Supporting kin, then, is not about ideological parity but about a sense of a familiar relationship. This might be encoded otherwise as being about long-standing alliances or good relationships. It is no surprise that many former British colonies have a kin relationship with the UK, and rally to their side in moments of need. Kin countries do not have to have such a colonial relationship, they just need to share a civilization.

See also: **colonialism, diaspora, realist paradigm**

Further reading: Bennett *et al.* forthcoming; Lepgold and Unger 1997; Nossal 1998; Ruggie 1998

KITSCH

See: **postmodernism**

KNOWLEDGE SOCIETY

Knowledge society is a contested concept, as it can mean many things. Although all societies are knowledge based, usually, the knowledge society refers to the situation where the transformation of societal structures by knowledge is seen as the core resource for economic growth and as a factor of production. Robert E. Lane (1966) was one of the first to recognize this specific place for knowledge in contemporary society and this reading is associated with Castells' (1996) theory of the information society. In this conceptualization, the knowledge society is seen as a new kind of society that is driven by new developments in communication and information technology. Some of the most important economic developments in **global capitalism** are related to the application of knowledge in technologies. According to Manuel Castells (1996) who has written the most comprehensive analysis, the knowledge society is also a global society in that it is less defined by the parameters of the national state. Acquiring the key attributes of a "knowledge society" has become the focus for many national and international economic development policies and is a key focus for many nations seeking an economic edge on the global market. The concept knowledge society refers to technical competencies but it also impacts upon **citizenship** and participation. The emergence of knowledge-based societies instigates new forms of relationships between citizens, on the one hand and between citizens and institutions on the other. Communication and information technology has acquired an increasingly prominent place in our society during the past two decades. This change is significantly affecting how we understand the nature of political life and citizenship. Some observers argue that technology is leading to a flowering of democratic principles; others maintain that this infrastructure is fostering entirely new forms of leadership and power. In terms of participation, those who have the recognized technical competencies are able to participate in the knowledge society in ways that those who do not, cannot.

See also: **experts/expert systems, human capital, income polarization, network society, risk**

Further reading: Beck 1992; Castells 1996; Giddens 1994; Stehr 1994

RM

KYOTO

A city in Japan often used as a shorthand for the Kyoto protocol, an amendment to the United Nations Framework Convention on Climate Change (UNFCCC) which is a treaty to manage and prevent global warming. It was negotiated in Kyoto December 11 1997, inviting all UN members to voluntarily agree to its terms. It came into force February 16 2005. While 141 countries have ratified the treaty, the US and Australia have not and have no intention of doing so.

There is much debate as to the soundness of the science underlying the thesis of greenhouse gases and global warming and the efficacy of the protocol itself. Arguments in both areas tend to cluster around environmental concerns (concrete results and sustainability) and economic ones (whether the protocol will impact negatively on developed nations to such an extent that their economies will go into rapid decline).

The Kyoto protocol highlights a number of ongoing issues relevant to the field of globalization. First, it clearly shows the enduring power of **nation–states** even in the face of what is often considered a global institution (the **UN**) and indeed in the face of **civil society** and **NGO**s. Second, it shows that for many nation-states, economic concerns may override environmental ones. While the former, economic concerns, is certainly part of a global discourse, economic decisions are still firmly rooted in national concerns, even though the national concerns might in turn be oriented to a global context. The latter, environmental concerns, are arguably more global and one of the central issues in concepts the **global village** such as. Third, the situation shows clearly that nation-states are not on an equal footing in the world. Certainly the convention of treating nations differently is fair, but it does draw attention to the discrepancies (both historical and contemporary) that endure. Finally, the Kyoto protocol highlights the need for attention to be given to the environment and the need to deal with the **risks** we face as humans.

See also: **balance of power, hegemony, nation–state, realist paradigm**

Further reading: Daly 1989; Gupta 2002; Houghton 2004; Legett 2001; Stokke *et al.* 2005

LANGUAGE RIGHTS

Language rights, like other rights, have various discourses attached to them including nationhood and **citizenship, human rights** and natural justice, identity and diversity. The dominance, or official status of a language is routinely defined by the **nation–state** and is usually part of a national cultural ideology. Such language dominance may also be encoded in legislation and similar state practices. Recently in the UK, for example, English language tests have been introduced as a part of qualification for citizenship.

Many see globalization as threatening minority languages; simply, this is an effect of **homogenization** and a perceived dominance of English especially. The results are thus **marginalization** of difference, loss of culture and history and oppression of minority speakers. While globalization can be argued to foster and indeed spread diversity, whether that diversity involves learning foreign languages is in question.

Language rights have increasingly been argued for from within a paradigm of human rights. This is advantageous because the concept of human rights has institutional support (through the **UN** for example). There are various ways of mounting an argument for language as a human right. Usually, language is tied to culture, or indeed, equated with it. Thus, loss of a language is said to result in a loss of culture. Some also tie language to political representation and identity. In both cases, language becomes a marker of difference. Indeed, the status of any language variety as a "language" has political implications.

However, while at an abstract level, or in terms of natural justice, one can argue that all people have a right to speak their own language (that is, their mother tongue), if there are no resources or support made available (such as translators and language instruction), this right may cease to be practically operable. In real terms, language rights and language policy go hand in hand. The question of language rights, if taken in the context of human rights, needs to be politically viable. While the discourse of human rights in law and international relations is a sturdy one, mechanisms of enforcement are far from consistent in content or application. Further, the issue of language rights cannot be seen in isolation from other human rights and indeed from other forms of cultural discrimination. While language may be indexical of a cultural identity, if a particular culture is marginalized, simple fluency in the dominant language will not always remove discrimination.

If a language has negative **cultural capital**, it may become "endangered." "Language death" and "endangered" languages evoke a discourse of environmentalism and biodiversity. Some scholars argue analogically employing a discourse of eco-linguistics. This argument rests on the premise that biological diversity (natural ecosystems, as the prime example) is good and therefore diversity is good in itself. Indeed, some argue there is a geographical link between diversity in nature and diversity in language; that is, where there are diverse natural ecosystems, there are also diverse languages. This argument has the advantage of tapping into established discourses around environmental protection. However, whether such an argument is politically motivating, that is, whether those in power will be swayed by it, is questionable (see **Kyoto**).

See also: **cultural imperialism, global English, global labor market, indigenous culture**

Further reading: Heller 1988; Kontra 1999; May 2001; Phillipson 1992, 2003; Skutnabb-Kangas and Phillipson 1995

LEGITIMATION CRISIS

The concept of "legitimation crisis" was made popular by the German philosopher Jürgen Habermas in his book *Legitimations-probleme im Spätkapitalismus* (*Legitimation Crisis* 1975) in the context of a broad evolutionary theory of history. In early "liberal capitalism" (i.e. at the time of **Marx**), Habermas argued, it was the dynamics of competitive markets which produced crises and thus fuelled class conflict. In the context of the 1970s, though, when growth rates were high and unemployment low, the locus of crisis had to be placed elsewhere. Habermas contended that the high degree of interconnectedness between the economic and the political sphere puts the strain of legitimation on the latter, since demands for state intervention and redistribution are continuously on the rise. Thus, it is no longer economic crises, but political ones which are the driving forces of "late capitalism." In Habermas's view, these are all the more threatening because politics has become a largely pragmatic affair. The reservoir of traditional or religious loyalty and legitimacy has been eroded by capitalist dynamics. The mass of the population feels no real commitment to the political system and readily becomes alienated from it if expectations are not met.

With the benefit of hindsight, we cannot but note the dependency of the notion of "legitimation crisis" on a particular time and circumstances. Today, different challenges have come to the fore, and general theories of the evolution of society have lost credit. However, at a second glance, there are aspects in Habermas's writing which are still relevant and can be found in contemporary globalization discourse, too. For one, Habermas has pointed to a general dilemma of complex societies, namely the tension between efficient governance on the one hand (demanding specialization, expert knowledge, etc.), and the need for orientation and identity beyond technocratic imperatives on the other. In other words, output-legitimacy cannot fully replace the positive identification of the addressees of decisions with the values projected by the institutions producing those decisions. Considered from this perspective, the **antiglobalization** movement in the West could also be described as a symptom of a "legitimation crisis," produced by a lack of responsiveness of the institutions of "**global governance**" for citizens' conceptions of justice and a good life.

See also: **antiglobalization, democracy, nation-state, welfare state**

Further reading: Held 1980

FO

LIBERAL DEMOCRACY

Liberal democracy first and foremost means the limitation and control of government. Its intellectual origins are to be found in notions like the "separation of powers" (Montesquieu) or of the "natural rights' of individuals (John Locke). The American and the French Revolution mark the advent of a modern conception of democracy at the historical scene. The term "democracy" has, since Antiquity, had been rather negatively connoted, only now has its global conquest begun. However, such success was only possible due to a considerable reinvention of democracy for it to suit the conditions of large-scale territorial states.

Today, the concept of liberal democracy is defined by a number of criteria such as the separation and control of state power (judicial review, the rule of law etc.), public accountability and control of government, the possibility of citizens' participation through elections and other means, the existence of a pluralistic society capable of articulating and organizing its interests, and the protection of basic rights and of minorities. Liberal democracy, thus, is not "radical" democracy; popular sovereignty is not exercised directly, but it is limited, mitigated and mediated by representation and a set of institutional "checks and balances." In a famous speech from 1819, Benjamin Constant defended such "modern" conception of democracy against its ancient Greek precursor: in modern societies, Constant argued, the individual citizen can only have a minimal influence on collective decisions, and, thus, the idea of collectively exercising political authority is unrealistic. Consequently, it is rather *individual* liberties and autonomy that have to be guaranteed in order to protect citizens from political oppression and collectivist, egalitarian tyranny.

Certainly, the devastating experiences with totalitarian political regimes in the twentieth century have strongly supported the basic ideas of liberal democracy. On the other hand, weaknesses of liberal democracy have also been experienced and have given rise to various criticisms. Throughout the nineteenth century, it was mainly the "social question" that fuelled discontent. As Karl Marx had put it, individual liberty appears rather cynical when the majority of the population cannot enjoy its promises due to a lack of material resources. Only in the twentieth century, the gradual expansion of the welfare state and thus the implementation of a "second generation" of basic rights, i.e. social rights, alleviated such tensions and led to the institutionalization of "class compromise" throughout Europe.

Contemporary criticisms of liberal democracy include social issues, but they cover a wider range of others. The alienation of citizens from politics, for instance, is a pervasive theme which goes together with a critique of liberal democracy falling short of "true" **democracy**. Elections, it is argued, have degenerated to a spectacle for the mass media, while other possibilities for effective political participation are lacking, and, thus, seem to be confiscated by a self-selected political class. In the context of globalization discourse, though, it is rather the *weakness* of the **state** vis-à-vis the economy that is deplored. Echoing arguments by the German philosopher Hegel, the state is seen as the key agent capable of acting for the common good, while the globalized market forces are perceived as anarchic, unjust and potentially harmful (both for the natural environment and for societies).

Such criticism points to the uneasy fit between liberalism on the one hand and democracy on the other with regard to contemporary challenges. Liberalism tends to belief in the existence of a harmonious order of things, i.e. a "natural" balance (e.g. Adam Smith's "invisible hand") between the individuals set free from traditional bonds and political oppression. Consequently, neither social nor natural "limits to growth" are perceived, and the global mobilization of market forces is thought of as beneficial by its very nature. The notion of democracy, on the other hand, underlines political autonomy, and thus the need to collectively define a just social order and to devise political institutions capable of implementing such order. To put it more pointedly: liberalism wants to limit political authority in order to liberate the individual; democracy wants to empower citizens to collectively govern themselves. Needless to say, from the latter perspective, the growing cultural **heterogeneity** of populations brought about in the context of globalization is perceived as a major challenge, since the unity and solidarity of the *demos* are seen as prerequisites of citizens' self-government.

See also: **cosmopolitan democracy, democracy, multicultural/ism, pluralism**

FO

LIBERAL HUMANISM

Liberal humanism is a philosophical tradition which emphasizes the political values of (1) **universalism**; (2) an essential (common and universal) human nature; and (3) individual autonomy. Liberal

151

humanism is not concerned with traditional modes of authority for their own sake (church, state and so on).

It is a tradition that emphasizes the role of Man as knowing subject. Thus values of rationalism and empiricism are central. The power of the liberal humanist mode of thought can be seen in the continuing ascendancy of these two values, even in the face of the intellectual challenges of **postmodernism**. It should be stressed that the liberal humanist view of the world and indeed of history is very much a Western ideal and construct. Liberal humanism has some positive outcomes, for example the emphasis on education as a means of Man developing his powers of reason and observation thus being better placed to be and act in the world.

As a concept it is most relevant to globalization in its construction of universal values by the West in the form of **human rights** agendas and infrastructures. It is possible to understand at least some of the more recent global institutions as founded on values from the liberal humanist tradition (e.g. the **UN**).

Liberal humanism is a tradition and set of values which tend to be oriented towards "the interests of the bourgeois class" (Belsey 1985: 7) and often seeing Man (male) as the norm. It is also a tradition which is more or less secular. In the creation and imposition of universal human values, spiritual and religious traditions are often effaced.

See also: **ethnocentrism, Marx/Marxism, reflexivity**

Further reading: Belsey 1985; Surber 1998; Tarnas 1991

LIBERALIZATION

Liberalization refers to a decrease in (usually) the intervention of the **state**/government in particular areas of social or economic policy. Thus while liberalization can refer to the way in which the state in some ways withdraws from the policing of individuals, liberalization, in the globalization context is normally used to refer to a more laissez-faire approach to economic matters. This classically involves **privatization** of previously state-run enterprises (postal services, water and energy supply) as well as the opening up of economic borders for the purposes of trade and foreign investment. Such policies and actions are also referred to as being **neoliberal**. When open markets (in terms of trade and finance) are prioritized, the economic infrastructure of the **state** does not necessarily improve. Indeed, given that privatization and general deregulation are core features of liberalization, the state may well be left with less control over financial and trade traffic and less access to financial stability in the form of taxes and the like.

Global financial institutions such as the **IMF** and the **WTO** are largely predicated on the positive value of liberalization.

Liberalization also refers to a modern view of society that can be seen as threatening social values, particularly those of social cohesion and community.

See also: **fair trade, Foreign Direct Investment (FDI)**

Further reading: Rodrik 1997; Tornell and Westermann 2005

LIFESTYLE

Lifestyle describes a new kind of social organization based on marketing theory which started in the 1970s. Lifestyle describes a category of person characterized by behaviors, consumer practices and opinions and attitudes. Market research links these up in order that products can be appropriately branded. We might separate lifestyle into individual style and social style. "Individual style" suggests that we behave based on who we are as individuals. "Social style" suggests that we behave in terms dictated by our membership of social groups such as gender or social class. In lifestyle we choose our own style using products and opinions that are packaged for us by marketers. So a beer or a newspaper, for example, will be produced to signify a particular set of attitudes, a particular set of behavioral characteristics. Chaney (1996) has said that lifestyle is fundamentally a visual phenomenon where people learn to publicly reveal the kind of person that they are through conspicuous acts of consumption, such as drinking a certain beer, carrying a certain newspaper. Global advertising companies now spread lifestyle marketing techniques around the planet.

See also: **choice (discourse of), consumerism, cultural capital, global media, lifestyle enclaves, localization, Transnational Corporations (TNC)**

Further reading: Chaney 1996; Machin and van Leeuwen 2005

DM

LIFESTYLE ENCLAVES

Mass media and other products are now produced for target audiences, that are not characterized, as before, by demographic qualities such as gender, age and social class, but by **lifestyle**. Members of society in this model are therefore thought about in marketing terms not as being "working-class," or as "women," but in terms of the lifestyle group, or enclave into which they fit. Lifestyle is a marketing concept that started in the late 1970s. It is a process in which market researchers gather information about behaviors, attitudes and consumer practices. They then use this information to describe particular lifestyle groups or enclaves for advertisers. They are then able to place products for these groups by associating the products with the attitudes and opinions of that group. This is important in the process of branding whereby products become associated with certain core values. Cars, beer, newspapers or magazines will be carefully branded so that they immediately signify something broader than their use value, something that makes them recognizable as being in the realm of a certain lifestyle enclave. A lifestyle enclave will be thought about as a "constellation" of behaviors and attitudes. Arguably this has an effect on the way that identity becomes displayed not by what a person thinks, but by aligning alongside a set of values through an act of consumption. As marketing and advertising practices consolidate around the world so too will society become characterized by lifestyle enclaves.

See also: **consumerism, global media**

DM

LIFEWORLD

Lifeworld is a concept from the philosopher Habermas which refers to the everyday experiential practice of living. It is a part of his broader concept of communicative action – it is in the lifeworld that communication action is possible. We are able to interact with others because of shared beliefs, values, cultural practices and the like. In turn, individuals are able to construct themselves using the resources of the lifeworld.

The lifeworld is defined in part by its opposition to the "system," though both the lifeworld and the system are aspects of society rather than discrete identities. The system "operates by way of the functional interconnection of action consequences and by-passes the action orientation of individual agents." (Cooke 1994: 5). The system is not concerned with the norms and values of the lifeworld, rather, the lifeworld is built up of language and culture (in the broadest sense).

In the context of globalization, our lifeworld is subject to great change because of the encroachment of other administrative, political and financial systems. The lifeworld in the period of globalization is one of **hybridity**. Having access to a lifeworld is essential for maintaining language and culture but also a sense of community. The system, however, is colonizing the lifeworld such that organizations (such as corporations, universities and other institutions) are driven not by individuals and communicative action but by the logic, demands and external viewpoint of the system.

See also: **antiglobalization, global sub-politics, habitus, structuration, theory**

Further reading: Bartlett 2001; Habermas 1987; Tomlinson 1999

LIMINAL/LIMINALITY

A term which originates with Turner (1974), "liminal" can be used to refer to a person or a space characterized by indeterminacy, openness and uncertainty. The liminal is outside stable categories, and defined by being outside rather than being a separate space in its own right. The concept of liminality was originally used to describe the transition state that individuals pass through in certain rituals. Thus, in initiation practices, one may be removed from society to undergo practices or processes to finally return to the group with a new social identity. In short, the liminal is the "betwixt and the between," a way of speaking about concepts and things that do not fall within conceptual, temporal or spatial boundaries and certainly not anything that is neatly described in terms of binary oppositions. Thus it is particularly present in **postmodern** and post-structural work.

In terms of globalization, liminal is used about spaces and identities or people. In the latter case, it is a partial synonym for marginalized.

Further reading: Rampton 1999; Turner 1974

LIQUID MODERNITY

A concept mostly used in globalization studies by Zygmunt Bauman (2000) to highlight differences of contemporary life when compared with **modernity**. Liquid modernity requires new ways of narrating human experience because, for example, identity is fluid rather than static. It is characterized by "boundary management" (Beck *et al.* 2003) as boundaries are not set as they were previously. In short, liquid modernity as a concept seeks to capture the changing nature of the world and identity at a time when traditional models and explanations no longer work.

A good example of the way in which boundaries have shifted is exemplified in the way power is now exercised. Bauman writes that we have moved "from a Panopticon-style to a Synopticon-style society" (2000: 85). There has been a shift away from surveillance by authority to constant monitoring by all. Bauman notes that conforming to rules and norms is more likely to be "through enticement and seduction rather than by coercion" (2000: 85–86). Further, the public is being colonized by the private, with private lives on show in a central domain which erodes (in a typically liquid way) the very division between public and private. The advent and popularity of reality shows and blogs are symptomatic of this shift. Bauman suggests that there are no longer citizens, only individuals. Thus, there can be little collectivity based on preexisting membership of groups.

Liquid modernity is similar to Beck's concept of second modernity (2002) or Giddens, notion of modernity (1990). The features of liquid modernity mean that **risk** is of prime concern.

See also: **civil society, master concepts, panopticon, postmodernity/ postmodernism, re-embedding, reflexivity**

LOCALIZATION

The concept of localization is key in globalization. It refers to both perspectives and practices which prioritize the particular and local rather than the global. In terms of perspectives, it recognizes that while the world is to some extent globalized and interconnected, people still live in particular places and have particular practices because of that. This does not mean that the local is immune from outside (global) influences. The concepts of **glocalization**, **hybridity**, **re-embedding** are ways of talking about the flows between the local and the global.

In terms of practices of localization, global corporations are a good example. Microsoft will localize their products in terms of language options, marketing and service strategies. The mass media, especially magazines and films, also localize their content and look. Thus while genres and formats may be common throughout the world, there is some variation in terms of content appropriate to local markets. There is a constant push–pull of flows and influences. Thus localization also refers to concern for and investigation into the local effects of global policies, particularly in the areas of sustainable development, **free trade** and **liberalization**.

See also: **antiglobalization, global English, global media, Transnational Corporations (TNC)**

Further reading: Hines 2000; Tunstall and Machin 1999

MACROANTHOROPOLOGY

This term was coined by Hannerz (1989), an anthropologist, who argued for an analytic perspective not normally associated with the discipline of anthropology that is capable of dealing not only with the local but also with other localities, flows, networks and connections. In his words macroanthropology is "a reasonably comprehensive view of the (relative) coherence and the dynamics of larger social and territorial entities than those which the discipline has conventionally dealt with" (1987: 5). This is clearly a response to the challenges of globalization as a perspective as well as a phenomenon.

See also: **glocal/glocalization, localization, network society**

MARGINALIZATION/CENTRALIZATION

Marginalization in globalization discourse is usually used as a short-hand for economic marginalization. The patterns of development, flows of products and concentrations of power mean that some actors (be they nations or corporations) will be pushed to the periphery of production, influence and accumulation of capital.

Marginalization may also be used to refer to the geographic marginalization of nations and corporations, particularly with respect to the north/south divide and the **core-periphery model** of **world systems theory**.

It is also used in contrast to enmeshment, that is, the complex interrelationship between economic actors at a global level. This is typical of the view of global transformationalists who see globalization as heralding a new order in the organization of the world (see Held and McGrew 2003).

MARKET SEGMENTATION

Market segmentation describes the way consumers are grouped into segments according to habits, interests, and consumption profile. George Day (1980) distinguished between two broad ways of doing such segmentation; bottom up and top down. The former takes an individual consumer and builds a group around them; the latter starts with the whole population and divides it into groups.

Given that many corporations operate globally, market segmentation occurs not only within a particular national demographic, but also within a global context. This is where **localization** of products and marketing campaigns becomes particularly relevant. Thus variables that contribute to profiles include income, nationality, education and occupation but also increasingly other more fluid identity markers, such as **lifestyle**, values and loyalty to brands.

See also: **consumerism, internet**

MARX/MARXISM

Karl Marx (1818–1883) bequeathed to the social sciences an encyclopedic theory that outlines the development, internal workings, and decline of the capitalist mode of production. His work was ground-breaking in two ways. First, Marx devised a method of research called dialectics to expose the processes underlying human history. The dialectical method is a way to develop an argument by exploring the contradictions within it and then devising a solution to those contradictions. Knowledge advances through a thesis-antithesis-synthesis process. A thesis consists of a theory, and its antithesis is the inconsistencies and problems internal to it. Synthesis is achieved when a solution is devised and integrated into a new system of ideas, which is the next starting thesis. In the realm of human history, Marx identified feudalism as the first thesis, which gave way under its own internal contradictions. **Capitalism** resolved many of those problems, but it too generates tensions, paving the way for a new synthesis called communism.

Second, Marx rejected the dominant notion of his time that ideas are the guiding force of history. Instead, he argued that the material conditions of life determine how history unfolds. The changing processes people use to meet their basic material needs constitute not only the engine of history, but also the foundation of society, and all other aspects of social life follow from them. Social analysis, then, should take as its starting point the prevailing economic relations of society. Marx merged these two intellectual strands to create "dialectical materialism," which focuses on dialectical relations within the material world.

Capitalism was the new prevailing mode of production in Marx's time. He witnessed the inequalities engendered by it, which inspired him to write his critical analysis of capitalism in the three volume work *Capital* [1972 [1867]]. Marx claimed that capitalism is unequal, because it divides people into two classes: those who own the means of producing material needs (bourgeoisie) and the majority who don't (proletariat). This latter group of people are paid subsistence wages for their labor, but what they produce is owned by the bourgeoisie. The gap between the value of their wages and the market value of the products they make is called **surplus value**, the profits that accrue to the capitalist employer. This inequality, in combination with the alienation that results when workers are forced to do demeaning and meaningless work over which they have little control, fosters class conflict. Marx theorized that the proletariat would rise up through a mass revolution to overthrow the owners of capital and instate the collective ownership of all means of production within a communist economic system.

In terms of globalization studies, contemporary Marxists are concerned with the world economic system that has developed as capitalism spreads across the globe, creating regions of "development" and "underdevelopment." Contrary to the received wisdom that "third world" countries lack the requirements necessary to develop as northern countries have, Marxists argue that underdevelopment is a consequence of a world capitalist system that, through imperialism and **colonialism**, has plundered southern resources and undermined their economies. Even now that most colonized countries are politically independent, their economies and workers are still dominated by capitalist forces which are largely out of their control. Marxists continue to analyze these processes, hoping that understanding will reveal important sites of class revolution.

See also: **capitalism, colonialism, hegemony, world systems theory**

Further reading: Gramsci 1971; Mandel 1969; Smith 1992

NC

MASS MEDIA CONGLOMERATES

In the early 1980s the introduction of 24-hour channels, the video cassette recorder and the deregulation of the global media market greatly increased profits made in the media. At the same time, a small number of vast **TNC**s expanded their global ownership of media outlets.

In today's **global media** market the largest media conglomerates (Time Warner, Disney, Bertelsmann, Viacom and News Corporation) own a wide range of companies around the world. These TNCs adhere to vertical and horizontal integration of their products. Vertical integration occurs when a TNC purchases companies that complement the original product, so film production companies (e.g. Viacom) purchase film distribution companies or video rental stores in order to distribute the films themselves. Horizontal integration occurs when companies purchase or develop other companies in order to expand their output. For example, a company like Disney purchases music companies, television networks, comic books or sports teams in order to sell/market their own products.

The concentration of the global media raises numerous concerns such as the threat to the diversity of public opinion, the effect of cross ownership on news programs and the potential self-censorship of journalists. One of the most serious concerns is the convergence of the media products resulting in a lack of diversity and in particular, the dominance of American-style programs around the world.

Concern about media ownership is not now. At the turn of the twentieth century owners such as the press barons Lords Northcliffe and Beaverbrook in the UK had significant influence over their newspapers, shaping both their content and layout.

See also: **Americanization, consumerism, cultural imperialism, global media, lifestyle, media imperialism**

Further reading: Herman and McChesney 1997; Williams 1998

DM

MASTER CONCEPTS

Traditionally, academic disciplines build on a core set of more or less unchanging theories that form a paradigm through which phenomena are viewed. Master concepts is a synonym for these fundamental theories and modes of analysis (also known as grand narratives). Master concepts outside academia also exist as general beliefs realized in, for example, gender roles and cultural practices.

Globalization arguably challenges the utility of these concepts because, as Tomlinson notes, master concepts "are bound to misrepresent globalization: lose the complexity and you have lost the phenomenon" (1999: 14). Thus, new concepts are being generated in order to capture complex phenomena more accurately. The new concepts often borrow from, extend and combine previous approaches.

Given the attention to this reassessment of master concepts in globalization literature, it is easy to believe that such attention is unprecedented. In fact, such master concepts are constantly undergoing shift within their disciplines of origin. The concept of "class" for example, has been problematized, reinterpreted and redeployed in perhaps every discipline in which it is relevant (e.g. economics, sociology, linguistics etc.), thus the problematization of master concepts in the field of globalization is as much a rhetorical as a theoretical turn.

See also: **counter-narratives, experts/expert systems, hybridity/ hybridization, postmodernity/postmodernism, risk**

Further reading: Blasco 2000

MATERIALISM

Materialism is often used as a virtual synonym for **consumerism** and consumer culture. Otherwise, materialism is most often encountered as **post-materialism**.

See also: **consumption rituals, lifestyle, liquid modernity, postmodernity/ postmodernism**

MCDONALDIZATION

This term was coined by George Ritzer in his book, *The McDonaldization of Society* (1993). For Ritzer, McDonaldization is the

161

process by which the principles of the fast food restaurant (efficiency, calculability, predictability and control) are coming to dominate several sectors of society and parts of the world. Thus it is the spread of these ways of working (highly "rational" ways of working) into new fields that Ritzer explores and critiques in his concept of McDonaldization. He argues that this is not a new phenomenon, in fact, Henry Ford's revolutionary production line system of manufacture is the example used for work practices in places like McDonalds. The problem Ritzer identifies is that these processes are entering new social and cultural realms.

This "rational" way of working requires that every task in a manufacturing process is broken down to its component parts. Each task is then made as simple as possible, and a strict order of tasks is decided upon. While this is in some ways completely rational, it also excludes the permissibility of things being done in any other order. Tasks at McDonalds in particular are designed to be "idiot proof." This way of managing processes is incredibly efficient. It also allows quantification of how many products are made in certain time frames (calculability), knowing exactly what the product will be like (predictability), and ensures very little variation and few mistakes (control).

Ritzer critiques the spread of this process on the grounds that it takes away control, creativity and autonomy of the individual. According to him, these kinds of work models are being used in places and in ways that were not previously subject to such "rational" modes of production. It is worth bearing in mind that this way of working is also enabling (mainly at the point of consumption) because efficiency means availability and affordability. Further, the features of "rational" working are not necessarily bad in all parts of life. Knowing that a car is well put together, that quality is controlled and that it is affordable is a good thing. Likewise, predictability and efficiency are desirable features of a government welfare system for example. The question is not so much whether working in a highly "rational" way is a good thing in itself, but whether such management of processes is always appropriate.

McDonaldization impacts not only those within the sectors that are being managed in this way but also upon those who interact with these sectors (e.g. consumers).

McDonaldization also is often confused with **homogenization** and this is often the way the tom is used and understood. The Mc-prefix has also been used to indicate that the concept attached to it is a *homogenized* version (e.g. McEnglish). In addition, **McDonaldization** has, for some people, because of the association with the United States, become synonymous with **Americanization** and **Coca-colonization.**

See also: **Americanization, Coca-colonization, cultural imperialism, homogenization**

Further reading: Ritzer 1997; Schlosser 2002

MEDIA IMPERIALISM

The mass media have spread around the world over the past 100 years from Western origins. This has had an impact in different ways at different times. The mass media as we now know them started in the wealthier Western colonial powers. These countries had developed a massive surplus from the exploitation of the less-developed world and were able to use this to finance industrial development. One area of development was the mass media infrastructure which was subsequently moved out into, or adopted by, the rest of the world at different times and in different ways, depending very much on the wealth available in that country and on their relationship to the dominant Western powers. The kinds of press, television, movies, magazines and radio, that people therefore enjoy around the world were mainly inspired by American models. Tunstall (1977) argued in fact that the media are American. All the recognizable media formats were pioneered there: television, radio, magazines, newspapers, space satellites, advertising. He says "the media are American in much the same way that spaghetti bolognese is Italian and cricket is British" (13).

What was designed in the USA has been changed as it has been localized and adapted to fit different societies. This has meant, for example, that the ex-European colonies, were often highly influenced, at least initially, by the ideas of public service broadcasting. Other countries, post-WWII, had their media designed by the US in its commercial privatized image. Others, in the Middle East, called in the US for their expertise, although state control has been dominant at least until recently. But importantly the basis for these media were Western models

Hollywood has been seen as one special example of media imperialism with its ability to send its movies and television programming around the world. This has led many countries to develop, or call for, regulatory protection, from what they see as a colonization by American values and lifestyles. Writers like Schiller (1971) have seen the large transnational media conglomerates that control Hollywood film production and dissemination as especially indicative of Western media imperialism.

Over the past decade there has been a massive wave of commercialization of the mass media. The demise of state control of media has been seen by many commentators as the true era of media globalization. Again, this trend has originated in the US, which, supported by the Western powers, has given the world the massive waves of deregulation and **privatization** that are now transforming the media landscape. This has led to large media conglomerates being able to expand their powers around the planet.

See also: **cultural imperialism, internet, localization, mass media conglomerates**

DM

METACULTURE

Metaculture refers to discourse about and representation of culture. Arguably the fullest account of the concept has been given by Urban (2001), however it is also used by some other scholars. Metaculture as a phenomenon is essentially reflexive as its object of consideration and action is culture itself. At the same time metaculture is also cultural and can be understood as a level of culture.

Urban refers to the "stories" or comments made about cultural objects as they are exchanged, passed on and undergo transformation. The concept of metaculture (itself cultural) accounts for how cultural products (documents, films, products etc.) are constructed as culture and circulated. In short, he argues that if we can't situate a new object in metaculture, that is, with some reference to cultural antecedents, we will not be able to make sense of it.

Urban argues that metaculture accelerates the flow and transmission of cultural objects and forms, especially those that are not simply replications ("β forms" of the original "α forms") but those that are innovative ("ω forms"). Urban seeks to account for new cultural forms in terms of this understanding of metaculture. Further, cultural innovation is essential to ideological change, and thus engages with hegemonic forms at least in the sense of attempting to overcome them (Urban 2001: 26).

See also: **aura (of cultural phenomenon), habitus, hegemony, life-world, localization, postmodernity/postmodernism, re-embedding, simulacrum**

Further reading: Johnson 1997; Mulhern 2000, 2002; Robertson 1988, 1992

MICROGLOBALIZATION

A view of globalization that understands the micro level as informing the macro level and vice versa. It is thus a form and perspective of analysis as well as a particular way of viewing actions that attribute agency to globalization. This perspective differs from a top-down approach, which sees local action as influenced primarily by global events and also from a bottom-up approach which sees global events as comprised of local action.

It is perhaps most well known in relation to the theorizing of terrorist groups operating in groups called cells. Such cells are local, but they take their cues (rather than orders) from a real or imagined global or higher order. Knorr Cetina writes "the micro in the form indicated instantiates the macro; micro-principles enable and implement macro-extension and macroeffects" (2005: 215).

See also: **glocalization, network society, structuration theory**

Further reading: Eade 1997

MICROSTATE

Independent states comprised of a very small geographic area such as the Vatican, Liechtenstein, Andorra, Monaco are considered microstates. Arguably, under the pressures of economic globalization, microstates may be under threat unless they have financial and or natural resources at their disposal. In theoretic terms, microstates do not always fit into theories of international relations or political economy and thus present challenges to such globalizing theories.

See also: **world systems theory**

Further reading: d'Argemir and Pujadas 1999; Griffin 1994; Simpson 1990

MIGRATION

Migration is hardly a new phenomenon, however in the period immediately following WWII, migration (forced and otherwise) happened on an unprecedented scale. Initially an east to west flow, migration is now arguably more south to north than anything else. Obviously this poses challenges for the **nation–state** and for dealing with **multiculturalism**. It should be remembered that migration can be forced and for all kinds of reasons, including political instability, natural disasters, economic duress and as a result of human trafficking. While globalization discourse speaks about flows of people and ideas, the breaking down time and space, *free* movement of people is limited to a global elite involved in international business and to those with the necessary capital (cultural and financial) to relocate at will. Immigration policy is still the preserve of the nation-state, notwithstanding the rhetorical and sometimes actual pressure that **human rights** law and discourse may place on this. In short, migration is not a choice for many even in the globalized borderless world (Ohmae 1990). The migration policies of developed countries show that they encourage only particular kinds of migrants based on employability, financial means, language skills and *cultural capital* generally.

See also: **core-periphery model, diaspora, global managerial class/ global elite, human rights, time-space compression**

Further reading: Featherstone 1990; Massey 1993; Richmond 1994

MOBILITY

While mobility is a key idea in globalization studies, it is an overarching consideration rather than any particular theory. The focus on mobility is linked to a central tenet in globalization that the mobility of people, products, ideas and money is occurring at an unprecedented rate. Thus there are concerns within globalization studies in relation to the mobility of capital, people, ideas and jobs (e.g. **offshoring**). Such mobility is made possible by computer technology (especially for finance and ideas), travel technology and the decreasing importance of class and social position (because of the move from traditional to modern societies, in Giddens' terms).

Such mobility can be overemphasized, however. It should be remembered that there are still, and arguably increasingly, barriers to the mobility of some people in particular. Thus while mobility is a key concept, it does not of itself have anything to say about the various causes and results of such mobility.

See also: **digital nomads, free trade, internet, liberalization, migration, modernity, nation-state, offshoring, time-space compression**

Further reading: Marchand *et al.* 1998; Wang 2004

MODERNISM

Modernism is a way of viewing the world and applies not only to sociological and political theories (and perhaps resultant actions) but also to artistic movements. It is connected to **modernity** in that modernism is concerned with representation and particularly changing experiences of time and space typical of modernity. However, modernism is not tied to any particular chronological period called modernity.

MODERNITY

Modernity refers to a number of periods in history. Some date modernity from the Enlightenment period (mid eighteenth century) because of the rise of rationalism and empiricism. Still others use modernity to refer to the changes brought by **industrialization**. In this sense, modernity is characterized by a move from rural to urban living, increasing intervention of the state (especially in relation to welfare, employment conditions and city planning), secularization, individualism, education, social mobility, the rise of the **nation-state** and the increasing importance of **capitalism** and trade. In the West, this was also a period of colonization, exactly to feed the demands of production and consumption, such as the sourcing of labor and materials and the creation of new markets which could consume the resulting products. This period of modernity is what Beck calls "first modernity." This first modernity was characterized by "the idea that *we live and act in the self-enclosed spaces of national states and their respective national societies*" (2000: 20, emphasis in original).

In terms of globalization, modernity is used differently by a number of scholars and must be considered in context of those scholars' views of history and theory. Giddens (1994a), for example, calls the present period modernity (or radical modernity or **reflexive modernity**). It is a period *and* a way of living and thinking that he contrasts with the "traditional" societies we used to inhabit. Giddens characterizes "modern" society (i.e. modernity) as one consisting of self-**reflexivity** and a break with traditional social order. This means that we are no longer bound by traditional roles or institutions such as the family, and the nation, and therefore are free to make choices regarding our roles and identities. Bauman, on the other hand, has coined the term **liquid modernity** to refer to a similar transition.

Some regard modernity as a time period that has already passed, and argue that we are living in a time they call **postmodernity**. This, like Giddens' modernity, is characterized by the critical reevaluation of **master concepts**, by self-reflexivity, **mobility** and **hybridity**. Jameson (1991) regards the current period as one of "late capitalism" clearly linking economic concerns to broader ideological issues. Albrow suggests that we are moving into a period of globalism, being "the next epoch after Modernity" (Albrow 1996: 8). As suggested, Beck distinguishes between first and second modernity. Beck suggests that second modernity is characterized by the declining relevance of the nation–state when making sense of the world. In political terms, he sees first modernity as a period of rule–governed politics, and second modernity as one of rule–changing politics (2000: 65).

While modernity (and postmodernity) are time periods, the related modernism (and postmodernism) are not strictly tied to chronology. While modernism can be understood as theories and practices typical of modernity, modernism does not need to be located in a specific time. These terms are not used consistently and their meaning is a site of struggle.

Further reading: Albrow 1996; Appadurai 1996; Gwynne and Kay 2004

MONETARIZATION

In short, this refers to conceiving of something in terms of money. Monetarization is a quantification of something in terms of a monetary unit and goes hand in hand with **commodification.** Thus there can be monetarization of work, that is, work defined in relation to whether and how much money is given for it. Similarly, environmental damage can be subject to monetarization. Such conceptions are not only theoretic, but can impact in unpredictable ways on social and cultural structures.

See also: **capitalism, exchange value, global labor market, Marx/Marxism**

Further reading: Carruthers *et al.* 1998; Michaud 1997; Reck 1993

MONTAGE

Meaning "putting together," montage is usually used in relation to the temporal arts, especially cinema and music. The static form especially may be called collage. It is related to melange (mixing) and the typically **postmodern** concepts of bricolage and pastiche. The term in full, "intellectual montage," was coined by the film maker Sergei Eisenstein to describe a break with continuity editing. The juxtaposition of different elements in montage is said to create new ideas and also to mirror the processes of the mind, hence the "intellectual."

See also: **postmodernity/postmodernism**

Further reading: Pryke 2002; Smart 2004

MORAL ECONOMY

First used by Thompson (1971) to describe the behavior of the eighteenth century crowd. Currently, references to the moral economy pertain to a continuum where morality, social custom and justice influence, for example, economic and legal processes.

Sayer (2004) defines the moral economy in one of its uses as referring to how much morality influences and structures economic activities. According to this, he claims, all economies are moral economies.

The moral economy does not always just refer to the ethics of economics. It can also be used to refer to the way society functions in general. Obviously legal, financial and other regulatory institutions are central to the organization of society. In the same way that economic activity can be more or less ethical, so too for other parts of society. Thus, a society which functions only according to natural justice can be said to be a completely moral economy.

However, nowadays, a moral economy is more of a relative concept or refers to an aspect of the way society works. In the West, the **welfare state**, the prohibition on certain kinds of contracts (for example those which are illegal only because they are immoral) can be said to form part of a moral economy which works alongside a more "conventional" economy of financial and material exchange.

Sayer writes:

> The moral economy embodies norms and sentiments regarding the responsibilities and rights of individuals and institutions with respect to others. These norms and sentiments go beyond matters of justice and equality, to conceptions of the good, for example regarding needs and the ends of economic activity. They might also be extended further to include the treatment of the environment.
>
> (2003)

Thus the moral economy is not just about the substitution of morals for money, rather, the moral economy may be used to refer to any process, rule or custom where moral justice overrides the action of the market.

The term is also used as a call to action, as Powelson (1988) does in his book so titled essentially arguing that our economy should be (more) moral.

"The moral economy," Powelson writes, "captures the benefits of technological invention through classic liberalism while using side-wise checks and balances to prevent environmental damage, ethnic and gender bias, and distorted distributions of wealth . . . In the moral economy, governments facilitate but rarely mandate" (1998: 19).

See also: **civil society, human rights**

Further reading: Heath 2005; Powelson 1998; Sayer 2000; Thompson 1991

MULTICULTURAL/ISM

Multiculturalism refers to a mix of cultures and ethnicities within a particular place or **nation–state**. It can be understood as another way of speaking about multinational states, but also refers to government policies, particularly with respect to immigration. Given that populations are arguably more mobile now, multiculturalism continues to be an issue in respect of education, social cohesion and social welfare systems.

Multiculturalism often refers to policies and practices in relation to how minorities are identified and dealt with by the majority culture. In this sense, multiculturalism can stand for an integrationist policy that seeks to accommodate different cultures and ethnicities, as opposed to assimilationist policies that argue minorities should conform to the majority culture. The latter is accompanied by policies enforcing learning and exclusive use of official languages of the **state**, and a general abandonment of expressions of minority culture such as religion, dress and social relations. Such assimilationist (or monocultural) practices receive support from so called "nationalist" organizations, who campaign for homogeneity and the maintenance of an "authentic" culture.

Multiculturalism is used by some as a synonym for "melting pot" and by others as an antonym, where "melting pot" connotes assimilation of new groups into the dominant culture in an automatic way, that is, without the intervention of the state.

The policy of multiculturalism has been critiqued on a number of grounds including gender (Moller Okin *et al.* 1999), the construction and reification of "communities," the **marginalization** and ghettoization of ethnicities (Bissondath 1994), the "threat" to dominant culture and reducing solidarity and unity (Barry 2001).

See also: **biculturalism, clash of civilizations, cosmopolitanism, cultural integration, diaspora, language rights**

Further reading: Alibhai-Brown 2000; Miller 1998

MULTINATIONAL CORPORATION (MNC)

See: **transnational corporation (TNC)**

NATION-STATE

The political organization of a nation in a single sovereign unit is called nation–state. Two principles are conjoined in this concept: the principle of the **state** as an organization of power claiming sovereignty in a distinct territory on the one hand, and the claim to represent a nation based on common history, culture, language and ethnicity on the other. Since the nineteenth century, nation–states have become the dominant forms of political organization, they are the main units of the international system, and, in the course of **decolonization**, an impressive proliferation of nation–states has reshaped the political map of all continents.

The process of nation-building has been interpreted as involving a series of developmental steps: firstly, the penetration of a territory by state power; secondly, cultural and linguistic standardization and assimilation; thirdly, the expansion of political participation of the population; and fourthly, the (re-)distribution of social and economic benefits. Throughout such processes, a powerful sentiment of collective identity, solidarity and **trust** emerges. Thus, a generalized reservoir of legitimacy is created, social antagonisms are transformed into political conflicts and institutionalized, and large-scale redistributive policies are accepted. At the symbolic level, a positive sense of belonging is created, and political power is experienced as representing values and way of life. Consequently, **active citizenship** and a vital **civil society** is fostered which participates in the political process and invests in public life.

On the other hand, such national and political unity and integration was derived, in many cases, from long and often violent processes of cultural **homogenization**, assimilation and oppression of minorities. Moreover, aggressive national imperialism and contempt for the other mark much of European history, the rivalry of nation-states ultimately leading to the catastrophes of the wars of the twentieth century. The civilization and "taming" of such dynamics is a major theme of postwar politics, i.e. in international law and **human rights** regimes. Recently, a new positive image of the nation-state emerged in the context of discussions on "failed states," where deliberate nation-building is used to achieve a degree of stability and integration as the basis of any further political process.

See also: **active citizens, decolonization, democracy, nationalism, state**

Further reading: Montserrat 1996; Paul *et al.* 2003

FO

NATION-STATE, DECLINE OF

Traditionally, the nation-state has been based on the territorial state and sovereignty over this. Contemporary social, economic and cultural activity, however, is not confined to the borders of such states. Beck notes that this change "is apparent in each of the pillars of sovereignty: in tax-raising, police responsibilities, foreign policy and military security" (2000: 4). In the **EU** this is most apparent in the cooperation members undertake in relation to police matters for example. The EU is also a good example of traditionally sovereign powers being surrendered, or at least ultimately monitored, by another organization, that is, the EU.

Strange (1996) argues that whereas previously **states** were masters of markets, now the reverse is true. This "declining authority of states is reflected in a growing diffusion of authority to other institutions and associations, and to local and regional bodies, and in a growing asymmetry between the larger states with structural power and weaker ones without it" (1996: 4). At the same time, Strange notes paradoxes, for example the increasing intervention of the state in the lives of individuals and the continuing desire of those societies without official nation-state status to achieve this. Strange does argue that the nation-state is declining, but also concludes that this decline is neither uniform nor without apparent contradictions.

Michael Mann, argues that a historical perspective is essential if claims are to be made about the decline of the nation-state. Mann describes four "threats" to the traditional nation-state: capitalist transformation, environmental limits, **identity politics** and **transnationalists**. He argues that some of these alleged threats actually strengthen the nation-state. It is impossible to generalize about the status of the nation-state because "Human interaction networks are now penetrating the globe, but in multiple, variable and uneven fashion" (1997: 495).

Further reading: Mann 1986, 1993a, 1993b; Ohmae 1990; Strange 1998

NATIONALISM

Narrowly conceived, nationalism is often understood as egoism writ large, i.e. a bias in favor of one's own nation, which can also be at the basis of political principles or programs. More generally, nationalism refers to the processes involved in the emergence of large-scale collective identities and the sentiments, aspirations, discourse and imaginary such processes are connected with. Most often, language, territory, and myth/shared experience are among the criteria employed to define nationality.

Historians of ideas have sometimes grasped nationalism exclusively as an ideological phenomenon of the nineteenth century, a product of the German philosopher Herder and the Romanticists. However, from an anthropological perspective, the construction of collective identities and solidarity, of common symbolic structures and a shared understanding of space and time appears as a general problem of human social existence. At the same time, the distinct features of nationalism in its modern form have to be stressed. Charles Tilly (1990) and Michael Mann (1993a), for instance, have explained it is an ideological complement to **state** building. Ernest Gellner (1983) and Eric Hobsbawm (1990) have, rather, stressed the role of certain political and cultural changes associated with **industrialization**. To be sure, the national integration of millions of people presupposed a set of powerful media and institutions like the printing press and newspapers, public education, administrations, census, maps etc. On the other hand, one can also stress the general human tendencies to affiliate in social groups, and then act in furtherance of these groups, such as, for instance, social identity theory in psychology has done.

Theoretical debates in the human sciences have for some time now revolved around an argument between "constructivism" on the one hand and "essentialism" or "primordialism" on the other. While the former stresses the social and historical processes by which nations are "invented" and "created," the latter insists on enduring traditions and ethnic bonds that are ancient or natural, i.e. predating nationalist mobilization. In concrete research, though, such dichotomous opposition is transcended by reconstructing a wide range of modes of group (re-)production in their specific historical and sociocultural contexts. Consequently, the metaphor of "construction" seems rather misleading: while social life, like a painting, is always made, it is never an autonomous, sovereign "construction."

In globalization discourse, perspectives on nationalism are ambivalent. On the one hand, the experience of "one world" and calls for solidarity within the ecological community of mankind seem incompatible with a nationalist worldview. States and nations are perceived as things from the past, and the missionary, imperialist tendencies of Western nationalism, most recently of the US, are readily recalled. On the other hand, perceived dehumanizing tendencies of economic globalization, domination by private interests and a non-transparent global "governance without government" recommend (national) self-determination as a counterforce which enables emancipation and social justice.

To reconcile such ambivalent views on nationalism, various writers resorted to a normative distinction between a desirable "Western" (civic) form of nationalism and an undesirable "Eastern" (ethnic) form. However, such dichotomous conceptions fall short of the complexity of the problems brought about by transformations in the course of globalization. Going far beyond finding the "right" type of nationalism, they rather seem to reframe the very fabric of political space and thus to pose once more the fundamental questions of political order, justice and legitimacy. Concerning such a major process of transformation, the sociopsychological dynamics of in-group/out-group relations represent an important variable that has to be taken into account.

See also: **colonialism, imagined communities, nation–state, one world paradigm**

Further reading: Smith 2001

FO

NATIONALIZATION/NATIONALIZED INDUSTRIES

A nationalized industry is one that is owned by the **state**. Nationalization was common in post-WWII and is connected to the **welfare state** model of government. In the 1980s, however, some governments privatized certain services such as transport, energy and water provision.

The contemporary trend is the exact opposite of nationalization, that is, **privatization**. Thus if there is to be nationalization of an industry now, it is more likely to be renationalization, that is, the state buying *back* a particular industry. For example, the New Zealand government bought back a majority (80%) of Air New Zealand in 2003.

What remain of nationalized industries are under pressure to privatize because of the economic imperative the **nation–state** faces in the global economy. The National Health Service (NHS, nationalized in 1948) in the UK is a good example of a nationalized health care system which is under increasing pressure to privatize in some form or another (e.g. by way of PPFIs: Public Private Finance Initiatives).

See also: **global capitalism, liberalization, nationalism, neoliberalism**

Further reading: Coulmas 2000; Pollock 2004

NEOCONSERVATISM

Neoconservatism is a controversial term the meaning of which is widely disputed. Coined by the American socialist Michael Harrington in the 1970s, it is generally agreed that neoconservatism as a political movement first emerged as a response to the social upheaval of the 1960s, and that the first neoconservatives were not originally very "conservative." Associated with American politics, neoconservatives are committed to corporate **capitalism**, and believe that big business has largely succeeded in providing unprecedented freedom and affluence for Americans (Kristol 1978). Yet they are not libertarians because neoconservatives are uncomfortable with the libertarian indifference to culture and do not believe that capitalism ought to act freely or in an unregulated manner. The strong role of culture means that neoconservatism is also hostile to social welfarism. With strong beliefs in the centrality of the family, as a political group, neoconservatism aims to revalue women's place within the family, particularly as mothers and mobilize the family as a solution to state dependency. It is also a movement founded on, and perpetuated by an aggressive approach to foreign policy, **free trade**, opposition to communism during the Cold War, and opposition to Middle Eastern states that are perceived to pursue terrorism or anti-Israel policies.

See also: **neoliberalism, social capital**

RM

NEOLIBERALISM

Neoliberalism is concerned with economic policy and action rather than being a broad political ideology like liberalism, which held the liberty of individuals as paramount. This requires at the very least protection of basic rights as well as the rule of law. Neoliberalism is usually more associated with trade, capital and the state regulation of these. It is characterized by a move to open markets, low state intervention, free movement of capital and goods and **privatization** of previously **nationalized industries.** The **state** still has a role to play in providing defense and financial infrastructure, but it is more laissez-faire than interventionist.

These conditions of free trade and free movement of capital and goods allow multinational and **transnational corporations** to flourish. Neoliberalism is also the macroeconomic template employed by the

176

major global financial institutions, i.e. the **IMF**, the **World Bank** and the **WTO**. Thus neoliberal values are at the core of economic globalization and have been increasingly popular with Western governments since the end of World War II though even more so since the 1970s with the turn away from **welfare state** models, unionism and Keynsian economics towards **trust** in the rule of the market and emphasis on individual responsibility (rather than community or state responsibility).

Neoliberalism can take many particular forms, prioritizing different economic measures but, as opposed to liberalism, economic action and reform are seen as the path to development. This is in contrast to a prioritizing of political development, specifically, democratization. Neoliberal and neoliberalization are used as synonyms for (especially) economic globalization and for globalization generally. Thus "neoliberal," like "globalization" are words that are sites of struggle.

See also: **antiglobalization, capitalism, IMF, liberal democracy, liberal humanism, WTO**

Further reading: Clarke 2004; Coburn 2004; Pieterse 2004; Sassen 1999; Stiglitz 2002; Wade 2004

NETWORK SOCIETY

This term is employed by Manuel Castells (1996) to encapsulate his groundbreaking, synoptic analysis of **global capitalism**. Castells believes information and the technologies that produce and transmit it to be at the center of the network society. It allows the creation of a global economy, whose distinguishing characteristic is its ability to function as a coherent unit in real time.

The foundations of the network society were laid down in the 1970s and 1980s with the emergence of the information technology (the PC and its networking), the deregulation of markets, the collapse of the Eastern Bloc, the move in many advanced economies away from manufacture to service, the emergence of an industrial base in the developing nations, and a growing emphasis in advanced economies on the well-being of the individual over the collective, a process that has resulted in a gradual contraction of the public sphere. Although initially independent, these elements have become interdependent, such that we now inhabit an unprecedented social system. The network society is not simply a matter of economics and technology; it has social, cultural and political dimensions. Thus its rise is commensurate with the movement of women into

177

the workforce and the general demise of patriarchy, the destabilization of the nuclear family, a weakening of community ties, and the gradual reduction of the **state**'s powers and influence.

The network society is "horizontally" rather than "vertically" integrated. This means that it is not centrally controlled or planned but is distributed across regions, institutions, and territories. This logic is reflected in a number of its features. For instance the decentralized nature of its emblematic technology the **internet**, which is without hierarchy, means that it is flexible enough to be able to continually generate new routes for information transmission. Similarly the multinational organizations that operate in this new environment exhibit an exceptional flexibility, **offshoring** their operations to developing countries where labor costs are low and selling their products in the advanced economies. Indeed, so decentralized are these operations that they seem held together only by a patchwork of contracts, a distinctive brand, and their shareholders.

An allied feature is its **hybridity**, it is a society where extremes coexist, and it appears to actively accentuate these differences. Castells notes that the network society is "structured around a bipolar opposition between the Net and the self" (1996: 3). Thus we witness at one and the same time a process of social and **cultural convergence**, as different populations are brought, through media technologies and consumption, into a homogenized "non-space." There is also a resurgence of local and ethnic identities, as more and more individuals choose to identify themselves with their racial, cultural or religious heritage in an exclusive manner. Often these communities are geographically discontinuous and linked by telecommunications.

This hybridity and spatial discontinuity can be seen in the distribution of economic sectors, for instance geographically proximate areas can be effectively distant, as when areas of deprivation are found within meters of vibrant, economic hotspots. These centers of production and consumption are in constant communication with each other via technology and transport, and form a global network which routes itself around zones of extreme deprivation. This Castells terms the "space of flows," in which space is subordinate to flows of goods, data and information. These flows reconfigure formerly unified territories, and often completely bypass entire populations. In this respect Castells talks of a geographically distributed "fourth world" made up of pockets of social exclusion in every nation.

For those excluded from these flows a number of elements of network society combine to make their position particularly precarious. These include the flexibility demanded by multinationals, which continually relocate operations in order to cut costs, the absence of trade unions, and the decrease in state provision and welfare. Moreover, it is these same populations that suffer the environmental fallout of the resource-intensive lifestyle of the first world. Thus the network society is the site of a growing polarization of wealth and poverty.

See also: **civil society, diaspora, glocalization, modernity, Transnational Corporations (TNC)**

Further reading: Castells 1997, 1998

JH

NEW LABOUR

New Labour is a term the Labour party in the UK began to use to identify itself (and be described) in the mid-1990s. This involved a move away from the traditional left wing concerns of the Labour party towards a more **centrist** politics, that of the **Third Way**.

See also: **neoliberalism, welfare state**

Further reading: Fairclough 2000; Monbiot 2001

NEW PUBLIC MANAGEMENT

See: **reform (political)**

NGO (NON-GOVERNMENTAL ORGANIZATION)

Technically, an NGO is any organization which is independent of and not founded by a **state**. Corporations are in this sense NGOs. However, the term is generally used for non-profit organizations. They can be very small (also known as a CBO – Community Based Organization) or operate at a global level, like the **UN**. The phrase first occurred in the UN Charter (1949) giving NGOs a consultative role in the UN.

The **WTO** and the **IMF** are NGOs, but usually when NGO is used it refers to advocacy and operational groups who foreground humanitarian and environmental concerns (rather than economic).

There are a number of other acronyms that have developed in the domain of NGOs to distinguish between various groups. These

179

include INGO (International NGO), BINGO (Business-oriented international NGO), RINGO (religious international) and ENGO (Environmental). Not completely independent of government are **QUANGOs** (quasi autonomous) and GONGOs (Government operated). There are also a number of "other" NGOs, including: the BRINGO (Briefcase NGO) which exists simply in name only without actually performing the functions normally associated with an NGO; and the CRINGO (Criminal NGO), that is, a front organization for illegal activities. These terms provided for these "other" NGOs here are not routinely used formally. However, the fact that they have been coined at all does illustrate the concerns about NGOs emanating either from government, other NGOs, donor organizations and society generally.

An NGO is given certain funding and advocacy opportunities but NGO status must be verified according to criteria set down by any particular funding body (or donor agency, which might also be an NGO). For UN recognition this requires that the organization is not involved in commercial (for profit) activity, or in violence (or advocating it), it cannot be under the control of a government or to want to replace an existing government. Truly independent NGOs are essential to the development of **civil society** globally and also especially for humanitarian aid in situations of crisis or warfare. While such NGOs exist, their independence does not mean that they are immune from national and international politics. **Nation–states** can and do regulate the work of NGOs either through explicit legislation or granting and withholding of funding opportunities (for example, legislation may determine whether it is possible to receive money from foreign donors).

There is also a hierarchy of NGOs, as the existence of INGOs would suggest. Thus larger and better financially resourced NGOs (often charities such as OXFAM or ActionAid) will provide funding to smaller NGOs to work according to their policy guidelines. It is also common for NGOs to work in partnership, especially when one is more affluent but not equipped with local expertise. NGOs also work in partnership more or less formally in networks of NGOs often for antiglobalist ends.

It has also been suggested that NGOs evolve along a path from providing relief (needs-based work) to becoming more involved in development, especially **sustainable development**, and advocacy (Korten 1990). Whether this is true depends very much on the kind of NGO that one is talking about. For example an NGO committed to lobbying and advocacy may never be involved in needs-based work in a local community at all.

The NGO sector has its own constantly evolving discourse. As in any other industry, there are more or less fashionable ways of framing and undertaking work. At the moment, there appears to be a continuing shift towards a **human rights** orientation. This is consonant with other global discourses and manages to take advantage of legal infrastructures at national and global levels.

See also: **civil society, global governance**

Further reading: Clark 2001; Dichter 2003; Hilhorst 2003; Iriye 2004; Jordan and van Tuijl 2000; Malhotra 2000; Pratt 2004

NON-ALIGNED MOVEMENT (NAM)

The Non-Aligned Movement is a group of nations who decided to band together on the basis that they were not allied to major powers in the international scene. The organization was first suggested by Indian Prime Minister Nehru in 1954 and founded shortly after. It is an organization of mainly southern and recently independent states who are not affiliated with major powers in the global context.

It is an alliance interested in development (especially in a post-colonial setting), mutual respect and nonaggression. Thus it is neither a trade nor a military alliance. While the organization was intended to have some of the cohesiveness of NATO, it has struggled in recent years to achieve or maintain this. Nevertheless, it has been instrumental in putting some issues on the global agenda, most notably a call for a new international information order (1955) and subsequently a new international economic order (1973). Both of these themes recognize unequal flows of each of these resources leading to many nations feeling culturally colonized (MacBride and Roach 1989). The NAM, however, potentially can make a great deal of difference in global forums (like the **UN**) not so much through putting their own consensus or particular policy forward but by drawing attention to their concerns in the global context. This becomes increasingly possible with the growing economic power of members like India, China and Brazil.

See also: **balance of power, colonialism, core-periphery model, cultural imperialism**

Further reading: Harris 2005; MacBride and Roach 1989; Roach 1997; Singham and Hune 1987

NON-MODERN

Usually used to describe organizations or nations in relation to a
concept of the modern and **modernity** without invoking notions of
the premodern, **traditional**, **postmodern** or hypermodern. In practice, it usually refers to societies which are agricultural and agrarian.
Thus it refers to something which is not traditional but at the same time
cannot be accounted for in any "modern" terms. The term surfaces in
Latour's (1993) work where the meaning is not straightforward but
rather gestures to an argument about contemporary society.

See also: **hybridity, networks, postmodernity/postmodernism, risk**

Further reading: Locink and Schultz 1997; Nolan and Lenski 1999; O'Brien *et al.* 1998

NORTH/SOUTH DIVIDE

This term refers to the unequal distribution of political and economic
power that exists between the countries located in the northern and
southern hemispheres.

See also: **core-periphery model, world system theory**

OECD (ORGANIZATION FOR ECONOMIC CO-OPERATION AND DEVELOPMENT)

The OECD is an alliance of developed countries accepting liberal
political and economic policies and as such can be seen as institutionalization of the power of the north. It is perhaps most well known
for its development, negotiation and drafting of the MAI (Multilateral Agreement in Investment) which was to outline the rights of
foreign investment by corporations. The agreement was subject to
concerted lobbying by a large number of NGOs and is, at the
moment, held in abeyance.

The organization is a direct descendant of the Organization for
European Economic Co-operation (OEEC), set up post-WWII to
implement the US-led Marshall plan for the rebuilding of Europe.
Thus while some rhetorical attention is paid to development and
quality of life, the predominant mode of action is macroeconomic.

The headquarters in Paris acts as a clearing-house for information on economic and social indicators at a global level. This information then provides the basis of discussion among the OECD members and indeed for their own domestic and business policy formulation. This research function is the foundation of the OECD whose publications, reports and statistics are considered thorough, reliable and authoritative.

It is also a forum in which issues and problems are discussed. This often results in informal agreements which may then become bilateral or multilateral agreements. An Anti-Bribery Convention, for example, which came into effect in 1999 was a result of such a process. The OECD positions itself as an institution with a global reach citing its collaboration with **NGOs, civil society** and nonmember nations.

Globalization **skeptics** (e.g. Hirst and Thompson 1996) argue that changes typically associated with globalization are only really happening in OECD states, which is hardly surprising given the organization's commitment to the core principle of economic globalization, **liberalization** of economies.

The OECD is most likely to be encountered as a way of grouping and describing countries. In short, 24 of the 30 members are classified as high-income nations (according to **World Bank** criteria).

See also: **hyperglobalist thesis, liberal humanism, Third Way**

Further reading: Mittelman 2000; OECD 2005

OFFSHORING

Offshoring is the transfer of business processes overseas, either by outsourcing to a third party or retaining control in-house. While outsourcing of production has developed with increasing trade **liberalization**, *service* outsourcing is more recent. The term has been particularly applied to the relocation of customer service and IT functions. One estimate suggests a loss of five million jobs from the US and UK by 2015.

Advances in technologies made it possible, by 2000, to integrate globally dispersed business processes. Effectively, call center and "back office" functions could be performed wherever there were adequate communications and a supply of qualified labor. Driven by competition at home, companies relocated work to countries such as India, where labor costs were lower (and labor rights inferior).

Initially a feature of the financial services, by 2005 there were examples of offshoring across the economy, including the public sector. Early growth was largely attributable to US and UK companies, who were able to exploit the global dominance of the English language. Subsequently, market pressure has seen other European economies follow.

The debate has been fraught with conflicting priorities. For advocates, offshoring represents a win–win solution: savings in one activity mean investment in more sustainable jobs elsewhere. For critics, unregulated **mobility** means a "race to the bottom." However, trade union responses have been tempered by international solidarity. It is likely that competition from still lower cost economies will prompt reevaluation.

See also: **digital nomads, global English, internet**

Further reading: United Nations Conference on Trade and Development 2004

GW

ONE WORLD PARADIGM

There are a number of ways in which the phrase "one world" may be used in the globalization discourse. Huntington, in his work on the **clash of civilizations**, claims that a one world paradigm, in the sense of a universal culture, is an "unreal alternative" (1993: 23). "One world" can also refer to arguments about **homogenization** in globalization. In terms of the interconnectedness implied by talk of "one world," the phrase may also refer to the responsibilities that result from living in a **global village**. It is more in line with this last sense that the philosopher Peter Singer argues for consideration of ethics in the global landscape of inequality (2004).

See also: **communities of fate, risk**

Further reading: Singer 2004

OPEN SOCIETY

Originally coined by the philosopher Bergson (1935), this term refers to a government which is flexible, transparent, open to change and tolerant of diversity and dissent. In that sense, it is the opposite of the authoritarian state. The term is usually used in the philosopher Karl Popper's (1945) sense, which is not radically different. It is based on his philosophy of science and general epistemology which claims that we do not have access to the truth; an open society is one which is open to change. Thus for a change of government a revolution is not required (as it would be in an authoritarian closed society).

An open society thus protects cultural and ethnic diversity with appropriate human and civil rights infrastructures. In a global age, flows of people especially in the form of migrants (economic, forced or otherwise) challenge the open society in terms of retaining tolerance and social infrastructure in the face of increasing diversity. An open society has to be aware of its contingent status to remain open and thus a measure of self-**reflexivity** is required.

See also: **liberal democracy, migration, multiculturalism,**

Further reading: Fuller 1999; Soros 2000

ORGANIZATION OF PETROLEUM EXPORTING COUNTRIES (OPEC)

OPEC is an economic alliance, and a cartel of petroleum-producing and exporting nations who coordinate policy and to ensure stability of price for the benefit of producing countries. Given the constant demand for oil, OPEC has a high degree of political and economic power. As oil comes largely from the south, this provides some redress to the domination by the north by restricting production, raising prices or refusing to sell to certain nations. The influence of OPEC is also part of a move away from the power of **nation–states**. It should be remembered, however, that while OPEC is an alliance, its constituent nations may act independently. However, global oil trade is conducted in US dollars and thus dependent on the performance of the US economy. Iraq is the only member to insist on being paid in Euros, thus the industry is still very much tied to the US.

Given ongoing **industrialization**, the demand for oil is not likely to abate without intervention. At a global level, especially because of environmental concerns, there are strong demands for the reduction in use of all fossil fuels. Here, the north is again at an advantage. Not only are northern countries not as industry reliant on fossil fuels, they also have capital and expertise to invest in alternative energy products. Partof OPEC's demands in the past have included technology transfer fromnorth to south. The south are more dependent on fossil fuels and thus more likely to suffer in cases of large fluctuations in prices and supply.

The geographic location of production and supply stores are also relevant, as transport also involves significant amounts of money and fuel.

Recent global negotiations regarding the reduction in fossil fuel use have been far from conclusive, especially given the reluctance of the US to ratify the **Kyoto** protocol.

See also: **balance of power, core-periphery model, global capitalism, nation-state**

Further reading: Buchan *et al.* 2004; Deffeyes 2003; Roberts 2005; Singh 2002; Stevens 2005

ORIENTALISM

In *Orientalism* (1978), Edward Said examines how the "Orient" has been represented in Western literary, scholarly, political, and popular writings of the colonial era. His central argument is that a Western style of thought has developed over many centuries to posit a radical opposition between the Orient (the East) and the Occident (the West). Said argues that Orientalism is a discourse that naturalizes the Orient as inferior to Europe and thus is in need of "improvement" by European superiors. He describes three interrelated aspects of Orientalism.

First, academic Orientalism is the knowledge produced by a group of scholars and government experts who study the Orient. Said insists that knowledge cannot be separated from the power relations within which it is produced. Therefore, knowledge of the Orient is infused with imperial power relations.

Second, imaginative Orientalism consists of the general public's images and fantasies about the Orient. Any cultural representation that posits a fundamental and hierarchical distinction between East and West is Orientalist. This distinction between self and other enabled Europeans to develop corporate institutions to describe, judge, settle, and rule over the inferior Orient. This is institutional Orientalism. Europeans employed **imperialism** and **colonialism** to dominate, restructure, and gain authority over the Orient.

As recent studies show, the discourse of Orientalism is still prominent in our ostensibly postcolonial world, structuring unequal relations between "East" and "West." Efforts to realize more just global social systems, then, must include attempts to dismantle Orientalism.

See also: **ethnocentrism, human rights, world systems theory**

Further reading: Butz 1995; Young 1990

NC

PANOPTICON

The name of a prison designed by the philosopher Jeremy Bentham (1995) in which the prisoners were constantly observed, but could not see their observer. It was an effective mode of surveillance in that the guard need not be constantly on duty. The term generally invokes Foucault's (1977b) analysis in *Discipline and Punish* where he uses the panopticon as a metaphor for the structure of any hierarchical (or indeed ideologically based) movement, group or society. As a result, because people don't know whether they are being watched or not, they behave as though they are. People monitor their own behavior according to the (internalized) values of the community. This is often encountered terminologically as "self censorship."

In terms of globalization, some argue that the technology now available to the state, in the mode of CCTV cameras, and allied recognition software, means that we live in a virtual panopticon.

See also: **ideological state apparatus, liquid modernity**

PARTICULARLISM

This term refers to the identification and advocacy of values and practices specific to a group, especially in the context of ethnicity and culture with respect to **multiculturalism** and in direct opposition to **universalism**. It is often used with the words "moral" or "ethical" or with regard to religion, to defend actions based on an appeal to a specific and contextual "good" (rather than to a universal good).

See also: **relativism, multiculturalism, moral economy, pluralism**

Further reading: Hooker and Little 2000

PERFECT KNOWLEDGE

This concept relates to what is referred to as *the problem of perfect knowledge*. The economist Hayek phrases this as "a problem of the utilization of knowledge which is not given to anyone in its totality" (1945: 520). It is a problem not limited to economics, but to any theory which would generalize about the world, especially those which advocate action on the basis of theory. That is, it is impossible to have complete knowledge about any set of circumstances. This leads to debates about whether it is possible to rely on theories (especially in the field of economics).

In the field of globalization the issue of perfect knowledge is relevant to **risk**, **expert systems** and the concept of the **knowledge society**. In what could well be an explanation of expert systems in the negotiation of risk, Hayek writes, "We make constant use of formulas, symbols, and rules whose meaning we do not understand and through the use of which we avail ourselves of the assistance of knowledge which individually we do not possess" (1945: 528).

See also: **modernism**

Further reading: Downs 1957; Peukert 2004

PERFORMATIVE CITIZENSHIP

This is a term coined by the sociologist Albrow (1996) to highlight that **citizenship** is an accomplishment, something done, enacted and performed, rather than a status assigned by the state. Albrow points out that citizenship and nationality are not synonymous. Rather than simply responding to decisions and actions emanating from a centralized state, people individually and in groups perform citizenship and construct a space in which it is possible to be a citizen.

While "Citizenship has itself become a highly complex, multiple and fluid identity" (Werbner and Yuval-Davis 1999: 23), performative citizenship turns attention to what was often implicit in theorizations of the **nation–state** and the social contract in particular: the surrendering of certain individual rights to the **state** contingent on the state acting for the interests of its members. The action of citizens in Albrow's model is, however, more interactive, contextual and not revolutionary in the way that some social contract accounts might suggest.

See also: **antiglobalization, citizenship, civil society, cosmopolis, globalization from below, identity thinking, structuration theory**

Further reading: Boudreau 2000; Butler 1988, 1990; Sheil 2001

PLACELESS GEOGRAPHY

Also known as placelessness, flatscapes, thin places, and McWorld.

Placelessness "describes both an environment without significant places and the underlying attitude which does not acknowledge significance in places" (Relph 1976: 143). Placeless geography is a way of describing places and space that are not significant to the people who use them. Placeless geography is related to the **homogenization** of "place," a process analogous to that of culture or products. Airports, expensive business hotels, multinational retail outlets, theme parks and other tourist spaces are good examples of placeless space. But, it is a relative concept. Space that is placeless (thin) for some people may be meaningful and useful (thick) for others because of the way the latter can and do interact with it. Thus a concrete plaza in the middle of a city may be thin for people who only pass through on their way to work; but it may be thick for skateboarders and the like who use it as a place of recreation and socialization. Thus placeless geography is not so much about a space as such, but people's relationship with space.

See also: **global managerial class/global elite, imagined communities, McDonaldization, postmodernity/postmodernism, simulacrum, territorialization (de & re)**

Further reading: Arefi 1999; Chatterton and Holland 2003; Knopp 2004; Massey 1994; Merriman 2004

PLURALISM

Pluralism can mean a number of things, but essentially it refers either to a social policy which accepts and encourages difference (usually language, culture or religion) or to the actual profile of a society. In relation to globalization, pluralism is relevant to **citizenship** and **democracy** as well as to identity and construction of self. The **liberal democratic** state allows difference to exist within its boundaries. Thus pluralism is sometimes a term present in the fields of **multiculturalism,** religion and politics. To understand pluralism properly, consideration of relativism is necessary. Relativism is an epistemological stance, that is, related to theories of knowledge and how we know things. In short, relativism holds that absolute truth either does not exist, but more usually, that even if it does, it is inaccessible from our limited human point of view. Thus relativism holds that points of view are true only in relation to their context, whether this be cultural, political or ideological. It is thus related to pluralism in as much as it provides a philosophical ground for advocating pluralism. Relativism should lead towards tolerance, acceptance and a move away from dogma. Some treat relativism as an "anything goes" stance, however this neglects the important role of context. The idea that relativism means anarchy is a misunderstanding of the insights of relativism (and indeed of **anarchism**).

Because pluralism can be simply a state of affairs (related, for example, to the profile of a society) it does not necessarily lead to tolerance. It is often used as being synonymous with relativism and the related multiculturalism, multilingualism and so on. The latter are usually used to advocate tolerant policies which positively encourage and support diversity.

See also: **language rights, open society, perfect knowledge, relativism**

Further reading: Hogan 2005

PLURALIST PARADIGM

See: **Realist paradigm**

POLICY AGENDAS

Policy agendas refer to the pre-decision-making phase of policy. In John Kingdon's (1995) work, *Agendas, Alternatives and Public Policies,* he lays out a model of agenda setting that includes three separate streams, each operating relatively independently from the other. First, the *problem* stream consists of the set of issues that government, the media and the public believe are pressing and in need of attention. He suggests that problems come into bold relief when indicators change (e.g. unemployment rises) or by a focusing event (e.g. a train crash). Second, the *policy* stream involves the set of alternatives, at any one time, that are being considered and debated. This set is drawn from a larger "policy primordial soup" made up of popular and less popular alternatives and ideas that are being circulated by specialists, academics, and think tanks. Finally, Kingdon discusses the *political* stream, or what others have called the political opportunity structure, that is, the extent to which decision-makers are receptive to new ideas and alternatives. Kingdon emphasizes the importance of "coupling" which refers to when the three separate streams (problems, policies and politics) come together with the help of policy entrepreneurs who take advantage of windows of opportunity. Policy agendas are a central issue of globalization because historically, the policy discipline was devised by nations to ensure the welfare of its citizens. In as much as globalization is understood to have a massive and detrimental effect upon human welfare, policy agendas, programs and outcomes become one of the only effective points of intervention and amelioration (George and Wilding 2002). Policy agendas are an important site of political debate in globalization. At its heart, the debate concentrates on the issue of large **NGOs** having the skills and resources to set the agendas of nations and international organizations to benefit the free flow of global capital and labor, thus accelerating and embedding globalization.

See also: **global social policy, policy cycle, policy evaluation, policy programs**

Further reading: Held and McGrew 2003; Kingdon 1995

RM

POLICY CYCLE

The policy cycle concept is based on an understanding that, under normal circumstances, a distinction can be made between the different phases in the policy-making process, that is, the decision-making process that leads to the implementation of the "policy" (in the form of laws, regulations, programs and the like). The public becomes aware of an issue as a problem and, because of demands being made by certain groups and dominant values in society, this problem is defined as a problem on which action needs to be taken (this is called "problem definition"). This problem then becomes a part of the political decision-making agenda, meaning that a decision has to be made as to when and who will deal with the problem and in what form (called "agenda setting"). Then, accompanied by lobbying and political argument, the process of formulating the political position takes place within the set of rules laid down by the individual political system and by the protagonists. This process ends with the laying down of an authoritative assignment of value in the form of a law, a provision or a program (called "policy creation"). This policy is then given its final structure during the implementation process involving subordinate political and administrative protagonists (called "implementation"). The results and effects of these policy and implementation decisions finally create political reactions of either a positive or negative nature, which, in turn, are also implemented politically and which lead to the continuation, change or end of the policy (called "restatement of policy" or "policy termination").

See also: **global social policy, knowledge society, policy agendas, policy evaluation, policy programs**

Further reading: Mishra 1999

RM

POLICY EVALUATION

The following definition of policy evaluation has been proposed by the British Cabinet, July 2003: "Policy evaluation uses a range of research methods to systematically investigate the effectiveness of policy interventions, implementation and processes, and to determine their merit, worth, or value in terms of improving the social and economic conditions of different stakeholders" (Cabinet Office 2003). Policy evaluation is an area in which the political aspects of globalization are debated. At one level, it is a crucial means for governments to identify the impact of specific policies that have been implemented in light of globalization. At another level, much non-government policy evaluation, particularly comparative policy analysis, is used to outline the transnational consequences of policies, such as trade **liberalization** upon human welfare (Mishra 1999; Kingfisher 2002).

See also: **policy agendas, policy cycle, policy programs**

Further reading: Rossi *et al.* 1999; Scriven 1991

RM

POLICY PROGRAMS

Policy programs are the organized set of financial, organizational and human interventions used to achieve an objective or set of objectives in a given period. A program is delimited in terms of a time scale and budget. Program objectives are defined beforehand; an effort is then made systematically to strive for coherence among these objectives. The three main steps in the life cycle of a program are design, implementation and ex-post-evaluation review. A program is always under the responsibility of an authority or several authorities who share the decision-making. The program cycle follows the same pattern as the **policy cycle**. It contains the following stages: agenda setting; planning/program formulation; program implementation; program monitoring; and evaluation and feedback. Public policy is a course of action by government designed to attain specific results. **NGOs** have policies too, but they cannot call on public resources or legal coercion in the same way.

The concept of a policy program is relevant to the discourse of globalization in a variety of ways. Policy programs are increasingly the medium through which social change is wrought and are linked to the rise in significance of technical solutions to political crises (Giddens 1998) such as the call for **nation-states** to be much more efficient and accountable in their use of public resources. For some, evidence-based (empirical) approaches are central to the identification, development, implementation and evaluation of policies is seen as a core strategy to develop rational, feasible, appropriate and practical responses to the effects of globalization. There has been an expansion in the use of policy program logic and method (such as evidence-based policy planning, implementation and evaluation) beyond the boundaries of nation-states into global policy networks such as the **WHO**. For others, the proliferation of policy programs marks a transformation from a political to technical mode of governance.

See also: **global social policy, knowledge society, policy evaluation, WHO (World Health Organization)**

Further reading: George and Wilding 2002; Policy Hub

RM

193

POLITICAL GLOBALIZATION

Refers to political action which takes place in a global context and is considered one of the key dimensions of globalization. A clear example of political globalization is the **UN**, as it brings together **nation–states**. However, political globalization is not limited to action involving traditional nation–state players. Indeed, political globalization is characterized by the nation-state becoming merely one of the players in the political sphere, having to compete with corporations, other global institutions (notably those concerned with economic issues), and **NGO**s. Thus other movements such as **feminism**, those with environmental concerns and indeed the **antiglobalization** movement are also examples of political globalization.

Such action is possible for a number of reasons, though there is no singular or simple cause. The existence of global institutions (such as the UN, the **IMF** and **WTO**) means that lobbyists, activists and interest groups orient to these existing structures. The increase in access to technology, especially in the area of communication, means that aligned action across the globe is also possible. Finally, some issues are of particular global importance and motivate people and groups around the world to cooperate in working towards a common goal. Perhaps the best example of this is to be found in environmental groups concerned with, for example, depletion of the ozone layer.

Indeed, NGOs are arguably some of the most important players in global politics. In terms of how democratic and representative they are of a global population, it is reasonable to suggest that in some areas they are more accountable and representative of people than nation–states. Part of political globalization is the very questioning of the centrality of the nation-state as it is marginalized by corporations, global institutions and other regional alliances.

See also: **active citizens, antiglobalization, citizenship, civil society, feminism, nation-state, performative citizenship, world systems theory**

Further reading: Ougaard 2003

POSTCOLONIALISM

See: **colonialism**

POST-FORDISM

Applied to the production process, to industrial organization, or to the economy as a whole, post–Fordism refers to the current phase of capitalist development, seen to be qualitatively distinct from the previous "Fordist" regime. Beyond this general point, there is little consensus on the causes and social consequences of this shift, or on the scope for human agency in directing or ameliorating change.

At the level of the workplace, "Fordism" is associated with the intensive, automated production techniques that spread throughout industry from the 1920s – notably the assembly line and with the specific forms of work and industrial relations that developed around these processes. At the level of the economy, Fordism can be thought of as the bringing together of mass production with mass consumption, which delivered sustained growth, notably in the three decades after 1945. Post-Fordism represents a disjuncture on both levels.

The crisis of Fordism followed both the failure of Fordist production methods to deliver sustained productivity gains, and also the failure of Fordist economic management. Key factors include the globalization of production and finance, domestic market saturation and changing consumer demands. Commentators differ as to whether post-Fordism constitutes a resolution of this crisis, rather than an incomplete process of adaptation in response to declining profits – a *neo*-Fordism.

Thus, in this broader sense, Fordism was a "mode of regulation": a socioeconomic framework within which a particular regime of production was sustained. If Fordist production was inseparable from the wider Fordist state, including Keynesian demand management, along with the institutional basis of industrial relations, then post-Fordism entails the dismantling of much of this regulation in pursuit of flexibility.

Amongst the first evidence of a new production paradigm came from northeastern Italy in the 1970s. Here, in contrast with the older industrialized regions, small firms were organizing as cooperative networks of subcontractors. The work process, divided and de-skilled by Taylorism, appeared to be reintegrated. And the focus was on "flexible specialization" in response to customer demand. Subsequently, various initiatives such as **offshoring**, just-in-time production and the growth of a peripheral workforce have been seen as symptoms of a more widespread trend.

The post-Fordist period, then, saw the adoption of new production methods, new forms of industrial organization, and a redefinition of work and managerial control. Niche production for diversified markets, it is argued, began to supplant the mass production of standardized products. Monolithic companies gave way to decentralized and vertically disintegrated structures. And, in some accounts, the new, consumer-led production gave rise to a new workforce, empowered and polyvalent, in place of Fordist automatons.

But the model has attracted criticism on several levels. The concept >is founded on a selective reading of the evidence, initially extrapolated from very specific developments. Modern production methods seem stubbornly similar to those of Fordism. Whilst **commodity chains** are dispersed, ownership of production capacity is concentrated. Whilst new technologies rely on "**symbolic analysts**," these coexist with a casualized, deskilled, and frequently unrepresented workforce. And where local "post-Fordist" change is observed, this needs to be seen in the context of an emerging "global Fordism."

More fundamentally, the concept of paradigmatic change can be seen as having promoted, rather than simply explained, new forms of organization and methods. In effect, post-Fordism may have acted, not as a theory, but as a template.

See also: **consumerism, global capitalism, industrialization, McDonaldization, modernity**

Further reading: Aglietta 1987; Amin 1994; Kumar 1995; Piore and Sabel 1984

GW

POST-INFORMATION AGE

The post-information age refers to a time marked by the evolution of digital technology after computers (often referred to as the information age) became a regular part of society. Digital technology allows information to be personalized and communication to happen in a way that is not synchronous therefore its relevance to globalization comes from its effect on space/time.

See also: **digital nomads, information age, internet, knowledge society, time–space compression**

Further reading: Negroponte 1995

POST-MATERIALISM

Post-materialism is a term derived from the work of Ronald Inglehart (1977, 1990). Basing his theory around the emergence of the **counter-culture** of the 1960s, Inglehart suggested that advanced societies were witnessing a shift from material to post-material values. He claimed that the predominant values of a culture were shaped by two factors: socialization and scarcity. The first refers to the ambient values of a culture, and these have their greatest impact on a given generation during its adolescence. The second describes whatever is missing in a given sociocultural context. Thus in the case of post-materialism, he maintains that the postwar generation has grown up in an age of material wealth (unlike their parents who had experienced the depression), as a result the scarcity that effected this generation was that of a "spiritual" or more intangible variety. This generation was the first to articulate a demand for the satisfaction of post-material needs (reflected in a concern for the environment, and a desire for self expression and fulfillment etc.). Inglehart suggests that as this generation assumed the mantle of power its post-material values would come to characterize the orientation of society in general. Critics have questioned the validity of this thesis, maintaining that there is little evidence of a mass reorientation to post-material values in Western societies.

In contemporary debate post-materialism is sometimes used more generally to describe the difference in values between developed and developing nations.

See also: **consumerism, moral economy, postmodernity/postmodernism**

JH

POSTMODERNITY/POSTMODERNISM

Postmodernity and postmodernism are fluid and contested terms that are often misleadingly conflated. Essentially they refer to a period of time in which cultural and political practices can be characterized as postmodern. Strictly, postmodernity is a historical era, whereas postmodernism is an artistic style. Thus one could live through postmodernity and practice postmodernism, but not vice versa. Both terms clearly signal a break from **modernity**, although scholars continue to argue about the precise differences between the modern and the postmodern, and sometimes question whether any differences exist at all.

The era of postmodernity is usually thought to have begun in the second half of the twentieth century, and many argue that it has not yet come to an end. The postmodern impulse is certainly a postwar impulse, and in this sense postmodernity shares its roots with post-structuralism, a mode of philosophy that seeks to topple the central pillars of Western thought, and which is often subsumed under the postmodern umbrella. Like post-structuralism, postmodernity presents a challenge to modes of thought that characterized the modern world. For the German post-Marxist philosopher Theodor Adorno, the Nazi concentration camps revealed the need to rethink the modern world completely: "a new categorical imperative has been imposed by Hitler upon free mankind: to arrange their thoughts and actions so that Auschwitz will not repeat itself" (1973: 465)

The rejection of the modern project is taken up in one of the central texts of postmodernity: *The Postmodern Condition: A Report on Knowledge* by the French philosopher Jean-François Lyotard. Lyotard characterizes postmodernity as a general "incredulity towards meta-narratives" (1984: xxiv). A metanarrative is simply a "story" or theory that seeks to explain the essential nature of human experience or the world in general. Religions, for example, are perhaps the most successful metanarratives because for thousands of years they have persuaded billions of people to hold certain beliefs about human experience without ever having any proof for those beliefs. In postmodernity, the legitimating discourses of modernity, concepts such as the **nation–state**, human progress, rationalism and scientific impartiality, are all irrelevant in the face of technological development and its capacity to allow knowledge to be controlled by **global capitalism**. Such all-encompassingconcepts have been replaced, according to Lyotard, by "little narratives," which function purely on a contingent, local and utilitarian basis. The collapse of meta-narratives necessarily challenges long-standing assumptions, and has thus led to a greater degree of self-**reflexivity** in many cultural and political endeavors. It has also encouraged the rejection of the distinction between "high" and "low" culture, and a celebration of diversity (difference) and **hybridity**. The end result of the disestablishment of aesthetic hierarchies and the rise of self-reflexivity is the triumph of irony as a postmodern mode of expression. Postmodern irony necessarily implies the cool detachment of the subject from the object, and it is irony that fuels postmodernity's engagement with nostalgia and kitsch, which is an engagement that celebrates those objects whilst simultaneously rejecting them. It is often said that postmodernity places everything in quotation marks. These hypothetical quotation marks reemphasize ironic distance, suggest that everything is open to question, and argue that the postmodern era is one in which all is quotation because originality itself is no longer possible.

For the Marxist theorist Fredric Jameson, the collapse of legit-imating discourses and the triumph of irony is a regrettable function of late capitalism. Postmodernity is, for him, a time in which political action (and specifically the critiquing force of parody) is inevitably frustrated because it is immediately reabsorbed into the "stupendous proliferation of social codes [...] and disciplinary jargons" (1991: 17). Jameson argues that parody is lost amidst the multiple competing discourses of postmodernity to become no more than one valueless style amongst many. For Jameson, the typical postmodern mode is not parody, but what he calls pastiche, a toothless mimicry that has lost its satirical edge and thus its capacity to question received judgments or ideological positions. French cultural theorist Jean Baudrillard is similarly pessimistic, and his related theories of **simulacrum** and **hyperreality** suggest that the postmodern world is one in which "reality" has been replaced by a series of empty signs.

See also: **liquid modernity, Marx/Marxism, modernity, reflexive modernization/modernity, Transnational Corporations (TNC)**

Further reading: Featherstone 1995; Jencks 1989; Turner 1990

CM

POST-TOURIST

First coined by Feifer in 1985, with reference to **postmodernism**, post-tourists see tourism as a game with many layers. They recognize not only that any place can become a tourist destination, but also that a tourist experience can be obtained anywhere, not necessarily at the destination itself but, for example, through the media. Post-tourists acknowledge, even enjoy, the inevitable inauthenticity of any tourist experience.

See also: **anticipation of pleasure, reflexivity, simulacrum**

Further reading: Urry 2002

SL

PRIMITIVE ACCUMULATION

Primitive accumulation describes the forced appropriation of surplus and resources (for instance in acts of enclosure or **colonialism**) prior to the emergence of **capitalist** economy. This emphasis on violence of accumulation was deliberate; **Marx** wished to distance his account of primitive accumulation from the "original" accumulation of Adam Smith, who proposed a gradual, peaceable consolidation of wealth by a certain class. In contrast Marx saw primitive accumulation as a theft, coercing the majority into giving up the goods and land held in common.

Marx seems to locate primitive accumulation firmly in capitalism's prehistory; once capitalism is realized, it does not require explicit force to generate surplus, since this can be done solely through its economic relations. But some have argued that primitive accumulation is an ongoing component of capitalism, for instance, in the developing world where native people are driven off the lands in the interests of "development." From this perspective so long as there are resources that can be appropriated by capitalism, "primitive" accumulation will continue.

See also: **consumerism, Marx/Marxism**

JH

PRIVATIZATION

A process by which industries and assets normally owned/run by the **state** are sold to private companies. Transport, post/mail, health care, prisons, water and energy industries have all been privatized in many countries in recent decades. The intention is to improve the economic position of a government and also to improve the provision of these services. The reasons given for improvement include increased competition and thus efficiency, but this does not always happen. While privatization means that shares in utilities are available for members of the public to buy, in fact the industries are more often than not bought by existing corporations or financial alliances put together for the purpose.

Privatization is a core feature of **neoliberal** economics and is often prescribed by global financial institutions (such as the **IMF**) as a precondition for financial aid. It is part of a general move away from the state providing services towards a minimal, noninterventionist state.

See also: **dependency theory, liberalization, nationalization, nation-state, Transnational Corporations (TNC), World Bank**

Further reading: Barnekov 1989; Macarov 2003; Mudambi 2003; Strange 1998

PROTECTIONISM (ECONOMIC)

Protectionism is instigating barriers to the international flow of goods and services. First advocated by the mercantilists in fifteenth-century Europe, economic protectionism is the practice of using tariffs or quotas to limit imports of foreign goods in order to protect native industry. The logic behind economic protectionism is to protect national economies from fluctuations in the market. Protectionism is associated with building up and sustaining internal economies through encouraging people to produce and sell goods locally in preference to importing (potentially cheaper) goods made elsewhere. This is done by, basically, restricting the amount and range of imported goods that are allowed to enter a particular economy and by making imports very expensive. Protectionist policies are located within mercantilist economics which sees government intervention as necessary for the stability of the economy. Protectionist policies are linked to policies for full employment and public spending. Public spending is an important regulator which can be used to stimulate the economy at a time of a slump or to suppress growth if it happens too quickly. Unemployment is unnecessarily wasteful. The English economist Maynard Keynes argued, the economy may correct itself; but in the long run, "we are all dead" (Keynes 1971: 65). Emerging from the worldwide political instability fanned by the early twentieth-century economic slumps, economic intervention by the **state** is often referred to by scholars as the historical compromise between capital and labor (Castles 1985: 1).

As protectionism favors national over global circulation of commodities, the protectionist doctrine stands and has always stood in opposition to the doctrine of **free trade**. For instance, the GATT (General Agreement on Tariffs and Trade) agreement was created and signed in 1947 at the zenith of Keynesian Welfarism.

See also: **Common Agricultural Policy (CAP), economic liberalization, fair trade/free trade, wage earner welfare states, WTO (World Trade Organization)**

Further reading: Keynes 1997; Overbeek 1999

RM

PSUEDO EVENTS

A pseudo event is staged and planned so that it can be construed as newsworthy by the public. In the first chapter of *The Image*, Daniel Boorstin (1961) gives four features of the pseudo event. First, it is not a spontaneous happening. Rather, and secondly, it is staged in a way that can be reported by the media. Thirdly, Boorstin argues, there should be some ambiguity as to the "underlying reality of the situation." Finally, the event is a self-fulfilling prophecy in that it displays and performs its significance and importance while exactly laying claim to such significance. Pseudo events are thus typical products of marketing and publicity professionals. Launch events for new products, celebrations of certain milestones and celebrity appearances in conjunction with a product are all such pseudo events. The **internet** and mass media make pseudo events more viable and accessible.

The political uses of pseudo events should not be underestimated as they are the foundation of propaganda and politics generally. Press releases, speeches, public debates are all staged and managed to produce certain effects. Some such events generate their own enduring significance by constructing a tradition for themselves; the Christmas Day Queen's Speech in the UK is arguably such an example. For a lengthy discussion of the first Gulf War and its status as a pseudo event, see Baudrillard's (1995) work. His argument was not that the war literally did not take place but that the war viewers saw on television ("the Gulf War") was in fact a pseudo event and not the war that was actually taking place.

See also: **bodily display, cultural economy, cultural tourism, embedded journalists, global media, lifestyle, postmodernity/postmodernism, simulacrum**

Further reading: Clarke 2003; Goffman 1969; Merrin 2002

QUANGO

QUANGO stands for Quasi-Autonomous Non-Governmental Organization and is generally pejorative. The term, and the corresponding organizations, are particularly common in the UK and flourished under Conservative rule in the 1980s. Technically they are not **NGOs** as they are the result of government devolving powers to bodies which are in theory independent of government but nevertheless appointments, funding and scope of power is defined by the government. They are often set up to monitor the actions of government especially how they perform with respect to particular legislative initiatives. For example, Equal Opportunities Commissions are QUANGOs. As members are not directly elected, there are concerns about democratic deficit and sometimes charges of "quango-cracy." The term is variously attributed to Alan Pifer, President of the Carnegie Corporation (in the US) and Sir Douglas Hague (in the UK). Non-Departmental Public Body (NDPB) is now often used instead of QUANGO. There are now bodies to monitor, among others, bodies like QUANGOs. In the UK, the Nolan Committee introduced the Committee on Standards in Public Life and the Office of the Commissioner for Public Appointments.

See also: **global governance**

Further reading: Gray 1994; Norris 1996; Ridley and Wilson 1995; Wilson 1995

RACIALIZATION (OF GOVERNMENTAL PROCESSES)

Racialization refers broadly to **identity politics** in governmental forms and more specifically, the role of identity politics in the reconfiguration of governance. Racialization of governmental forms seeks to recognize the ways in which modes of government draw upon concepts of race and ethnicity to achieve rule. For instance modes of government driven by concepts of homogeneity and universality draw upon racialized discourses in a particular way. Using ideas of cultural homogeneity and universality to define populations of particular **nation-states** serves to define what are recognized (white, heterosexual, Western etc.) and unrecognized identities (non-white, non-heterosexual, non-Western etc.). An effect of this is the racialization of access to and benefit from social provision and leads to the racialization (as well as feminization) of poverty.

Racialization (of governmental processes) also has a more specific meaning, which is the role of identity politics in the reconfiguration of governmental forms. This reading refers to the era of global relations and the theoretical move away from homogeneity and universality toward fragmentation and **hybridization**. The racialization of governmental forms seeks to recognize that **heterogeneity** and complexity play a key role in the contemporary governmental form of advanced liberalism. There are multiple sets of governmental practices at any one time, thus the articulation of different discourses of rule can and do have contradictory and disjunctive consequences. A key contribution that the idea of racialization of governmental forms allows is that it can recognize and elaborate on emerging paradoxes and counter trends. For instance, the increased racialization of poverty as a result of restructuring across and between nations (Kingfisher 2002) at the same time as an increased formal recognition of indigenous rights (Larner 2002).

See also: **feminization of the workforce, homogenization**

Further reading: Cohen and Shirin 2000; Havemann 2000

RM

RADICAL MODERNITY

See also: **modernity, liquid modernity, reflexive modernization/modernity**

RATIONALITIES OF RISK

Counter to Beck (1992) and Giddens (1990), genealogical studies analyze **risk** as part of a *"particular style of thinking* ... (which) entailed new ways of understanding and acting upon misfortune *in terms of risk"* (Rose 1999: 246). Rationalities of risk are assemblages of practices, techniques and rationalities concerned with how we govern. It is a form of reasoning that allows us to make events calculable in specific ways. The concept is associated with Ewald who posits that risk is a way of thinking about and representing events (Ewald 1991). For instance, in insurance, risk is a form of calculation based on a statistical table that establishes the regularity of events and a calculus of probabilities in order to evaluate the chances of that event actually occurring. Rationalities of risk are technical, they rely on particular calculative techniques and are themselves technical in their own right – risk cannot be separated from the practices of insurance and the techniques that allow us to intervene in a world amenable to risk calculations. Rationalities of risk are plural and hybrid. Accident insurance risk, epidemiological risk, case-management risk, clinical risk, comprehensive risk management and their proliferation can all be placed in a framework for analyzing current forms of government

(Dean 1999b). Rose suggests that there have been transformations in the rationalities of risk. Previously we had a collectivization of risk in the social state. This "is being displaced: individuals, families, firms, organizations, communities are being urged by politicians to *take it upon themselves* the responsibility for the security of their property, and their persons, and that of their own families" (Rose 1999: 247).

Beck and Giddens' thesis on the risk society is a means to comprehend "globalization" as a focus of fear and anxiety – and also untrammeled possibility. The concept of rationalities of risk refers to the globalization of risk as a technology of governance. Rationalities of risk is linked to globalization through offering an alternative, **counter-narrative** to Beck's totalizing, realist, uniform conception of risk based on a narrative of the emergence of risk society. Limits of the concept are that this approach cannot account for how, where and under what conditions, rationalities of risk change.

See also: **governmentality, hybridity, risk**

Further reading: Dean 1999b; Lupton 1999; Rose 1999

RM

REALIST PARADIGM

The realist paradigm claims that the way to understand international relations is to look at how **states** interact with one another. Other internal and cross-border groups are of no or little significance, rather, states seek power and position themselves primarily in relation to each other. This is in contrast to the pluralist paradigm which argues that other players, such as religious groups, multinational corporations and the like are not peripheral players, as realists would have it, but need to be considered to understand the international scene.

Pluralists do not see the state as homogenous, but rather as complex entities and are thus more in line with current views of the nation-state as of waning importance in the global climate. Finally in the inter-paradigm debate, structuralists argue that social, political and economic structures need to be considered. Most structuralists are Marxist in some way or another and focus largely on economic structures.

See also: **Marx/Marxism, nation–state, pluralism, political globalization**

Further reading: Snow 2004; Turner 1998

RE-EMBEDDING

Dis-embedding and re-embedding relate to the way in which capital, cultural practices and products are lifted out (dis-embedded) from one context and placed in another (re-embedded). The significance is that these terms seek to describe the changes in space and time which are characteristic of globalization. The terms are commonly associated with Giddens who writes, "The image evoked by disembedding is better able to capture the shifting alignments of time and space which are of elementary importance for social change in general and for the nature of modernity in particular." (1990: 22). Further, in what is typical of **postmodern** thought (not withstanding that Giddens claims we live in a period of **modernity**) the concept of origins and authenticity are thrown into question by these processes of embedding.

See also: **postmodernity/postmodernism, territorialization (de & re), time–space compression**

REFLEXIVE MODERNIZATION/MODERNITY

A term used by Beck, Giddens and Lash (1994), however the three theorists give the phrase different definitions and accord it varying levels of importance in relation to the process of globalization. Broadly, reflexive modernization refers to the way in which we are in a stage of **modernity** which questions the very foundations of modernity. Modernity refers to various time periods and theoretical approaches. The general consensus is that the world has moved past the first modernity (as Beck calls it) into another stage of modernity. While some theorists call this current period **postmodernity**, others seek to draw more explicit connections with what is often called the modernist project. In this second stage of modernity, it is argued, we need to think about the premises of modernity and reframe these. "'Reflexive modernization' means the possibility of a creative (self-) destruction for an entire epoch: that of industrial society" (Beck *et al.* 1994: 2).

The differences between the three theorists are significant. Beck understands reflexive modernization as linked to the move to the **risk** society. The reflexivity for Beck is more the working out of a process than a conscious reflection on states of affairs. He writes "it is not knowledge but rather non-knowledge which is the medium, of 'reflexive' modernization" (1994: 75). Thus, he highlights the automatic process of reflexive modernization: "modernization *undercuts* modernization, unintended and unseen, and therefore also reflection-free, with the force of autonomized modernization" (1994: 176). The formulation of new questions is informed by and in turn influences the risk society that Beck identifies. Indeed, one of the fundamental differences is another risk inherent in this fracturing of modern foundations, and that is the threat of neo-nationalism and neo-fascism. While on the face of it such responses might seem reactionary, they are a way of containing uncertainty.

Giddens' concept of reflexive modernization is more cognitive. However, he prioritizes institutional reflexivity over reflexive modernization. He argues that "Reflexive modernization tends to imply a sort of 'completion' of modernity, the bringing into view of aspects of social life and nature that were previously dormant" (1994: 185). The "clear 'direction' of development supposed" in such an idea does not capture, for Giddens, the uncertainty and difficulty of contemporary life.

Lash claims that reflexive modernity moves beyond both modernity and postmodernity. For Lash, what "underpins reflexivity . . . [is] an articulated web of global and local networks of *information and communication structures*" (1994a: 120–21). He focuses on "life chances" in reflexive modernity and argues that becoming a "reflexivity winner" or "reflexivity loser" is "a question of access not to productive capital or production structures but instead of access to and place in the new information and communication structures" (1994a: 121).

Globalization is linked to this reflexive modernity as it too is characterized by the changing nature of interaction in the world. If **nation-states** were still primary actors, or individuals primarily defined by their nation-state, then a discourse of the international would be able to account for action. Those working in globalization studies argue that this is not the case. They point to the proliferation of transnational actors and actions including corporations (**TNC**s), **NGO**s, **civil society** and the **network society**. Modernity was characterized by **industrialization**, but the world is (at least in parts) now in a postindustrial stage and even a **post-information age**. Further, the concept of linear progress that was central to modernity is no longer present. Giddens argues that there "is no obvious 'direction' to globalization at all" (1994: 96).

Reflexive modernity is sometimes also called second modernity (by Beck), **late modernity** (by Giddens) or **liquid modernity** (by Bauman 2000). While postmodern theory highlights the problems with the modernist project, it does little to solve them. Different theorists foreground different aspects of reflexive modernity. While

Beck is concerned with politics and Giddens with culture and social structures, Lash is perhaps more abstract and theoretical.

Giddens warns that reflexive modernization should not be understood as some kind of resolution of modernism or its inherent crises. While modernity sought answers to questions, reflexive modernity seeks to reframe the questions.

See also: **experts/expert systems, fundamentalism, global sub-politics, nationalism, reflexivity**

Further reading: Beck 1992; Beck, Giddens and Lash 2003; Giddens 1990; Lash 2002

REFLEXIVITY

Reflexivity is not a straightforward concept in that it is applied to different agents and situations for different reasons. For example, while Bourdieu uses reflexivity in relation to the practice of sociology, Beck Giddens and Lash (1994) locate their reflexivity squarely within the bounds of globalization studies, theorizing a **reflexive modernity**. Bourdieu (1992a) and Beck (1994) have used the term most widely.

Bourdieu's reflexivity can be seen as a response to what he saw as a structuralist sociology, especially in the work of Claude Lévi-Strauss (1994 [1969]). Being reflexive as a sociologist means paying attention to "the unthought categories of thought which limit the thinkable and pre-determine what is actually thought" (1992a: 40). This mode of reflexivity is not restricted to the sociologist, however.

Beck, Giddens and Lash each take a very different approach, focussing on what "reflexive modernization" means and what the implications of this are. For Beck, reflexivity does not mean active thinking or reflecting. The reflexivity is rather *self-confrontation* (1994: 5). The reflexivity does not require an agent; the reflexivity that Beck describes happens of itself. Beck writes, "Let us call the autonomous, undesired and unseen, transition from industrial to risk society *reflexivity*" (1994: 6). This automatic reflexivity is firmly connected to and part of Beck's **risk** society.

Giddens' use of reflexivity is perhaps more familiar. It involves being aware of choices and is symptomatic of the move from traditional societies to modern ones. For Giddens, reflexivity is cognitive and is connected to disembedding, his theory of **structuration** and the necessary "project of the self." For Giddens, it is institutional reflexivity that is more important than that reflexive modernization. The institutions that Giddens deals with include the family, intimate relationships, sexuality and indeed anything that is part of traditional society.

Lash distinguishes between structural reflexivity and self-reflexivity. In the former, "agency, set free from the constraints of social structure, then reflects on the 'rules' and 'resources' of such structure" (1994a: 115). In self-reflexivity, agency reflects on itself. Lash further identifies three modes of reflexivity: the cognitive, the aesthetic and the hermeneutic. Lash sees Beck and Giddens as dealing with cognitive reflexivity. Though this is arguably true of Giddens' reflexivity, Beck's take on reflexivity does not involve the reflection that is necessary for it to be cognitive. Lash argues instead for the importance of aesthetic reflexivity. Hermeneutic reflexivity is related to the community and aesthetic more with **postmodern** theory.

See also: **confluent love, habitus, modernity, re-embedding**

REFORM (POLITICAL)

Political reform refers to the procedures and strategies to change political systems. In globalization studies it refers to the widespread reform of public management (the way that governments manage the services they provide) first referred to as **New Public Management** (NPM) by Louis Gunn and Christopher Hood in the mid-1980s. These reforms have sought to replace traditional rule-based, authority-driven processes with market-based, competition-driven tactics.

Sometimes referred to as the global reform movement, because of the number of nations that have taken up the reform agenda in such a short time and because of how similar their basic strategies have been, NPM has six core characteristics: increasing productivity; using market mechanisms to change the behavior of program managers; the shift to a service orientation by seeing citizens as "clients"; decentralizing programs to lower levels of government; and separating policy function (government's role as purchaser of services) from service-delivery function (its role in providing service). Finally, there is an increasing ethos of accountability: governments are trying to replace top-down, rule-based accountability systems with bottom-up, results-driven systems, seeking to focus on outputs and outcomes instead of processes and structures. The management reform movement builds on the notion that good governance in the global age, a sorting out of mission, role, capacity, and relationships, is a necessary (if insufficient) condition for economic prosperity and social stability. The concept is relevant to the discourse of globalization because governments have used public management reform to reshape the role of the state and its relationship with citizens and these changes are seen as part and parcel of the profound social changes associated with globalization and the concomitant rise in **neoliberalism**.

See also: **economic liberalization, policy agendas, policy cycle, policy evaluation, policy programs, privatization**

Further reading: Common 1998; Pollitt and Bouckaert 2004

RM

RELATIVISM

This term is often used in the context of "cultural relativism" which relates to evaluation of practices. In short, relativism holds that truth, knowledge and goodness can only be assessed relative to a particular standpoint, whether this be that of an individual, a culture or a historical period. Relativism is related to knowledge, how we can know things and what we can know. It holds that absolute truth is not accessible as we are limited by our points of view, whether these are cultural, scientific or human. It is, however, also an antidote to **ethnocentric** assessments and can represent a stance of tolerance and understanding, especially when made a central tenet of social policy. It is often seen as typical of both **reflexive modernity** and **postmodernism** in that absolutes are questioned. Relativism is invoked in many forms and can mean anything from "anything goes" to the acceptance that truth and knowledge are essentially contingent and contextual. The former, the notion that relativism means something akin to anarchy, is a misunderstanding of the concept.

See also: **particularism, perfect knowledge, pluralism**

Further reading: Feyerabend 1975, 1987

RE-LOCALIZATION

See: **localization, re-embedding**

REVITALIZATION MOVEMENT

This refers to political and/or religious movements based on an agenda of removing what is perceived as domination from "the outside," that is of another they perceive as persecuting or preventing the group from achieving its goals in some way. Such movements may focus on political, economic, cultural or linguistic rights. It is in relation to these areas that the outside (and thus the inside) are defined. They often develop in oppressed indigenous nations, religious or ethnic groups which are in a minority or somehow disenfranchised. Such movements are often politically and economically marginalized and, rhetorically at least, appeal to a traditional culture or ethnicity in which to ground themselves.

See also: **clash of civilizations, diaspora, ethnolinguistic, fundamentalism, language rights, multicultural/ism, social movements**

Further reading: Carroll 1975; Lechner 1984; Ramet 2004

RISK

Risk is a common theme in contemporary society. Public anxiety about a risk often disregards its scientific calculation of the risk, which is the probability of an event multiplied by its severity. As such, the social sciences and natural science most often analyze and understand risk in different ways.

The conventional discourse on the public understanding of risk is that voluntary risks are regarded as more acceptable than coerced risks. For example, the public are less concerned about the risks from smoking, a "voluntary" activity, but are more concerned about the risks from air pollution, a risk they have no control over whether they are exposed to it.

Academics such as Mary Douglas (Douglas and Wildavsky 1982) analyze risk from a sociocultural perspective; emphasizing the social and cultural contexts in which risks are understood and negotiated. Douglas argues concepts of risk are shared within cultures or communities and are not simply products of individual knowledge and perceptions. German sociologist Ulrich Beck and British sociologist Anthony Giddens' risk society theories have attracted most attention from a range of academic fields and in wider society, including politicians. Giddens' risk society thesis (1990) primarily concentrates on the changing nature of **trust**. He argues traditional forms of knowledge have been abandoned in contemporary society and this, combined with societies becoming more complex, has forced the public to become more reliant on trusting others, such as experts and institutions, to inform them about risks.

Beck's *Risk Society*, first published in Germany in 1986, received a great deal of attention when it was published in English in 1992. Beck argues the results of **industrialization**, the "dark sides of progress" such as global warming or pollution, were not envisioned during the industrial revolution but they now dominate social debate. In a risk society the effects of this progress cause anxiety and worry. Beck believes **reflexivity** or **reflexive modernity** is inherent to a risk society. Reflexivity occurs when a society reflects on the events around them and responds by actively looking for reasons or effects. The result of this reflection is that new risks are perceived and a new form of **modernity**, a risk society, is created.

Beck criticizes science for having an "idealized model of risk" where scientists assume they can control variables of risk. In a risk society scientific calculations of risk are challenged by political groups, individuals and politicians (see for instance the MMR debate in the UK or global warming in the USA) with the result being that scientists have lost some of their authority.

In Beck's theory, risks are invisible (e.g. unemployment) and carry the potential for being catastrophic and irreversible (e.g. nuclear accidents). He assumes the lay public does not possess knowledge and need to be made aware of the risks by those who are the traditional holders of knowledge; scientists and institutions. Lay people are thus dependent on **expert** knowledge to inform and warn them about risks and he is optimistic that this means the public can themselves become knowledgeable. This idea that the public depend on themselves for knowledge and expertise relates to Beck's idea of "side effects." In a much quoted idea, Beck regards the public, not science or other institutions, as those who can be depended on to be the "voices, faces, eyes and tears" in a risk society and see "coughing children. . . . farmers' cows turning yellow" (1992: 61). Scholars argue that this belief that side effects outweigh the benefits of scientific innovation is now entrenched in Western culture.

Many media studies scholars (e.g. Kitzinger 1999) criticize Beck for being undeveloped and vague about the media's role in a risk society as it is not based on empirical research nor does it consider the media production processes.

See also: **experts/expert systems, knowledge society, perfect knowledge, postmodernity/postmodernism, symbolic analysts**

Further reading: Giddens 1990; Lupton 1999a, 1999b; Mythen 2004

TB

SEATTLE

It was on 30 November 1999 in Seattle that the **antiglobalization** movement first came to worldwide attention. An estimated fifty thousand activists gathered on the streets of Seattle, to protest the meeting of the **WTO**, which had met to launch a new Millennial round of trade negotiations. The protests successfully disrupted the meeting leading to the opening ceremony being cancelled with no agreement as to future trade **liberalization** plans being reached. Seattle is often referred to as "the coming out party" of the antiglobalization movement, and became the first of many large summit demonstrations against the international organizations generally associated with economic globalization and **global governance** (e.g. the WTO, the **IMF**, the **World Bank**, the **G8**), with others later taking place in Prague, Quebec City and Genoa among others. The participants (as with other demonstrations) were made up of a loose knit nonhierarchically organized international coalition of people and **social movements**, with no leadership. They came from a diversity of backgrounds, such as environmental groups, labor unions, religious groups, campaigners for the rights of indigenous peoples, student groups and anarchists. The majority of media coverage, rather than focusing on the substantial issues of many of the campaigns, focused instead on the violent **direct action** tactics of a small group of anarchist protesters known as the "black bloc." These protesters attacked the buildings and property of some of the more symbolic multinational corporations, such as McDonald's and Starbucks, while the vast majority of the protesters who favored a variety of nonviolent methods of protest were entirely peaceful.

See also: **anarchism**

HB

SEMI-PERIPHERY COUNTRIES

Within **world systems theory**, countries are sometimes labeled as core, periphery or semi-periphery. Semi-periphery countries are said to act as a buffer between the core and periphery. They often produce natural resources (e.g. fossil fuels) and act as both suppliers and markets to the core countries.

See also: **core-periphery model**

SERVICE WORK

Service work includes forms of work which involve working with people rather than manufacturing things and for which qualifications required are minimal such as working in the hospitality industry, retail and personal services.

Especially in developed countries, which are generally post-industrial, knowledge-based economies, manufacturing jobs and other menial labor is not readily available as a form of employment. Such work is often non-unionized and primarily undertaken by those most marginalized in a society (e.g. women, immigrants or illegal workers). In addition, because of the nature of certain service work (it can be done over the phone or through computer-mediated means) companies set up offices in foreign countries where labor is cheaper (e.g. call centers). As such, work in these sectors can be particularly exploitative.

See also: **export processing zone (EPZ), feminization of the workforce, industrialization, knowledge society, offshoring**

Further reading: Hodson 1997

SIMULACRUM

This term, the plural form being simulacra, is used by French cultural theorist Jean Baudrillard to refer to a copy of something that has no connection to an original object or to reality. Baudrillard argues that in a **postmodern** era simulacra (sometimes, although by no means always, in the form of digitised media) come to replace originals so much so that it is impossible to tell the difference between what is "real" and what is a simulacrum. Simulation and **hyperreality** are related concepts; in his essay "Simulacra and Simulation," Baudrillard describes simulation as "the generation by models of a real without origin or reality: a hyperreal" (1988: 166). Thus hyperreality is a mode of reality overtaken by simulacra produced by a process of simulation.

Further reading: Baudrillard 1995

CM

214

SKEPTICS

Held and McGrew identify a "crude" dualism between globalists and skeptics. The former "consider that contemporary globalization is a real and significant historical development" while skeptics "conceive [globalization] as a primarily ideological or mythological construction which has marginal explanatory value" (2003: 2). It is important to note that there are two possible dimensions to both the globalist and keptic position, as alluded to in Held and McGrew's orienting definition. First, there is a question of whether there are real changes occurring in the world. This is largely an empirical question. Second, though obviously related to the first, is if there are changes happening in the world, is a discourse and theory of globalization the best way to account for them.

See also: **heterogeneity, hyperglobalist thesis, IMF (International Monetary Fund), internationalization, OECD (Organization for Econcomic Co-operation and Development), traditionalist, Transnational Corporations (TNC), war of position**

Further reading: Bourdieu 1999; Hirst and Thompson 1996

SOCIAL CAPITAL

The term "social capital" was first coined by Karl **Marx** in the nineteenth century (1972: 636) and there have been many different independent usages since, especially in the last 30 years. Broadly, the concept in its modern use refers to networks of personal connections, social ties, norms and affiliations (e.g. girl/boy scouts, bowling leagues) that can bring benefits for individuals and society, other than their perceived intrinsic value, by underpinning and strengthening the social fabric of the community.

Despite the small but distinct sociological literature using the concept focusing on social networks since the mid–1980s, and the better known work of James Coleman (1988), the wider prominence of the concept is due to the work of Robert Putnam (2000). For Putnam, social capital is defined as "features of social organization, such as **trust**, norms, and networks, that can improve the efficiency of society by facilitating coordinated actions" (1993: 167). Putnam was part of a 20-year project exploring the development of new regional governments in Italy. Social capital as a concept helped to explain the radical difference Putnam saw in the quality of the different regional governments.

Putnam points out the reciprocity and mutuality involved in social capital as well as the possibilities for communal action. Putnam distinguishes between "bonding social capital" and "bridging social capital." The former applies between members of groups with something already in common, while bridging social capital describes connections across and between different social groups. Social capital refers not only to the resources available to individuals but more significantly (for globalization studies at least) to the resources that communities can develop and hold in common. It is possible to talk about the social capital that a society has. Helena Kennedy, for example, notes, "[t]raditionally Britain has been rich in social capital, with high levels of voluntary work, and lots of networks from the Women's Institute to youth groups and social clubs, all based on mutuality and trust" (2005: 19). Putnam argues that the changes in society over the last 30 years, especially in the USA, have resulted in the decline of social capital.

Putnam's work has attracted audiences internationally in both academic and in government circles. *Making Democracy Work* was the most cited social science work of the 1990s and his work on the United States helped inform Clinton's 1995 state of the union address. He has also had audiences with Bush, Blair, and Brown. Social capital has also been used by the **World Bank** and informs some development policy as well as having performance indicators at a national level, including some local governments in Britain.

Morrow, however, is concerned that social capital (in Coleman's and Putnam's formulations) is just another way to dismiss the disadvantaged, by claiming that they have no social capital and that this is somehow their fault: "[t]here is a danger that 'social capital' will become part of what might be termed 'deficit theory syndrome', yet another 'thing' or 'resource' that unsuccessful individuals, families, communities and neighborhoods lack." (1999: 760). Putnam's formulation in particular appeals to the **neoliberal** right and the concept has been taken up as way of absolving the **state** of responsibility for social exclusion.

On the other hand, grassroots community movements have adopted it as a strategy for community building and empowerment. This appeal across the political spectrum is indicative of its diverse applications but also its theoretical vagueness. Ultimately, Putnam's work on social capital raises as many questions as it answers.

Pierre Bourdieu has also used the term social capital when accounting for the reproduction of social inequality. Social capital is but one of Bourdieu's many forms of capital and is of a different nature than Putnam's. In "The Forms of Capital," Bourdieu identified three kinds of symbolic capital: economic, cultural and social.

Economic capital has straightforward monetary value (1986: 243). **Cultural capital** is less tangible and while it may be converted into economic capital, it cannot be bought in a straightforward transaction (1986: 243). Finally, social capital consists of "social obligations ('connections'), which is convertible, in certain conditions, into economic capital and may be institutionalized in the form of a title of nobility" (1986: 243).

While he never wrote a great deal on social capital, he did, unlike Putnam, link social capital to levels of resources. Bourdieu defines social capital as:

> the aggregate of the actual or potential resources which are linked to possession of a durable network of more or less institutionalized relationships of mutual acquaintance and recognition.
> (1986: 248–49)

While the number of connections matter, far more important is that a person is connected to others who have a great deal of economic or cultural capital and that this capital is available to the person (1986: 249). Portes notes how key this focus on resources is, in particular making a distinction between "the resources themselves [and] the ability to obtain them by virtue of membership in different social structures" (1998: 5). It is important that Bourdieu clearly links social capital to other types of capital.

While Bourdieu clearly outlines and defines social capital, Putnam's approach to the concept has a certain heuristic value. It is arguably more important in that it has stimulated debate. Further, Putnam's conceptualization of social capital appears more amenable to metaphorical and policy applications than others.

See also: **civil society, cultural capital, global sub-politics, NGO (Non-Governmental Organization), symbolic capital**

Further reading: Fukuyama 1995; Halpern 2001

AC

SOCIAL MOVEMENTS

Social movements are complex modes of collective action that are politically motivated and aim at achieving or resisting specific kinds of social and cultural change. Typical examples of social movements are that of labor movements, the women's rights movement, the gay rights movement, the environmental movement, and the newly emerging **antiglobalization** movement. They are commonly seen as employing a diversity of means through which to achieve their aims, from political lobbying to more confrontational and socially disruptive tactics, such as **direct action**. The increased influence of both **multinational corporations** and the institutions of global governance such as the **WTO** and **IMF**, whose power in many cases exceeds that of local or national governments, has meant that a number of social movements have undergone a number of significant changes in their forms of organization and modes of operation. Social movements have increasingly focused their attention away from seeing problems and issues in purely local or national terms to seeing them within a global context. In this way international coalitions have been forged that maintain locally focused resistance while building bridges across national borders – a process captured in the environmental movements slogan "Think globally, Act locally." These changes have been greatly facilitated by the growth of global communications networks, especially that of the **internet**, as well as an increase in affordable travel opportunities, which have allowed social movements to coordinate and mobilize their actions with more speed and efficiency both within and across national borders.

See also: **feminism, global governance**

HB

SOCIETIES OF CONTROL

The concept of the society of control was put forward by the French philosopher Gilles Deleuze (1990). Recently it has been developed by, amongst others, Hardt and Negri (2000) and Alex Galloway (2004). Deleuze starts from Foucault's analysis of the nineteenth-century "disciplinary" regime of **bio-power**, that is, regulated individual bodies and populations through a range of institutions, and argues that this formulation, has, under the combined pressures of information technology, the mass media and globalization, undergone a fundamental shift. It has moved from the rigid form of disciplinary power mediated by institutions to a subtle, immanent form of "control" that operates within the cognitive processes of the individual. Thus the emergence of the society of control is marked by a general crisis of the institutions of the disciplinary regime. Factories, prisons, hospitals, and even the state, are deregulated and their functions outsourced. In this manner their boundaries are blurred and they are no longer self-contained forms. The multinationals, in their flexibility exemplify the logic of control. At the same time, there occurs an internalization of the power within the thought processes of subjects themselves, which blurs the boundary between self and the outside. In this manner, control corresponds to the interplay between self and network, which other commentators have identified as characteristic of contemporary capital. Galloway (2004) argues that the protocols that coordinate data transmission in the decentralized system of the **internet**, offer another example of this general logic of control.

See also: **hegemony, liquid modernity, network society, panopticon**

Further reading: Deleuze 1990; Galloway 2004

JH

SOFT POWER

See: **hard/soft power**

SOVEREIGNTY

Sovereignty means a single and supreme locus of political authority. As a principle of political order and philosophical doctrine, it marks the beginning of political **modernity**, i.e. the transformation of the medieval system in Europe into a system of centralized, territorial states, a process that culminated in the Treaty of Westphalia in 1648. In the international system, sovereignty means the supreme control of **states** over their internal affairs, and the principle of nonintervention is a cornerstone of international society.

The sixteenth-century French thinker Jean Bodin was the first to employ the concept of sovereignty to conceptualize political authority fundamentally transcending earlier theological or traditional explanations to legitimate political power. The state, he argued, cannot be traced back to any religious or natural foundation, but it is solely a product of human will, built to serve human ends. The first and foremost of these ends is security, internal peace. To guarantee security, a single, final, and legitimate source of power – sovereignty – is the key.

Writing in the context of religious conflicts, Bodin, like Thomas Hobbes 100 years later, wanted to separate the legitimation of political authority from any religious claims. The law should be obeyed because it is the law, and not because it was perceived as true or just. *Auctoritas non veritas facit legem* (authority not truth makes law), is the famous formula coined by Hobbes. Sovereignty, thus, implies a purely formal conception of justice (legitimacy equals legality). Here, later achievements of constitutional limits to sovereignty, like fundamental rights, have been decisive for reintroducing substantial conceptions of justice into legal and political reality.

Nowadays, recent trends of globalization have undermined the effective control of states over their territories. Sovereignty, however, should not be confused with freedom of action. On the other hand, the density of international obligations and regimes has massively increased, political spaces and competence tend to overlap and intermingle, and political loyalty is diversified. The **European Union** is the most impressive example of such trends, and it renders a strong reading of sovereignty rather fictitious. A new complex geometry of power replaces the idea of self-contained, sovereign entities. However, the basic question of sovereignty, i.e. how to guarantee security and legitimate order given a pluralistic society and the absence of common beliefs, becomes all the more pertinent.

See also: **human rights, nation–state, state, statist paradigm**

Further reading: Philpott 2001

FO

STATE

Specialized organizations of territorially defined domination are no recent phenomenon in history, but they characterize human relations since the transition from nomadism to settled forms of existence. The modern state, though, is a specific set of institutions that gradually emerged from the Middle Ages, involving above all the centralization, territorialization and bureaucratization of power. In a process of several hundred years, the unclear boundaries of mediaeval, overlapping systems of domination were transcended and unitary, centralized, permanent institutions were established which guaranteed security, justice and stable administrative structures.

Among the main features of modern states are: a standing army, the ability to tax inhabitants effectively and to regulate large areas of social and economic life, trained civil servants and a centralized **bureaucracy**, a system of permanent diplomatic embassies, forms of data collection and identification (census, passports, etc.), and extensive means of social control such as police forces and schools. However, the formation of modern states did not only bring about internal peace, rational administration and social discipline, but also elicited a thoroughgoing process of cultural **homogenization** (e.g. of language) and assimilation. Political loyalty was accumulated or even monopolized by the state, which thus came to be a source of moral authority, identity and emotional attachment (patriotism).

Throughout the twentieth century, the number of states has risen enormously due to **decolonization** and the break-up of large-scale, multinational empires. Today, the international order rests on states as the subjects of international law, and achieving political autonomy basically equals achieving statehood. For many political movements, thus, the notion of the state represents a promise of freedom and self-government. At the same time, the establishment of new states often goes together with the violent oppression of minorities and the confiscation of power by corrupt elites.

Scientific studies of the state have mainly concentrated on analyzing its complex and heterogeneous internal composition as well as its relation to society and social interest groups. Studies in the tradition of Michel Foucault have broadened the focus of research on the "microphysics" of state power, on how it projects certain forms of organization of daily activities and how it imprints on mentalities and subjectivities.

With the advent of globalization discourse, the focus has shifted. Since the 1980s, the crisis of the state vis-à-vis global social and economic forces has been emphasized, and both the end of the state and the coming of a world-state have been predicted. However, the continuous proliferation of statehood, the central role of states in international politics, and the pervasive domestic state power have rather refuted such theses. However, the imaginary of the state as closed "container" or integrated whole was weakened indeed. More and more, states appear as actors among other actors, who are situated in a complex web of interdependencies, and who have ceased to appear as strictly bounded entities. At the same time, identities and loyalties of the populations shift, and citizens are engaged in political movements transcending the arena of national politics. As Martin Albrow put it in 1997, both social relations and transnational practices of administration transcend the realm of state boundaries. Thus, the modern fusion of state, people, society, government, nation and culture loses credit.

Insofar as such trends are stable, the questions of power, legitimacy and justice, too, are posed in new ways in political spaces beyond the state. Popular movements, for instance, are challenging the legitimacy of decisions of a new political class managing "global" institutions such as the **WTO**. At the same time, state actors are struggling with decreasing scopes of action, while being confronted with rising demands to secure jobs, welfare and security. Clearly, such trends underline the contingency of the current state of affairs. The stability and legitimacy of the modern state, contemporary observers realize, rested on a whole host of favorable conditions. The ongoing decoupling of state, society and identity thus implies a major potential for conflict, discontent and disorientation.

See also: **democracy, global managerial class/global elite, nationalism, nation–state, statist paradigm**

*Further reading*s: Albrow (1996), Pierson (2004)

FO

STATIST PARADIGM

The modern **state** is not only a historical reality that constitutes a rupture with the political landscape of the Middle Ages and establishes a vertical organization of power and a distinct set of institutions. It is also a "paradigm" that provides a certain political language, imprints on people's imagination and sense of identity, and is realized in modern law or the practices of international relations. Even the human sciences, themselves products of the modern age, for a long time served to organize, naturalize and reproduce such conception of a "world of states."

Until now, the bulk of our political language, its grammar, syntax and vocabulary, are distinctly modern and thus revolve around the state. Sovereignty, people, law, society, nation, government, constitution, **democracy**, build a grid of closely related terms which share a common underlying "logic": the state is imagined as a unitary structure of vertical authority dominating a bounded territory, the law expresses the will of the people which thus governs itself, society coincides with the population of the state, which politically and culturally is understood as a unitary subject, the nation.

Arguably, the image provided by contemporary maps of the world, with their mosaic of differently colored territories, is a "product" of such, paradigm which informed the fundamental structure of international law and diplomacy from 1648 until today. States are the subjects of international law; at the same time, the structure of international law serves to reproduce a "statist" conception and order of politics. Most of the time, the human sciences reproduced such structure, since they tended to presuppose the state and the nation as basic frames of reference and categories of analysis. Historians wrote national histories, sociologists worked with a territorially bounded notion of society and used the data provided by state censuses, economists devised models of "national economies" as closed systems, and so on. It is only major processes of change which bring the "constructed" character of such a "statist world" to the fore. For instance, tourism, political interdependence, economic globalization, mass media, etc. gradually eroded the naturalness of national identities. Only then was science able to point to the discursive, narrative, social and symbolic processes involved in its (re-)production. However, sensitivity for the "constructive" nature of social and political life must not equal de-legitimizing such structures. On the contrary, since construction is acknowledged as an ubiquitous and defining characteristic of human existence, "deconstruction without reconstruction," as Jacques Derrida (1994) has put it, is irresponsible.

See also: **sovereignty, state**

Further reading: Philpott 2001

FO

STRUCTURAL ADJUSTMENT PROGRAMS

See: **IMF (International Monetary Fund)**

STRUCTURATION

Outlined by Giddens in *The Constitution of Society* (1984) structuration attempts to strike a middle ground between the roles of agency and structure in determining society and events. For example, individuals can be understood as having agency or being influenced by their social context in a more or less determined way. Structuration attempts to recognize both forces and suggests a duality of structure. Giddens writes, "One of the main propositions of structuration is that the rules and resources drawn upon in the production and reproduction of social action are at the same time the means of system reproduction (the duality of structure)" (1984: 19).

There are further key terms in Gidden's theory relating to resources, types of structure and interaction, as both agency and structure are retained. Structure can be described by identifying the rules and resources that individuals have access to and with which they can interact within a system. Resources can be authoritative (which seek to control people) or allocative (which seek to control objects). There are three kinds of structures, though they are perhaps better viewed as facets and features of structures rather than a typology. The signification aspect of structures involves language and other codes. Thus certain languages, systems of signs and ways of communicating will be resources available to individuals in any particular structure. Legitimation is that part of structure which is more authoritative in the sense that it seeks to impose a moral or social order. Finally, structures also have a domination aspect. Those with control of objects (the ability to access and change allocative resources) will have power within the structure insofar as they have indirect or direct control of objects. Obviously those with power over signification also have significant power as they can manipulate the resources available for interaction.

Structuration helps explain how societies can be relatively stable or at least continuous and also how change is possible, whether this be in the form of social evolution or revolution.

Giddens' structuration has also been used in the field of technology. This is hardly surprising as technology, especially digital, is a key resource in the context of globalization. The notion of structuration is essentially an attempt to account for interdependence between social structures and individuals. "Society only has form, and that form only has effects on people, insofar as structure is produced and reproduced in what people do" (Giddens and Pierson 1998: 77).

See also: **modernity, reflexivity**

Further reading: Giddens 1990; Sewell 1992

SUBALTERN

While this is a term in the military for a junior officer, it is used within **postcolonialism** studies to refer to marginalized people

(Gramsci 1971). It has also been used more recently, especially by Spivak (1985), to mean a person without agency by virtue of such marginalization. It should be noted that subaltern is not simply a synonym for "oppressed."

Spivak points out that the subaltern can speak, but not in a meaningful way as their voices are not heard. The logic of the system which marginalizes them means that their voices cannot be heard. This is where the difference between the oppressed and the subaltern can be made clear. The oppressed speak the language of the oppressor, share it in fact, they are oppressed because they are not given time or space to speak but the possibility of such space being alloted is there. For the subaltern, what wants or needs to be said will not be understood because their concerns are incompatible with the ideology of those in power.

Homi Bhabha, following Gramsci, foregrounds the issue of power and describes subaltern groups as "oppressed, minority groups whose presence was crucial to the self-definition of the majority group: subaltern social groups were also in a position to subvert the authority of those who had hegemonic power" (1996: 210). Indeed, the concept of the subaltern is related to some of Bhaba's other concepts. **Hybridity** is, for example, the mixing of dominant and subaltern cultures while "mimicry" occurs when subaltern voices appear (though not in their original form) in dominant discourses.

See also: **colonialism, cultural imperialism, hegemony, indigenous culture**

Further reading: Bhabha (1996)

SUBSISTENCE PERSPECTIVE

A perspective from the sociologist Maria Mies developed in the 1970s which argues for the prioritization of human needs over commodities and production when making economic, political and social decisions. Mies is clear that this perspective is not just a new way of approaching economics but applies to culture, gender relations and other aspects of society. The subsistence perspective focuses on "life production" rather than "commodity production."

Mies also points out that women's work in the home being unpaid does not figure in **capitalist** views of economy. The same is true of subsistence industries like farming. The subsistence perspective thus argues for a turn away from commodities and a turn (or return) to needs-based, environmentally sustainable, cooperative and local industry. It is only if this is done that a sustainable future is possible, they argue.

See also: **antiglobalization, basic needs, consumerism, feminism, IMF**

Further reading: Bennholdt-Thomsen *et al.* 2001; Mies and Bennholdt-Thomsen 1999

SUPERMODERNITY (OR HYPERMODERNITY)

A term used by Augé (1995) to distinguish a continuation of **modernity** that is different from **postmodernity**. The central reason for this is to foreground the idea that some of the concerns of modernity are still relevant. Supermodenity for Augé is the result of three (super) abundances in relation to: (1) time history and events; (2) conceptions of physical space; and (3) personal identity. In relation to time and history, Augé argues that because of an abundance of information in the form of, for example, mass media and the **internet**, it is impossible to make sense of the world or its representations. In relation to space, there are two related concerns. One is the argument that we have a new understanding of the space that we inhabit. Rather than only being concerned with the limits of our immediate environment, we are aware of events in other parts of the world and their potential relevance to our lives. Second, Augé suggests that our immediate environments, local spaces, are becoming more like other local spaces. Part of this is the prevalence of **placelessness** which Augé regards as symptomatic of supermodernity. Thus the concern with space is also one of **glocalization**, **homogenization** and networks. The implications that Augé outlines for time and space are both related to the concept of **time–space compression**. Finally, in relation to identity, Augé suggests that our concept of personal identity is at once excessive and deficient. It is excessive in the sense that people have an abundance of choices in relation to the identities they can assume. It is deficient if and when consumption of identity markers (such as clothes, music) stand in for identity, that is, when a person becomes only what they consume.

See also: **choice (discourse of), consumerism, global village, imagined communities, information age, lifestyle, liquid modernity, modernity, placeless geography, postmodernity/postmodernism, reflexive modernization/modernity, simulacrum**

Further reading: Augé (1995), Merriman (2004), Tomlinson (1999)

SURPLUS VALUE

The concept of surplus value is a crucial component of **Marx**'s analysis of **capitalism**. Marx averred that all societies involved the creation of a surplus (understood as the production of goods or wealth beyond that necessary for the survival of its members), and that class conflict arose from the production and appropriation of this surplus.

Surplus value describes the form of surplus characteristic of the capitalist mode of production. Here the capitalist has appropriated the means of production and the product, and buys the worker's labor, which the worker, owning neither tools nor materials, is forced to sell. However, in order to generate profit, the capitalist must increase the difference between the cost of labor, materials, and means of production, and the market value of the product. This difference is surplus value. Put simply, workers must labor longer for less and less in order to generate more and more profit, and capitalism is based around the production of this surplus, which is accumulated in the form of capital. Since this capital is in turn invested in other means of generating profit (other forms of production, stocks, markets, banks etc.) surplus value as capital becomes increasingly independent of its origins in the labor of workers. However, as Marx was keen to stress, all surplus is derived from the exploitation of the worker by the capitalist, who exists as a parasite upon the laboring classes. For Marx this relationship could only be corrected by the collective ownership of the means of production, which would of itself negate the need for generating surplus value.

Further reading: Singer 2000

JH

SUSTAINABLE DEVELOPMENT

This is a form of industry which does not irrevocably harm the resources it requires and therefore can continue more or less indefinitely. The Bruntland Commission defines it as follows, "development that meets the needs of the present without compromising the ability of future generations to meet their own needs" (Bruntland 1987). A good example of sustainable development with respect to the environment is logging in such a way as to harvest only an amount of wood which can be regenerated by the ecosystem or replaced by replanting.

This approach has been ratified and promoted by, among others, the **UN** beginning with the 1992 Earth Summit. Whether it is possible to mandate such development depends in part on the will of **nation-states** and the global community to insist on penalizing or prohibiting development that is disadvantageous to people or places. This can be particularly difficult when there is little or no public attention directed to such ventures. The mining of precious metals and fossil fuels often occurs in remote locations and impacts disastrously on local (often indigenous) populations who are already marginalized and without access to official channels of protest or public organs of dissent. On the other hand, some global networks, particularly INGOs such as Greenpeace, perform a vital monitoring and publicizing role in such cases.

"Sustainable" also refers to markets, available labor, urban environments or any other kind of resource necessary for production or entity impacted on during and after production.

See also: **capitalism, indigenous culture, IMF, (International Monetary Fund), Kyoto, NGO (Non-Governmental Organization), subaltern, World Bank**

Further reading: Elliott 1999; Gustav Speth 2003; Haas 2003; Timmons and Thanos 2003; World Commission on Environment and Development 1987

SWEATSHOP

See: **Export Processing Zones (EPZ), service work**

SYMBOLIC ANALYSTS

An occupation or category of work named by the political economist Robert Reich (1992) and defined by Thompson and Warhurst as follows:

> Symbolic analysts solve, identify, and broker problems by manipulating symbols. They simplify reality into abstract images that can be rearranged, juggled, experimented with, communicated to other specialists, and then, eventually, transformed back into reality. The manipulations are done with analytic tools, sharpened by experience.

> (1998: 177–78)

Consultants (in many fields) are a good example of such symbolic analysts, but symbolic analysts can be found in nearly all industries. What is essential is that they don't manufacture goods. Peter Drucker's (1969) concept of the "knowledge worker" can be understood as a forerunner to Reich's symbolic analyst. Symbolic analysts play a central role in **expert systems** and the **knowledge society**.

See also: **global managerial class/global elite, placeless geography, risk, service work**

SYMBOLIC CAPITAL

This concept comes from the sociologist Pierre Bourdieu and accounts for the power some people have which derives not from money but from other accomplishments or attributes. Such symbolic capital functions like economic capital (money) in the sense that it can be exchanged and converted for concrete or abstract things. Symbolic capital endows an individual with symbolic power. However, "symbolic power is that invisible power which can be exercised only with the complicity of those who do not want to know that they are subject to it or even that they themselves exercise it" (Bourdieu 1992b: 164). It should be noted that Bourdieu referred to a number of different kinds of capital in his various writings, and there is some overlap between these different kinds.

It is important to remember that what counts as symbolic capital in a particular society or place depends on what is valued in that locale.

See also: **autonomization (of culture), cultural capital, global managerial class/global elite, hegemony, habitus, social capital, structuration, symbolic analysts**

Further reading: Bourdieu 1985, 1989

TERRITORIALIZATION (DE– & RE–)

Territorialization is associated with the ways in which space in the world is imagined. As Robertson (2002) outlines, many have argued that a critical feature of the dynamics of globalization, as a feature of **capitalism**, is the idea of scale and its social construction. Different scales are thus different levels of territory to be either fought over or carved out anew; spaces to be commanded and governed according to a new discourse and set of practices. Since the 1980s, scale changes have been particularly pronounced. According to Swyngedouw (2004)

> an important discursive shift took place over the last decade or so which is an integral part of an intensifying ideological, political, socioeconomic and cultural struggle over the organization of society and the position of the citizen. The pre-eminence of the 'global' in much of the literature and political rhetoric obfuscates, marginalizes and silences an intense and ongoing socio-spatial struggle in which the reconfiguration of spatial scale is a key arena.

Shifting scales involves the active construction and reconstruction of territories for the purposes of governing. The terms de- and re-territorialization are associated with post-structural discursive constructions of scale, space and territory. De-territorialization/re-territorialization are used to refer to the processes whereby existing spatial scales (like **nation-states**) are shattered and new-scaled configurations emerge.

See also: **counter-narratives, individuation, time–space compression**

Further reading: Harvey 1990; Robertson 2002; Swyngedouw 1996, 2004

RM

THIRD WAY

The Third Way refers to a political program and ideology concerned with renewing social democracy in a world changed by globalization. It is a "third way" in that it claims to move beyond the ideas advocated by the "old" left and "new right," offering policies that are presented as being pragmatic and nonideological: "pragmatic," in that they are unavoidable responses to a changed set of circumstances; "nonideological," in that they transcend existing ideological divisions in pursuit of the national interest. The ideas surrounding Third Way thinking developed in the 1990s, and have been championed by various left-of-center political leaders and social thinkers, including Tony Blair, the German Chancellor Gerhard Schröder and Anthony Giddens (Giddens 1998, 2001; Blair and Schroeder 1999; Finlayson 1999).

At the heart of the idea of a Third Way is an assumption that the traditional categories of left and right no longer have the same purchase as they once did. As a result of globalization, old style social democracy is rejected and policies such as **nationalization**, and commitments to full employment and equality of outcome (as opposed to equality of opportunity) are dismissed as anachronistic. Third Way theorists begin from the premise that there is "no ... [longer] any alternative to **capitalism**" (Giddens 1998: 43). However, though a positive role is accorded the market, Third Way thinking rejects the idea of a minimal **state**; "[b]ig government doesn't work, but no government works even less" (Blair 1998a). The so-called permanent revolution brought about by market forces and celebrated by the new right does not guarantee growth with a measure of social justice. The Third Way argues that both can be achieved, provided the state adopts a facilitative role. To "remain ahead of the race," the state must encourage flexibility in the labor force and improve competitivity by investing in education and infrastructure. As such, Third Way theory believes that intervention and the market are not antithetical, the former precluding the proper operation of the other. This idea touches on an important theme in Third Way thinking, relating to the "reconciliation of antagonistic themes." In an age of globalization, the market and public sector, individualism and the community, and in foreign affairs, commercial, security and ethical policies are seen as complementary, in that one does not necessarily jeopardize the realization of the other.

Guided by a set of leftist values or "ends" the approach claims to be social democratic in nature, only differing with traditional social democrats on the appropriate means rather than ends; "[w]hat counts is what works" (Blair 1998a). The particular blend of values or ends differs amongst Third Way theorists. For Blair, those values considered as timeless and defining of social democracy include a belief in equal worth, opportunity for all, responsibility and community (Blair 1998b). Others maintain the importance of equality of outcome and some stress the continuing relevance of Keynesian demand management (see White 1998).

Third Way theory has come in for considerable criticism with much of the debate focussing on whether there can in fact be a "third way" (see Driver and Martell 2002). Those critical of the idea reject that it is social democratic, portraying the approach as "primarily a rationalization for political compromise between left and right, in which the left moves closer to the right" (Hall 1998). Others argue that the Third Way functions as a sop to economic globalization, a sort of "Thatcherism lite" (Hay 1999). Nevertheless, the Third Way has contributed to the debate on what social democracy is or should be. With its view of possibly reconciling the **state** and market in a manner that promotes both growth and social justice, Third Way theory offers a novel program based on a view of what is achievable in an age of globalization.

See also: **centrism, neoliberalism**

Further reading: White 1998; Fairclough 2000

CW

THIRD WORLD WAR (WWIII)

Whether WWIII has occurred or is merely an imagined event depends very much on how the term is used. The Cold War is referred to in some quarters as WWIII; the "war on terror" takes the title in other quarters. When purely imagined, WWIII refers to an intended or accidental nuclear war, or, more figuratively, to some apocalyptic event such as an asteroid colliding with the earth.

Frank (2004) argues that the start of the Third World War was marked by the first US intervention in Iraq and that this can be understood as part of a broader, ongoing campaign against the third world. He writes:

> It was the third in two senses, after the first and second and now against the Third World. Since then that WAR has continued against Yugoslavia [miscalled the Kosovo War], against Afghanistan, and now again against Iraq; and who knows where next.
>
> (2004: 607–8)

Subcomandante Insurgente Marcos of the Zapatista National Liberation Army (EZLN) is an example of those who call the Cold War the Third World War. From his perspective, since then the Fourth World War has begun and is directly connected to globalization and the spread of **capitalism**. In that sense, the **antiglobalization** movement can be understood as involved in the Fourth World War against the "agents" of globalization.

See also: **antiglobalization, risk**

Further reading: Frank 1992; Neill 2001

TIME-SPACE COMPRESSION

The geographer David Harvey (1990) is credited with introducing the notion of time-space compression, the idea that in the globalized world time and space are not the barriers that they once were. This seems to be primarily because of improvements in technologies of communication and transportation. It should be clear that Harvey does not see time and space collapsing completely, but rather compressing in relation to the speed at which travel and communication can occur and thus influencing humans' experience of the world. Further, Harvey argues that the speed of life has also increased. Events, transactions and travel all happen more quickly. Harvey's argument is based not just on perceptions of space and place but also on changes in the markets of production and consumption. Money itself has been "de-materialized" while in relation to commodities, the "values" of instantaneity and disposability are emphasized.

Levine (1997) deals with this in his comparative study of tempos of society; the tempo (or pace) being linked to the level of economic activity. These changes in tempo are tied directly to the move from a world based largely on industrial production to one based on service industries and commodity consumption.

Giddens has coined the phrase "time space distanciation," referring to "the conditions under which time and space are organized so as to connect presence and absence" (Giddens 1990: 14). The distanciation of time and space allows for **transnational** practices and for the intersection of the local and the global and various locales and actors with each other.

See also: **glocal/glocalization, hybridity, network society, placeless geography, postmodernity/postmodernism, re-embedding, simulacrum, territorialization (de & re)**

Further reading: Roudometof 1997

TOBIN TAX

The Tobin tax was proposed in 1978, but has not been implemented. The economist James Tobin (after whom the tax is named) suggested a small tax, less than half a percent, on transnational transactions which would be payable on speculative trades. Thus if buying and selling, of a currency for example, occurs quickly (within a week) the tax would be payable. This means that proper trading would not be effected. There are two distinct advantages. First, national economies would be more secure without the potentially devastating effect of speculators on currency values and thus on the capacity for nations to stop sharp devaluation of their currency. Second, though the tax is small, indeed proposals are for somewhere between 0.1 and 0.25 percent the income generated from the tax would amount to billions annually global as trade is a large industry. This money could be used for particular development or emergency projects, for example to aid those subject to natural disasters. Legislative frameworks for the tax could be implemented nationally but to be effective there would need to be multilateral agreements.

See also: **financialization, global capitalism**

Further reading: ATTAC (Association for the Taxation of Financial Transactions for the Aid of Citizens), Tobin 2000; Wachtel 2000

TRADITIONALIST

This is another way of referring to **skeptics** in the globalization debate. As opposed to "globalists" and "transformationalists," traditionalists are suspicious of the claim that the world is changing in the way that the globalist scholars suggest. While impossible to capture all the nuances of the arguments here, many suggest that the changes occurring are not unprecedented and are perhaps better described in existing terminology of imperialism, internationalism the ongoing importance of the **nation–state** and an increasing division between north and south.

See also: **core–periphery model, cultural imperialism, hyperglobalist thesis, internationalization**

Further reading: Introduction to Held and McGrew 2003; Robertson 1992

TRANSNATIONAL

This concept was introduced by the sociologist Raymond Aron (1966). The transnational can be understood firstly by what it is not, that is, international and multinational. The international and the multinational prioritize the agency or relevance of the nation (state). In this sense, they fit into a **realist paradigm** of international relations. The transnational approach, on the other hand, seeks to understand events, people and groups without prioritizing the role of the **nation–state**. This is done when the nation–state is a marginal or nonexistent influence in the areas under consideration. However Sklair argues that the state is nevertheless given primary importance by many in the field (2002: 6)

Sklair writes that the transnational approach "is not a specific theory but more of an injunction to pay more attention to non-governmental entities, particularly when they are interacting with governments" (2002: 6). The work of Keohane and Nye (1972) particularly has brought the transnational approach to the broad sphere of globalization.

A transnational approach may aid in accounting for the activities of **NGOs**, **civil society** and indeed some more local issues, such as internal **migration** (Sassen 1996). Thus it is an important focus to maintain in the fields of economics, trade, politics and international relations. Dealing with a world that is not simply a sum of nations but rather comprised of other groups, agents and communities, means that concepts such as **citizenship**, **nationalism** and nationality and anything traditionally associated with the nation–state will need to be reexamined as part of the process of **reflexive modernization**.

At the same time cultural and material flows do occur at a transnational level mostly because of technology, mass media, migration and mobility. In this sense, the concept of the transnational is at the core of globalization studies even though it is often lexicalized in terms of networks, de-**territorialization**, **hybridity** and embedding. It should be remembered that transnational **social movements** are an important force in the global landscape as they are not tied to nations and increasingly are given space and voice at international and global fora such as the **UN** and indeed at the national level of government and law.

This concept is also known as transnational relations approach, TNP (transnational practices), transnationalism, or transnational society.

See also: **antiglobalization, cosmopolitanism, diaspora, re-embedding**

Further reading: Aron 1966; Moghadam 2005; Sassen 2002; Smith 2002

TRANSNATIONAL CORPORATION (TNC)

A company is often called a transnational corporation if it operates in at least two countries. However, there is some debate over what the definition of transnational corporation is, especially when considered in relation to the multinational corporation (MNC). The terms TNC and the MNC are often used interchangeably. While there is a general consensus that MNCs exist, there is some debate over whether TNCs do and what they look like.

While the MNC can be accounted for by taking an international perspective, that is, understanding the world as comprised of **nation-states**, the TNC is more considered to be properly global as it should ideally be absolutely mobile, moving to whichever locale offers it the largest competitive advantage. In reality, most corporations, while having arms and branches internationally in terms of both production and dissemination of product, are firmly based in one country; this may not be the home country of the company. This base country also tends to be in the developed north. Such a corporation may more properly be said to be multinational rather than transnational. The characterization of corporations as multinational leads the so called globalization **skeptics** to argue that such companies are not really globalized but rather an example of the north/core colonizing and behaving in an imperialist manner towards the south/periphery (see Hirst and Thomspon 1996). On the other hand, the transnational corporation has no home state; it is stateless. They cannot be understood in the context of the world as a set of nations. In response to the argument that so called TNCs are simply MNCs by another name, Sklair writes: "You cannot simply assume that all 'US', 'Japanese' and other 'national' TNCs express a 'national interest'. They do not" (1999: 147). Rather, it is the interests of those who own the corporations that matter, and this **transnational capitalist class** does see itself as globalized.

TNCs do exist, however, and they are central to globalization, especially economic globalization. It is for the TNC that EPZs are created. Government policy about **FDI** and tax concessions are aimed at the TNC. Enough investment by a large corporation in a country can stabilize a national economy; withdrawing the investment can weaken it. While TNCs need to be described in economic terms, they are also central to other "kinds" of globalization. Without distribution, marketing and retail arms in many places, the consumption of the same product globally would not be possible. The infrastructure that is needed for a product to be consumed globally is economically and culturally significant. Further, the cultural reach of the TNC is not only linked to the end product and consumer, but also those who work for it. The **cultural imperialism** that is often attributed to the West may more properly be corporate imperialism

(Girvan 1976) as it is the TNC (or MNC) who is the agent of such imperialism (if it happens at all).

Thus the significance of TNCs needs to be understood in relation to what they do as well as what they are. The increasing tendency for corporations in certain industries to merge, while not limited to TNCs, plays an important part in their power. Even if not actually merging, some scholars describe the way in which TNCs coordinate activity and strategy with similar corporations, leading to an "alliance capitalism" (Dunning 1997; Sklair 2002). Further, the level of **state** (that is government) control of TNCs appears to be relatively low in terms of restricting actions. This can be explained in a number of ways. Obviously, governments will be interested in investment and in job creation. TNCs are able to offer this. Which nation will be the beneficiary may depend on the benefits to the TNC. Thus the power of the TNC may be significant, especially when it is remembered that many corporations have budgets which far exceed the economies of the countries in which they work. Sklair (2002) also argues that the role of the TCC (transnational capitalist class) should not be overlooked. After all, this class (or social network of people) is usually that which allows TNCs and governments to talk to each other and broker agreements.

See also: **Export Processing Zone (EPZ), FDI, transnational, world systems theory**

Further reading: Barnet and Muller 1975; Coleman 2003; Girvan 1976; Kristensen and Zeitlin 2004; Morriesy and Yogesh 1995

TRANSNATIONALIST CAPITALIST CLASS (TCC)

Robinson and Harris argue that the TCC "is a global ruling class. It is a ruling class because it controls the levers of an emergent transnational state apparatus and of global decision making" (2000: 11). This group is defined not so much by their specific roles as by their ideology, which is one of **capitalism** and particularly **consumerism**. Sklair describes the TCC as those whose interests are "best served by an identification with the interests of the capitalist global system" (2002: 9), particularly, their interests are in alignment with **TNC**s. Sklair argues, "Members of the transnational capitalist class often work directly for TNCs and their lifestyles are exemplary for the spread of consumerism" (2002: 85). Sklair sees the TCC as

transnational in a number of ways (2002: 98) and including at least four groups, including TNC staff, bureaucrats and politicians, technical professionals and consumerists (merchants and media) (2002: 99). The TCC is linked not only to the production of goods, but also to government, media and even local practices.

See also: **consumerism, World Economic Forum, hegemony**

Further reading: Robinson 2004, 2005

TRUST

One of the defining features of the contemporary world, according to globalization studies, is the need to rely on **expert systems**. We are more or less forced to trust expert systems because many of the facts and circumstances which impact our lives are simply unavailable and unknowable. Giddens writes, " ... *the nature of modern institutions is deeply bound up with the mechanisms of trust in abstract systems*, especially trust in expert systems" (1990: 83).

We also must trust the individuals (**symbolic analysts**) who negotiate the expert system for us, and those who are the face of the system. These individuals may only be known by sight, that is, the relationship only exists because of the necessity of trust and negotiating the expert system.

This trust "becomes a project ... to be 'worked at' by the parties involved ... [T]rust [in modern societies] has to be won, and the means of doing this is demonstrable warmth and openness" (1990: 121). Because of past performance we are likely to believe some expert systems more than others. For example, governments have to work harder at gaining trust than those perceived as impartial. Trust is symptomatic of **modernity** but also essential to it.

See also: **abstract systems, liquid modernity, perfect knowledge, risk**

Further reading: Giddens 1991

UNITED NATIONS (UN)

The United Nations was established in 1945 with initially 51 member nations. Members now number 191. It was founded on four principles: to maintain peace and security, to develop positive relations between nations, to solve problems and promote human rights and generally to be a center for an agent of peace and harmony (www.UN.org). The UN was established as a reaction to WWII. Because of this, the UN has six parts: the General Assembly (in which all participate); the Security Council; the Economic and Social Council; the Trusteeship; and the Secretariat. The International Court of Justice (primarily for human rights offences) is also part of the UN but its members are only bound by decisions on a voluntary basis.

The Security Council makes resolutions and declarations on military matters, as Habermas notes it "take[s] actual power relations into account" (2001: 106). The five permanent members of the Security Council (China, France, Russian Federation, the UK and the USA) have special voting and veto rights. Under the UN Charter the Security Council can make decisions rather than just the recommendations of the Assembly.

The UN comprises a number of other agencies with particular interests and goals. For globalization, the UNDP (UN Development Program) is one of the most important. It monitors development globally and supports initiatives especially to aid developing countries, their governments and NGOs. Indeed, there are around 1,500 NGOs connected in some way to the UN currently (Sklair 2002: 97). The UN Environment Program (UNEP) may also be increasingly visible in the light of current debate on global warming and climate change.

The UN is central to the promotion of the discourse and indeed action in relation to human rights. They were involved with such issues in the former Yugoslavia and Rwanda. Its Commission on Human Rights can receive, examine and investigate (though the process is secret) allegations of human rights abuses. Governments and NGOs can also "name and shame" abusers at Commission meetings (Sklair 2002: 306). There is also a High Commissioner for Human Rights (installed under Kofi Annan's leadership). While there is at the very least a rhetorical commitment to human rights, the UN faces difficulties in intervening in states, even in the form of peace-keeping missions. This is because of the ongoing **sovereignty** of states and indeed the difficulty of marshalling appropriate and adequate resources and personnel with which to conduct interventions. However, since the 1990s, the UN has been increasingly willing to be involved in the affairs of states such as monitoring elections and humanitarian interventions (the former requested, the latter regardless) (see Matthews 1997).

While the UN might seem to be a global institution, it is in one way more international than global because countries are members by virtue of their **nation–state** status. In the work conducted with **NGOs**, however, and by UN agencies, it is easier to see transnational practices simply because the main agents are not nation-states. When nation-states are not involved as players or by virtue of issues involved, the UN can be quite global indeed. In terms of issues, anything which directly threatens the status and sovereignty of nation–states individually or collectively is likely to be resisted. Thus in matters where involvement does not involve blaming or singling out nation–states, the UN can be particularly effective. Thus HIV/AIDS can be addressed by the UN agency UNAIDS, and terrorism can also be taken up as an issue exactly because the terrorists are not (as such) representatives of a nation.

See also: **human rights, universal human rights**

Further reading: Drori 2005; Felice 1999; Gareis and Varwick 2005; Robertson and Merrills 1996; Weiss 2004

UNIVERSAL CIVILIZATION

The idea of a universal civilization is closely tied to the argument that globalization homogenizes. There appear to be more voices against the prospect of a realization of a universal civilization than predicting it. The once conservative John Gray argues that free market trade is the latest attempt to create a universal civilization. He writes, "The inexorable growth of a world market does not advance a universal civilization. It makes the interpenetration of cultures an irreversible global condition" (1998: 193). Presumably this leads to the "**clash of civilizations**" discussed by Huntington.

See also: **cosmopolitanism, cosmopolitan democracy; homogenization, one world, world culture theory**

Further reading: Ricoeur 1961; Riese 1995

UNIVERSAL HUMAN RIGHTS

The concept of universal human rights finds its central champion in the **UN**'s *Declaration of Human Rights* (1948). There are, however, significant issues that need to be addressed in terms of both the content and application of these rights. Many argue that the UN declaration is **ethnocentric**, concentrating on civil and political rather than economic and social rights. Cultural relativism also needs to be taken account of in terms of drafting "universals." Quite obviously, if the rights that are institutionally ratified are not deemed culturally acceptable, their enforcement is hardly likely. In a sense, the challenges facing universal human rights are the same central issues of debate in the globalization field and also connected to the processes of globalization itself.

If globalization means that the world and people are becoming more alike (**homogenization**) then the question of what will constitute an acceptable set of universal human rights should resolve itself. If this homogenization is ethnocentric, that is, by and large synonymous with **Westernization** for example, would such universality be acceptable? If, on the other hand, globalization rather complicates local cultures because of flows, networks and a plethora of cultural and material interactions, perhaps the concept of human rights itself needs to be considered as an evolving, even hybrid, concept. Further, if and when there is agreement as to what constitutes universal human rights, who should defend and uphold them? The role of the **nation–state** as traditionally taking on this task is under question if the authority of the nation-state itself is in doubt (as in some versions of globalization).

At the same time, the understanding that we all occupy the same space may provide a necessary commonality for taking rights seriously. In this case, **civil society** would have an extended role and would be performing rights (as well as **citizenship**).

See also: **cosmopolitanism, cultural defense plea, fundamentalism, human rights, indigenous culture, relativism, UN**

Further reading: Alaug and Chase 2004; Clayton 2004; Markowitz 2004; Richards 2005; Woodiwiss 2002

UNIVERSALISM

Universalism can refer to religions which are explicitly tolerant of other denominations, seeking common ground rather than differences. It may also refer to moral universalism, which as opposed to relativism, holds that there is one set of moral standards applicable to all. In globalization studies, universalism is likely to be used to mean universalization or **globalism** in the sense of **homogenization**.

URBANISM, TRANSNATIONAL

The role of the city (that is, the urban) in globalization is connected to a number of phenomena. **Global cities**, the **cosmopolis**, the **network society** and indeed many **transnational** activities and practices take place in cities (such as trade, financial business and their related support services). During **industrialization**, urbanization was necessary for the provision of manual labor; now, people are more likely to be involved in the service industry which is also concentrated in urban settings.

The rise of the city is significant in that it challenges the primacy of the **nation–state** both in international relations and in terms of being a prime identity tag for individuals. Cities too can have an agency with respect to global events because of (often devolved) control they may have over urban planning, decision-making and spending. Holston and Appadurai comment, "cities are challenging, diverging from, and even replacing nations as the important space of citizenship – as the lived space not only of its uncertainties but also of its emergent forms" (1996: 198).

See also: **citizenship, cosmopolis, cosmopolitanism, placeless geography, service work, world cities/global cities**

Further reading: Holston and Appadurai 1996; Sassen 2002; Smith 2001

WAGE EARNER WELFARE STATES

The term "wage earner welfare state" was coined by Francis Castles (1985) to identify a distinct "demand-led" welfare capitalism found in Australia and New Zealand. Castles was at pains to show that Australia and New Zealand's dubious reputation as social laboratories marked by periods of rapid reform and meager welfare provision was due more to the way they were categorized than with the limits of their "demand-led" welfare system. This perplexing reputation, as explained by Castles in *The Working Class and Welfare* (1985), is the result of welfare models and typologies that group and rank countries in terms of their levels of 'universalism' and 'citizen entitlement' so diminishing 'demand-led' welfare systems. Demand-led welfare systems work on the Keynesian logic that if an outside agency, such as a government, steps in and increases demand through public expenditure, this pushes the economy into a cycle of high demand and high employment. Demand-led economies are also "wage earner welfare states" when welfare is distributed through high wages rather than services for the dependent and poor. New Zealand and Australian governments achieved consistently high wages and secure employment through protectionist economic policies, centralized wage regulation, industrial arbitration and guaranteed minimum wages. This welfare system works very well if unemployment remains low. The wage earner welfare state is seen to be a casualty of globalization as the effects of the social, economic and technological changes attributable to the expansion of global markets lead to a rapid and persistent unemployment. This puts pressure upon the ability of the state to uphold "family wages" and leads to a rapid dismantling of the "wage earner" system of welfare provision.

See also: **family wage (decline of), protectionism (economic)**

Further reading: Castles 1985, 1996; Tennant 2004

RM

WAR OF POSITION

This is part of Gramsci's (1971) proposal for a way for **civil society** to challenge state power in order to bring about socialism. Although such a war of positions is usually associated with intellectuals and academics, for Gramsci the important distinction is between the **state** and **civil society** rather than between those who would call themselves intellectuals and others. In terms of globalization, there is an ongoing war of positions, for example, between globalists and antiglobalizers, but also between globalists, **skeptics** and transformationalists.

See also: **antiglobalization, counter-narrative, hegemony, hyperglobalist thesis**

Further reading: Rose 1990

WELFARE STATE

The theory or practice of the state providing some kind of assistance or safety net for those less able to provide for themselves. This most commonly takes the form of income provision in the event of unemployment, but may also include nationalized health services, tax policies and income regulation.

In globalization, the welfare state is most usually represented as being threatened by the values of **neoliberalism**.

See also: **nationalization, privatization, wage earner welfare states**

Further reading: Mishra 1999; Pestieau 2005

WESTERNIZATION

In globalization, Westernization is often used as a variant for **Americanization** or **homogenization**. There are an increasing number of such terms, including **McDonaldization** and Derrida's globalatinization (though this refers particularly to the influence of Christian values on other cultures and religions). Jameson (2000) notes that some in Iran call Westernization, "Westoxification." Seeing Westernization as synonymous with globalization is a particular view of globalization which is hotly debated. To take this view is to see globalization as a continuation of **colonialism**. Thus it should be remembered while some argue that globalization is simply colonialism with a new label attached, the terms are not necessarily equivalent.

Further reading: Derrida 1998; Jameson 2000; Latouche 1996; Sen 2002; Tomlinson 1996

WORK RICH/WORK POOR

This concept refers to the distribution of work across households. A household where all members are working is called "work rich" while a household where few or none of the members are working is called "work poor." The concept was developed in response to the descriptive limitations of **income polarization** and its concentration on disparities between individual incomes because analysis of labor market shifts based only on individuals disguises the distribution of work across households. As Callister notes (2001: 3), overseas research has identified that, over the long term, there has been a simultaneous growth of households where all prime working aged people are in paid work (work-rich) and households where no prime working aged person is employed (work-poor). This has led to a reduction in households containing a mixture of people in and out of paid work. One mixed work household that has declined substantially is that of a male in a couple working full-time and his female partner staying home full-time and looking after children.

The concept of work rich/work poor households also allows us to examine in more detail the impact of increasing levels of casual (part-time) employment, associated with global employment trends and largely affecting women. In reference to New Zealand, which was previously a **wage earner's welfare state** that relied on a gendered division of labor embodied in the **family wage**, the majority of women in paid employment work part time, yet part-time work has spread to both men and women in a wide range of age groups and living arrangements. In New Zealand, it appears that as part-time work has spread to men as well as women, so more households are totally relying on part-time work, rendering them work poor overall.

See also: **feminization of the workforce, global labor market**

Further reading: Borland and Sheehan 2001

RM

WORLD BANK

One of the central global financial institutions established post–World War II in 1945. It is not actually a bank as such, but one of the arms of the **United Nations** and a group of five agencies. Arguably the two most important of these are the International Bank for Reconstruction and Development (IBRD) and the International Development Association (IDA). The World Bank's primary role is to provide low-interest loans, interest-free credit and grants to developing countries. It was envisioned that such aid would primarily be used to develop infrastructure such as dams, roads and transport links, power generation and storage, health and education. The money for the loans and grants comes from members (who "own" the Bank) and also from investments on international markets. To become a member of the Bank, membership in the **IMF** is required. Thus the two institutions are linked.

Because of the poor financial situation of the borrowing countries, it became clear that not all loans could be repaid. In the 1950s, the IDA was established to provide soft loans, that is, loans with little or no interest.

There are three other relevant agencies that make up the World Bank. The International Finance Corporation (IFC) provides support for private sector investment in Bank-approved projects. Thus, for example, a private company may invest in power generation as a profitable project on their part. Such investment is encouraged by the IFC supporting high-risk industries and sectors.

The Multilateral Investment Guarantee Agency (MIGA) provides risk insurance to those investing in and lending to countries that the Bank is working with. Finally, the International Center for Settlement of Investment Disputes (ICSID) does as its name suggests: settling disagreements between foreign investments and host countries.

While the World Bank is the largest long-term financier of HIV/AIDS programs globally (www.worldbank.org), it often attracts criticism, especially from antiglobalizers. The Bank's various programs do not always work harmoniously. Altman writes:

> There is an irony in the World Bank putting increasing sums of money into AIDS work in countries such as Brazil and India where the Bank's own policies had helped weaken the health structures that might have already helped prevent the spread of HIV.
>
> (2002: 565)

Such criticisms stem largely from the Bank's **neoliberal** policies, that is, decreasing state spending, encouraging foreign investment and opening up trade.

See also: **antiglobalization, Foreign Direct Investment (FDI), global health policy**

Further reading: Bello 2004; Lawson 2003; Mallaby 2005; Owusu 2003; Peet and Born 2003; World Bank 2005

WORLD CITIES/GLOBAL CITIES

What makes a city a world or global city is a collection of factors including the presence of most or all of the following: large global corporations (in the form of headquarters or large offices); siting of an institution of political importance, such as the UN; transport infrastructure, both international and local; cultural and educational institutions; and a diverse population.

The term global city was introduced by Saskia Sassen (2001) in contrast to a city that is simply large (a mega-city). She argues that the decentralization of production in a spatial sense (**offshoring**, and subcontracting, for example) has not led to a decentralization of ownership or control. The phrase "world city" has a longer history, originating with Friedman (1982).

Derudder (2006) argues that "global city," "world city" and "global city region" are distinct terms which are not consistently treated as such. The concept of a "world city" is linked to **world systems theory** where the world city is a node in the network. The "global city region" is found in Sassen, but taken up by Scott (2001). Derudder distinguishes between the three concepts on the basis of their function, agents, structure and territorial basis (2006). What all three have in common is that they are characterized by postindustrial corporations.

There is an emerging concept of a world city, sometimes called a "world-class city." Making changes to cities in order to bring them world status is something states are increasingly interested in because of the rewards this can bring in marketing the city to business, organizations and institutions and tourists. Thus the presence of "world class" facilities in sports, the arts and for business (for example convention and exhibition centers) can then be used as a marketing strength. Obviously some cities will emphasize some facilities over others in order to attract a certain kind of visitor, whether this is in the form of **FDI** or tourism dollars.

Sassen argues that the changes brought by globalization mean that cities are changing. This is largely due to the **mobility** of capital, people and production. Cities have become important sites of industry and production. The latter refers not so much to actual goods, but rather, to services such as banking, marketing, financial institutions and indeed support to the needs and desires of the global elite. "Being a city becomes synonymous with being in an extremely intense information loop" (Sassen 2001: xx). **TNC**s and MNCs may offshore their manufacturing processes and thus need support services locally. This does not necessarily mean that the local manufacturing area sees this development, but somewhere in the nation or the region must be able to support the management of these industries.

Global cities provide attractive places for service industries and their employees to work. Advances in technology, especially communication and ICT, facilitate this. Further, nations may provide incentives for such service industries to locate in their larger cities in the form of tax concessions, for example. Thus the legal profile of a nation, or indeed a city, may be instrumental in its developing into a global city.

Sassen suggests that gentrification is also important in understanding the structural and infrastructural changes occuring in global cities.

> Gentrification emerged [in the 1980s] as a visible spatial component of this transformation [in advanced capitalism]. It was evident in the redevelopment of waterfronts, the rise of hotel and convention complexes in central cities, large-scale luxury office and residential developments, and fashionable, high-priced shopping districts.
>
> (2001: 261)

At the same time, these cities, at least in terms of business function, are oriented to the global context rather than to the local. However, those who work in global cities are not all the global elite. The kind of manual labor that is involved in especially the construction of the global city should not be forgotten. The rise in homelessness, exploitative working practices including the use of illegal immigrant labor, suggest that such groups are forgotten. Abu-Lughod (1999) draws attention to the inequalities present in the global city, however she suggests that to posit globalization as a single monolithic cause of this ignores the fact that global cities differ. That is, if globalization were the single factor in the creation of the global city, one would not find the variation between cities in different regions that one does.

Indeed, Sassen does distinguish between the global city and the global city region: "..the global city is more attuned to questions of power and inequality. The concept of global city-region is more attuned to questions about the nature and specifics of broad urbanization patterns" (2001: 351–52).

Beaverstock and colleagues in the Globalization and World Cities Study Group & Network (GaWC), based at Loughborough University have published a scale of world cities. They rank cities into Alpha-, Beta- and Gamma-cities on the basis of four areas "accounting, advertising, banking and law." Thus what global city or world city means depends on who is using the phrase and for what purpose.

See also: **cosmopolis, global capitalism, global managerial class/ global elite, global media, lifestyle, migration, network society, off-sharing, placeless geography, symbolic analysts**

Further reading: Beaverstock Smith and Taylor 1999; Gugler 2004; Knox and Taylor 1995; Scott 2001; Taylor 2004

WORLD CULTURE THEORY

Attributed to the sociologist Roland Robertson, world culture theory refers to the realization that we all live in the same place. Essentially, it is a consciousness of the physicality and unity of the planet on which all people live, regardless of their life differences. For Robertson, globalization is "the compression of the world and the intensification of consciousness of the world as a whole" (1992: 8). The changes that globalization brings means that not only are we aware of the fact that we live in a single world, we can also behave in that way. Advances in communication technology, ICT, transportation, production and consumption have relatively recently made this **globality** real to an increasing number of people. Further, we are all confronted with what it means to live in one place, that is, with the features and consequences of the now present fact of globality.

Obviously not everyone will answer these questions in the same way, hence globalization also leads to the "comparative interaction of different forms of life" (Robertson 1995: 27).

This interaction and comparison is not without its problems and conflict. Being confronted with different forms of life may lead to **reflexivity**, or to assert claims over particular forms of life (such as religious beliefs or **nationalism**). World culture theory as a way of thinking about globalization could be compared with **world system theory** and **world polity theory**.

See also: **clash of civilizations, cultural fate, globality, global village, glocalization, reflexive modernization/modernity, time-space compression**

Further reading: Caldwell 2004; Hannerz 1990

WHO (WORLD HEALTH ORGANIZATION)

Founded in 1948, the WHO describes itself as a

> specialized agency of the **United Nations** with primary responsibility for international health matters and public health. WHO promotes international cooperation to tackle health problems and carries out programs to control and eradicate disease. WHO has four main functions: to give worldwide guidance in the field of health, to set global standards for health, to cooperate with governments in strengthening national health programs, and to develop and transfer appropriate health technology, information, and standards. WHO leads the world alliance for Health For All, a **global health policy** that seeks to create conditions under which people have, as a fundamental **human right**, the opportunity to reach and maintain the highest attainable level of health.
>
> (WHO 2005)

There is considerable debate over changing role and authority of WHO. Forty years ago, activities in international health were the domain of WHO, governments (based on bilateral agreements), and **NGOs**. However, today, new players (such as the **World Bank** and, increasingly, the **World Trade Organization**) have an influence on international health. As globalization of trade and markets takes hold, new coalitions and alliances are forming to examine and deal with the direct and indirect consequences on health. Although WHO is struggling to maintain its precedence in the new political context, WHO's activities, are, in the discourse of globalization, the institutional embodiment of global health policy in the sense that it attempts to lead emergent coalitions; are instrumental in identifying global health problems; and instigating, coordinating and evaluating the national health agendas and policy programs of member countries. WHO is arguably a key political organization for those who seek to identify and off-set the harsher effects of globalization as it claims to value development and improvement in the health field for their own sake rather than because of the financial rewards such development may bring.

See also: **global health policy**

Further reading: Koop *et al.* 2002

RM

WORLD HEGEMONY

See: **hegemony, world systems theory**

WORLD POLITY THEORY

This theory (linked to Meyer 1980, 1997) draws attention to what we have in common rather than emphasizing difference. These similarities come about because of shared scripts or frames, that is, ways of doing things and ways of thinking about things. It is not quite the same as homogenization as there is still room for difference, so, as in **world culture theory**, world polity theory does not entail homogenization. It does acknowledge that actors are diverse. There is no "central actor [rather], the culture of world society allocates responsible and authoritative actorhood to nation states" (Meyer *et al.* 1997: 169). In this, world polity theory (WPT) can resemble an international approach (see **realist paradigm**). However **states** are not the only actors as they are not the only entities that can deploy the common frames and scripts which themselves help to legitimate the **nation–state** (Meyer 1980). Other actors include **NGO**s, voluntary associations and experts and even individuals. The relationship between actors and the polity can be explained in terms of **structuration** theory; that is, the relationship is recursive.

The paradigm of the nation-state, education and health institutions and the general supremacy of values of rationality and science are examples of ways of thinking that are global, regardless of important differences between regions and states. Adopting the model of a nation-state, for example, brings with it certain rights with respect to other nations, most significantly, **sovereignty** and territoriality. The model is globally recognized and adopted. The advantage of identifying such shared scripts and frames (which theoretically exist at a cognitive level) means that communication and action can take place even in the face of conflict.

The organizational frame established post-WWII and the kinds of actors it identifies are crucial in seeing WPT as a theory of globalization rather than simply a way of talking about **internationalization**. "The development and impact of global sociocultural structuration greatly intensified with the creation of a central world organizational frame at the end of World War II" (Meyer 1980: 163). The organizations that developed at this point play a central role in legitimating actors. The UN, for example, defines what counts as various actors (such as

NGOs). The end result is that actors tend to construct themselves in similar ways because, as WPT claims, all are drawing on the same models of thinking and legitimation. At the same time, the variety of actors and the ability to interpret shared models in different ways, by prioritizing different values, for example, means that there is still conflict, competition and conversation. For example, an NGO may interpret and champion protection of the environment in terms of progress and sustainability while a nation-state may argue for a particular dam in terms of economic progress and development.

See also: **global governance, world systems theory**

Further reading: Boli and Thomas 1997; Jackson 2001; Meyer *et al.* 1997

WORLD SYSTEMS THEORY

In his book *The Modern World-System* (1974), Immanuel Wallerstein makes his most significant contribution to both sociology and globalization studies in the form of world systems theory. Unlike most other Marxist historical work concerned with analyzing the development of capitalist economic inequalities, world systems theory does not concentrate on the relations between social classes or between the state and workers. Rather, it focuses on a large economic entity that is not constrained by sociopolitical boundaries. Wallerstein calls this entity the "world-system." This mutable system is most notably characterized by an unjust division of labor that produces unequal exchange relations between different geographical areas of the world. The world system, then, is not maintained through consensual agreement, but rather through social forces that are in constant conflict, threatening to collapse the system.

Wallerstein argues that the modern capitalist world economy is the current type of world system. Rather than relying on political domination as did an earlier system, this one operates on the basis of economic exploitation through an unjust global division of labor. The world system comprises three main geographical areas: core, periphery, and semi-periphery. The core is the geographical region that dominates the world economy. It exploits the peripheral region, which provides raw materials and cheaply produced commodities to the core while being forced to import expensive finished products from the core region. The semi-periphery are the remaining areas that are simultaneously exploited by the core and exploiting of the periphery.

As the world system gradually expands across the globe, it exerts a pressure on individual nations to become part of the world economy. Nations remain independent as states, as long as they integrate themselves into the "interstate" system. Otherwise they risk being taken over by states already incorporated into that political system. Once states become part of the world system, they must employ various strategies, including the cultural denigration of "others," to protect their economies from outside influence.

In terms of an agenda for social justice, Wallerstein argues that more equitable global exchange relations can be achieved through the formation of a third world system, which he calls a socialist world government. A socialist world economy, based on collective control and ownership of economic resources, would both amalgamate the political and economic sectors that capitalism separates and eliminate economic exploitation between geographical regions and among laborers across the globe.

See also: **Marx/Marxism**

Further reading: Bergesen 1984; Wallerstein 1980, 1989

NC

WTO (WORLD TRADE ORGANIZATION)

The WTO was established in 1995 as a successor of GATT (the General Agreement on Tariffs and Trade) as a result of the 1986–1994 Uruguay round of negotiations. There are 149 members who are responsible for 97% of world trade. There are also countries currently negotiating for membership. The four largest members, Canada, **European Union**, Japan and the United States are known as the Quadrilaterals or the Quad. The EU is a member as well as individual countries within it also being members.

Decisions about new trade agreements are made by "consensus" through negotiation. However, **antiglobalizers** argue that many meetings take place between larger and more powerful members (usually from the north) which lead to an agreement which members excluded from these initial negotiations have very little power to change. These initial meetings are unofficial and not recorded.

At the top of the WTO is the Ministerial Conference which meets every 2 years. The conference is more usually identified by the city in which it meets (Seattle, Doha and so on). The General Council meets every year in headquarters in Geneva. The WTO also consists of committees, working groups and working parties to deal with specific agreements (such as TRIPS and TRIMS; the Agreement on Trade-Related Investment Measures and the Agreement on Trade Related Intellectual Property Rights, respectively). The working parties and committees report to the General Council.

The WTO negotiate trade rules globally and bilaterally (between nations), and provide dispute settlement about the terms of these and also in relation to the broad principles which underpin global trade, such as the concept of "most favored nation." This concept is directly related to the principle that **free trade** means that trade should be nondiscriminatory. The most favored nation principle means that all nations should be treated equally, that is, as well as the "most favored" nation. Further, members also gave a right to "national treatment" that is, a nation has to treat one's own nationals and foreigners equally when it comes to trade. (There are similar agreements and principles within trade zones such as the EU).

The WTO covers trade in goods and services as well as intellectual property. It should be noted that the agreements do allow implementation periods for developing nations, for example if legal or administrative infrastructure needs to be put in place to uphold the agreement.

As well as members, however, the WTO is at least indirectly influenced by other players, such as MNCs and **TNC**s. Corporations will lobby their home nations or those in which they do business, in an attempt to have their own interests taken into account. In the sense that the WTO operates according to political and economic concerns it represents an important aspect of globalization. While **nation–states** (and similar legal entities) are members, decisions are not always made because of political ideology but because of economic concerns, whether these be those of the state (direct interests) or those of corporations working within the state (indirect interests).

The WTO says of itself that it is the only "international organization dealing with the global rules of trade between nations" (www. WTO.org). It makes sure that "trade flows as smoothly, predictably and freely as possible" (ibid.). The WTO is predicated on the value of free trade, or at least equal trade and this is part of the ideology of the nation-state. They argue that this of itself makes life better contributing to "a more prosperous, peaceful and accountable economic world."

See also: **antiglobalization, fair trade/free trade, European Union (EU), free trade, global capitalism, nation-state, Seattle**

Further reading: Guan 2001; Hoad 2002; Wheeler 2000

WORLD WORKS COUNCIL

A World Works Council (WWC) is a forum that brings together employee and management representatives within a **TNC** to discuss company-specific business.

The first wave of global union organization was in the 1960s–1970s, when over 50 "World Company Councils" were set up. These were organized by the International Trade Secretariats (later renamed **GUFs**), although initiated by US trade unions. In most cases these failed to develop a constructive bargaining role. The more recent growth of WWCs has been based on the extension of existing European Works Councils. Prominent amongst these are those at Volkswagen, SKG and Danone. These latter examples are based on formal agreement between central management, including undertakings on the provision of information.

A prerequisite for effective WWC organization is a relatively stable, vertically integrated company structure. In TNCs characterized by outsourced **commodity chains**, bargaining has generally been coordinated by the GUFs, and has focused on developing rights-based Global Framework Agreements.

The impact of WWCs should not be overstated. Some meet infrequently, and the scope of discussions can be very limited. Although they provide the basis of global solidarity, they have tended to be Eurocentric, and they have yet to deliver substantive benefits to workers in poorer countries. Whether they are capable of transforming themselves into something more will depend, in part, on the willingness of national unions.

See also: **Global Union Federations (GUFs), IFA (International Framework Agreements)**

Further reading: Rüb 2002

GW

BIBLIOGRAPHY

Abercrombie, N., Hill, S. and Turner, B. S. (1994) *The Penguin Dictionary of Sociology*, London: Penguin.

Abu-Lughod, J. L. (1991) *Before European Hegemony: The World System A.D. 1250–1350*, Oxford: Oxford University Press.

—— (1999) *New York, Chicago, Los Angeles: America's Global Cities*, Minneapolis, MN: University of Minnesota Press.

Addison Posey, D. (ed.) (2000) *Cultural and Spiritual Values of Biodiversity*, London: ITDG Publishing.

Adorno, T. W. (1973) *Negative Dialectics*, trans. E. B. Ashton, London: Routledge and Kegan Paul.

—— (1991) *The Culture Industry: Selected Essays on Mass Culture*, London: Routledge.

Aglietta, M. (1987) *A Theory of Capitalist Regulation: the US experience*, London: New Left Books.

Ahmed, S. (2003) 'The Politics of Fear in the Making of Worlds', *International Journal of Qualitative Studies in Education*, 16 (3), 377–98.

Alaug, A. K. and Chase, A. T. (2004) 'Health, human rights, and Islam: a focus on Yemen', *Health and Human Rights*, 8 (1), 115–37.

Albrow, M. (1970) *Bureaucracy*, London: McMillan.

—— (1996) *The Global Age, State and Society Beyond Modernity*, Cambridge: Polity Press.

Ali, T. (2003) *The Clash of Fundamentalisms: Crusades, Jihads and Modernity*, London: Verso.

Alibhai-Brown, Y. (2000) *After Multiculturalism*, London: Foreign Policy Centre.

Alleyne, M. D. (1995) *International Power and International Communication*, New York: St. Martin's Press.

Almond, G. A., Appleby, R. S. and Sivan, E. (2003) *Strong Religion: The Rise of Fundamentalisms Around the World*, Chicago, IL: University of Chicago Press.

Alston, P. and Robinson, M. (eds) (2005) *Human Rights and Development: Towards Mutual Reinforcement*, Oxford: Oxford University Press.

Althusser, L. (1977) *Lenin and Philosophy and Other Essays*, London: New Left Books.

Altman, D. (2002) *Global Sex*, Chicago, IL: University of Chicago Press.

Amin, A. (1994) *Post-Fordism: A Reader*, London: Blackwell.

Amin, A. and Hausner, J. (eds) (1997) *Beyond Market and Hierarchy: Interactive Governance and Social Complexity*, Cheltenham: Elgar.

Anderson, B. M. (2004) *News Flash: Journalism, Infotainment and the Bottom-line Business of Broadcast News*, San Francisco, CA: Jossey Bass.

Anderson, B. R. (1983) *Imagined Communities*, London: Verso.

Ang, I. (1994) 'Globalisation and Culture', *Continuum*, 8 (2), 323–25.

Appadurai, A. (ed.) (1986) *The Social Life of Things: Commodities in Cultural Perspective*, Cambridge: Cambridge University Press.

—— (1990) 'Disjuncture and Difference in the Global Cultural Economy', *Theory, Culture and Society*, 7, 295–310.

—— (1996) *Modernity at Large: Cultural Dimensions of Globalization*, Minneapolis, MN: University of Minnesota Press.

Archibugi, D. (ed.) (2003) *Debating Cosmopolitics*, London: Verso.

Archibugi, D. and Held, D. (eds) (1995) *Cosmopolitan Democracy: an Agenda for a New World Order*, Cambridge: Polity Press.

Archibugi, D., Held, D. and Kohler, M. (eds) (1998) *Re-Imagining Political Community: Studies in Cosmopolitan Democracy*, Cambridge: Polity.

Arefi, M. (1999) 'Non-place and placelessness as narratives of loss: rethinking the notion of place', *Journal of Urban Design*, 4 (2), 179–93.

Aron, R. (1966) *Peace and War: a Theory of International Relations*, trans. R. Howard and A. Baker Fox, London: Weidenfeld and Nicolson.

Arrighi, G. (1994) *The Long Twentieth Century: Money, Power, and the Origins of Our Times*, London: Verso.

ATTAC (Association for the Taxation of Financial Transactions for the Aid of Citizens). Available at: www.attac.org (accessed 27 March 2006).

Augé, M. (1995), *Non-places: Introduction to an Anthropology of Supermodernity*, trans. J. Howe, London: Verso.

Bangasser, P. E. (2000) 'The ILO and the informal sector: an institutional history', *Employment Paper* 9, Geneva: Publications of the International Labour Organisation.

Barber, B. R. (2001) *Jihad vs. McWorld,* New York: Random House.

Barlow, M. and Clarke, T. (2001) *Global Showdown: How the New Activists are Fighting Global Corporate Rule*, Toronto: Stoddart.

Barnekov, T., Boyle, R. and Rich, D. (1989) *Privatism and Urban Policy in Britain and the United States*, Oxford: Oxford University Press.

Barnet, R. J. and Muller, R. E. (1975) *Global Reach: The Power of the Multinational Corporations*, London: Jonathon Cape.

Barnett, M. (2003) *Eyewitness to a Genocide: The United Nations and Rwanda*, Ithaca, NY: Cornell University Press.

Barratt Brown, M. (1993) *Fair Trade: Reform and Realities in the International Trading System*, London: Zed Books.

Barrett, M. and Macintosh, M. (1982) *The Anti Social Family*, London: Verso.

Barry, A., Osbourne, T. and Rose, N. (1996) *Foucault and Political Reason: Liberalism, Neo-liberalism, and Rationalities of Government*, Chicago, IL: University of Chicago Press.

Barry, B. M. (2001) *Culture and Equality: an Egalitarian Critique of Multiculturalism*, Cambridge, MA: Harvard University Press.

Bartlett T. (2001) 'Use the Road: The Appropriacy of Appropriation', *Language and Intercultural Communication*, 1 (1), 21–29.

Baudrillard, J. (1975) *The Mirror of Production*, St Louis, MO: Telos Press.

—— (1988) *Selected Writings*, ed. M. Poster, Stanford, CA: Stanford University Press, pp. 166–84.

—— (1994a) *The Illusion Of The End*, trans. C. Turner, Oxford: Polity Press.

—— (1994b) *Simulacra and Simulation*, trans. S. Faria Glaser, Ann Arbor, MI: University of Michigan Press.

—— (1995) *The Gulf War Did Not Take Place*, trans. P. Patton, Bloomington, IN: Indiana University Press.

—— (1996) *The System Of Objects*, trans. J. Benedict, London: Verso.

Bauer, L. and Trudgill, P. (1998) *Language Myths*, London: Penguin.

Bauman, Z. (1993) *Postmodern Ethics*, Oxford: Blackwell.

—— (2000) *Liquid Modernity*, Cambridge: Polity.

Beaglehole, R. (2003) *Global Public Health*, Oxford: Oxford University Press.

Beasley-Murray, J. (2000) 'Value and Capital in Bourdieu and Marx', in N. Brown and I. Szeman (eds), *Pierre Bourdieu: Fieldwork in Art, Literature and Culture*, Lanham, MD: Rowman and Littlefield, pp. 100–19.

Beaverstock, J. V. and Boardwell, J. T. (2000) 'Negotiating Globalization, Transnational Corporations and Global City Financial Centres in Transient Migration Studies', *Applied Geography*, 20 (2), 227–304.

Beaverstock, J. V., Smith, R. G. and Taylor, P. J. (1999) 'A Roster of World Cities', *Cities*, 16 (6), 445–58.

Beck, U. (1992) *Risk Society*, trans. M. Ritter, London: Sage.

—— (1994) 'The Reinvention of Politics: Towards a Theory of Reflexive Modernization', in U. Beck, A. Giddens and S. Lash (eds), *Reflexive Modernization: Politics, Tradition and Aesthetics in the Modern Social Order*, Cambridge: Polity Press, pp. 1–55.

—— (1998) *Democracy Without Enemies*, trans. M. Ritter, Oxford: Polity Press.

—— (2000 [1997]) *What is Globalization?* trans. P. Camiller, Oxford: Polity Press.

Beck, U. and Beck-Gernsheim, E. (2001) *Individualization: Institutionalized Individualism and its Social and Political Consequences*, trans. P. Camiller, London: Sage.

Beck, U., Bonss, W and Lau, C. (2003) 'The Theory of Reflexive Modernization: Problematic, Hypotheses and Research Programme', *Theory, Culture and Society*, 20 (2), 1–34.

Beck, U., Giddens, A. and Lash, S. (eds) (1994) *Reflexive Modernization: Politics, Tradition and Aesthetics in the Modern Social Order*, Cambridge: Polity Press.

Becker, G. (1994) *Human Capital: A Theoretical and Empirical Analysis, with Special Reference to Education*, 3rd edn, Chicago: University of Chicago Press.

Becker, H. S. and Horowitz, I. L. (1970) 'The culture of civility', *Trans-Action*, 7 (6), 12–19.

Belk, R. W. (1996) 'Hyperreality and Globalization: Culture in the Age of Ronald McDonald', *Journal of International Consumer Marketing*, 8 (3–4), 23–37.

Bell, A. and Strieber, W. (2000) *The Coming Global Superstorm*, New York: Pocket Books.

Bell, D. (1973) *The Coming of Post-Industrial Society: a Venture in Social Forecasting*, New York: Basic Books.

Bell, D. and Kristol, I. (eds) (1971) *Capitalism Today*, New York: Basic Books.

Bellah, R., Madsen, R., Sullivan, W. M., Swidler, A. and Tipton S. M., (1985) *Habits of the Heart: Individualism and Commitment in American Life*, Berkeley, CA: University of California Press.

Bello, W. (2004) *Deglobalization: Ideas for a New World Economy*, London: Zed Books.

—— (2005) *The Anti-Development State: The Political Economy of Permanent Crisis in the Philippines*, London: Zed Books.

Belsey, C. (1985) *The Subject of History*, London: Methuen.

Benjamin, W. (1968) *Illuminations*, New York: Harcourt, Brace and World.

Bennett, A., Joseph, L. and Unger, D. (eds) (1997) *Friends in Need: Burden Sharing in the Gulf War*, New York: St Martin's Press.

Bennholdt-Thomsen, V., Faraclas, N. G. and von Werlof, C. (2001) *There is an Alternative: Subsistence and Worldwide Resistance to Corporate Globalization*, London: Zed Books.

Bentham, J. (1995) 'Panopticon', in M. Bozovic (ed.), *The Panopticon Writings*, London: Verso, pp. 29–95.

Berger, P. (1974) *Pyramids of Sacrifice*, Harmondsworth: Allen Lane.

Bergesen, A. (1984) 'The Critique of World-System Theory: Class Relations or Division of Labour?', in R. Collins (ed.), *Sociological Theory – 1984*, San Francisco, CA: Jossey-Bass, pp. 365–72.

Bergson, H. (1935), *The Two Sources of Morality and Religion*, trans. R. Ashley Audra and C. Brereton with W. Horsfall Carter, London: Macmillan.

Berman, M. (1983) *All That is Solid Melts into Air: the Experience of Modernity*, London: Verso.

Bhabha, H. K. (1994) *The Location of Culture*, London: Routledge.

—— (1996) 'Unpacking my library ... again', in I. Chambers and L. Curti (eds), *The Post-Colonial Question: Common Skies, Divided Horizons*, London: Routeldge, pp. 199–211.

Bissondath, N. (1994) *Selling Illusions: the Cult of Multiculturalism in Canada*, London: Penguin.

Blair, T. (1998a) 'The Third Way', speech to the National Assembly, Paris, France, 24th March.

—— (1998b) *The Third Way: New Politics for a New Century*, London: Fabian Society.

Blair, T. and Schroeder, G. (2000 [1999]) 'Europe: The Third Way – Die Neu Mitte', in Hombach, B. (ed.), *The Politics of the New Centre*, Oxford: Oxford University Press, pp. 157–77.

Blasco, J. S. (2000) *Signs, Solidarities and Sociology: Charles S. Peirce and Pragmatics of Globalization*, Oxford: Rowman and Littlefield.

Bleich, E. (2005) 'The Legacies of History? Colonization and Immigrant Integration in Britain and France', *Theory and Society*, 34 (2), 171–95.

Bocock, R. (1993) *Consumption,* London: Routledge.

Boli, J. and Thomas, G. M. (1997) 'World Culture in the World Polity', *American Sociological Review*, 62 (2), 171–90.

Boorstin, D. J. (1961) *The Image: A Guide to Pseudo-Events in America*, New York: Vintage.

Boote, A. R. and Thugge, K. (1997) 'Debt relief for low-income countries: the HIPC initiative', *IMF Working Papers* 97/24, Washington, DC: International Monetary Fund.

Borland, J., Gregory, B. and Sheehan, P. (2001) *Work rich, Work poor: Inequality and Economic Change in Australia*, Melbourne: Centre for Strategic and Economic Studies, Victoria University.

Boudreau, J. (2000) *The Megacity Saga: Democracy and Citizenship in This Global Age*, Montreal: Black Rose Books.

Bourdieu, P. (1977) *Outline of a Theory of Practice,* trans. R. Nice, Cambridge: Cambridge University Press.

—— (1979) *Algeria 1960: The Disenchantment of the World, the Sense of Honour, the Kabyle House or the World Reversed*, trans. R. Nice, Cambridge: Cambridge University Press.

—— (1985) 'The Social Space and the Genesis of Groups', *Social Science Information*, 24 (2), 195–220.

—— (1986a) 'The Forms of Capital', trans. R. Nice, in J. G. Richardson (ed.), *Handbook of Theory and Research for the Sociology of Education*, New York: Greenwood, pp. 241–58.

—— (1989) 'Social Space and Symbolic Power', *Sociological Theory*, 7 (1), 14–25.

—— (1992a) *An Invitation to Reflexive Sociology* (with Loïc Wacquant), London: Polity Press.

—— (1992b) *Language and Symbolic Power*, Cambridge: Polity.

—— (1999) *Acts of Resistance: Against the New Myths of Our Time*, Blackwell: London.

Bourdieu, P. and Passeron J.-C. (1973) 'Cultural Reproduction and Social Reproduction', in R. Brown (ed.), *Knowledge, Education and Social Change*, London: Tavistock, pp. 71–112.

Bourdieu, P. and Passeron, J.-C. (1977) *Reproduction in Education, Society and Culture*, trans. R. Nice, London: Sage.

Bovard, J. (1991) *The Fair Trade Fraud*, New York: St. Martins.

Braidotti, R. (1994) *Nomadic Subjects: Embodiment and Sexual Difference in Contemporary Feminist Theory*, Columbia, NY: Columbia University Press.

Brecher, J., Costello, T. and Smith, B. (2000) *Globalization from Below: The Power of Solidarity*, Cambridge, MA: South End Press.

Brewer, M. B. (1991) 'The Social Self: On Being the Same and Different at the Same Time', *Personality and Social Psychology Bulletin*, 17 (5), 475–82.

Brookes, R., Mosdell, N., Threadgold, T. and Lewis, J. (2005) *Shoot First And Ask Questions Later: Media Coverage of the 2003 Iraq War,* Oxford: Peter Lang.

Brown, J. (2005) 'The Compelling Nature of Romantic Love: A Psychosocial Perspective', *Psychoanalysis, Culture and Society*, 10 (1), 23–43.

Bruntland, G. (ed.) (1987) *Our Common Future: The World Commission on Environment and Development*, Oxford: Oxford University Press.

Buchan, D., Hoyos, C., Khalaf, R. and Morrison, K. (2004) 'Terror Attacks, Capacity Shortages and a Herd of Speculators: How Can OPEC Bring Calm to the World Oil Market?', *Financial Times*, 3 June, p. 15.

Burchell, G., Gordon, C. and Miller, P. (eds) (1991) *The Foucault Effect: Studies in Governmentality*, Chicago, IL: University of Chicago Press.

Butcher, M. (2003) *Transnational Television, Cultural Identity and Change: When STAR Came to India*, London: Sage.

Butler, J. (1988) 'Performative Acts and Gender Constitution: An Essay in Phenomenology and Feminist Theory', *Theatre Journal*, 49 (1), 519–31.

—— (1990) *Gender Trouble: Feminism and the Subversion of Identity*, New York: Routledge.

Butz, D. (1995) 'Revisiting Edward Said's Orientalism', *Brock Review*, 4, 54–80.

Byrne, D. (1998) *Complexity Theory and the Social Sciences*, London: Routledge.

Cabinet Office. (2003) *The Magenta Book: Guidance Notes for Policy Evaluation and Analysis*, London: Government Chief Social Researcher's Office, Prime Minister's Strategy Unit.

Calbucura, J. (2003) 'Investing in Indigenous People's Territories, a New Form of Ethnocide? The Mapuche Case', *Research in Rural Sociology and Development*, 9, 229–55.

Caldwell, M. L. (2004) 'Domesticating the French Fry: McDonald's and Consumerism in Moscow', *Journal of Consumer Culture*, 4 (1), 5–26.

Callister, P. (2001) 'A Polarisation into Work-rich and Work-poor Households in New Zealand? Trends from 1986 to 2000', *New Zealand Department of Labour Occasional Paper Series*, 2001/3.

Campbell, C. (1997) 'Modern Consumerism and Imaginative Hedonism', in N. R. Goodwin, F. Ackerman and D. Kiron (eds), *The Consumer Society*, Washington, DC: Island Press, pp. 238–41.

—— (2003) 'Traditional and Modern Hedonism', in D. B. Clarke, M. A. Doel and K. M. L. Housiaux (eds), *The Consumption Reader*, London: Routledge, pp. 48–53.

Cantwell, J. (1991) 'A Survey of Theories of International Production', in C. R. Pitelis and R. Sugden (eds), *The Nature of the Transnational Firm*, London: Routledge.

Carew, A., Dreyfus, M., van Goethem, G., Gumbrell-McCormick, R. and van der Linden, M. (eds) (2000) *The International Confederation of Free Trade Unions*, Bern: Peter Lang.

Carroll, M. P. (1975) 'Revitalization Movements And Social Structure: Some Quantitative Tests', *American Sociological Review*, 40 (3), 389–401.

Carruthers, B. G. and Espeland, W. N. (1998) 'Money, Meaning, and Morality', *American Behavioral Scientist*, 41 (10), 1384–1408.

Carter, A. (2004) *Direct Action and Democracy Today*, London: Blackwell.

Castells, M. (1989) *The Informational City*, Oxford: Blackwell.

—— (1996) *The Rise of the Network Society*, Oxford: Blackwell.

—— (1997) *The Power of Identity*, Oxford: Blackwell.

—— (1998) *End of Millennium*, Oxford: Blackwell.

—— (2000a) 'The Contours of the Network Society', *Foresight*, 2, 151–57.

—— (2000b) 'Grassrooting the Space of Flows', in J. Wheeler, Y. Aoyama and B. Warf (eds), *Cities in the Telecommunications Age; The Fracturing of Geographies,* London: Routledge, pp. 18–27.

—— (2000c) 'Materials for an Exploratory Theory of the Network Society', *British Journal of Sociology,* 51, 5–24.

—— (2000d) 'Toward a Sociology of the Network Society', *Contemporary Sociology,* 25, 693–99.

Castells, M. and Hall, P. (1993) *Technopoles of the World: The Making of Twenty-First-Century Industrial Complexes,* London: Taylor and Francis.

Castles, F. (1985) *The Working Class and Welfare,* Sydney: Allen and Unwin.

—— (1996) 'Needs-Based Strategies of Social Protection in Australia and New Zealand', in E.-A. Gosta (ed), *Welfare States in Transition: National Adaptations in Global Economies,* London: Sage, pp. 88–115.

Castles, S. (2002) 'Migration and Community Formation under Conditions of Globalization', *International Migration Review,* 36 (4), 1143–68.

Castoriadis, C. (1991) *Philosophy, Politics, Autonomy,* New York: Oxford University Press.

—— (1997) *The Imaginary Institution of Society,* Cambridge: Polity.

Castro-Gomez, S (2002) 'The Social Sciences, Epistemic Violence, and the Problem of "Invention of the Other"', *Nepantla,* 3 (2), 269–85.

Césaire, A. (1972) '*Discourse on Colonialism*', trans. J. Pinkham, New York: Monthly Review Press.

Chaney, D. (1996) *Lifestyles,* London: Routledge.

Chatterton, P. and Holland, R. (2003) *Urban Nightscapes,* London: Routledge.

Clark, A. M. (2001) *Diplomacy of Conscience: Amnesty International and Changing Human Rights Norms,* Princeton, NJ: Princeton University Press.

Clark, I. (1997) *Globalization and Fragmentation: International Relations in the Twentieth Century,* Oxford: Oxford University Press.

Clarke, J. (2004) 'Dissolving the Public Realm? The Logics and Limits of Neo-liberalism', *Journal of Social Policy,* 33 (1), 27–48.

Clarke, J. L. (2003) 'How Journalists Judge the 'Reality' of an International "Pseudo-Event"', *Journalism,* 4 (1), 50–75.

Clayton, J. (2004) 'Universal Human Rights and Traditional Religious Values', *Society,* 41 (2), 36–41.

Clifford, J. (1992) 'Travelling Cultures', in L. Grossberg, C. Nelson and P. Treichler (eds), *Cultural Studies,* New York: Routledge, pp. 96–116.

—— (1997) *Routes: Travel and Translation in the late Twentieth Century,* Cambridge, MA: Harvard University Press.

Coburn, D. (2004) 'Beyond the Income Inequality Hypothesis: Class, Neo-Liberalism, and Health Inequalities', *Social Science and Medicine,* 58 (1), 41–56.

Cohen, J. L. and Arato, A. (1992) *Civil Society and Political Theory,* Cambridge, MA: MIT Press.

Cohen, L. R. (1993) 'A Futures Market in Cadaveric Organs: Would it Work?' *Transplantation Proceedings,* 25 (1), 60–61.

Cohen, R. (1997) *Global Diasporas: An Introduction,* London: UCL Press.

Cohen, R. and Shirin, R. M. (2000) *Global Social Movements,* London: The Athlone Press.

Coleman, D. (2003) 'The United Nations and Transnational Corporations: from an inter-nation to a "beyond-state" model of engagement', *Global Society*, 17 (4), 339–57.

Coleman, J. S. (1988) 'Social Capital in the Creation of Human Capital', *American Journal of Sociology*, 94, 95–120.

Common, R. (1998) 'Convergence and Transfer: A Review of the Globalisation of New Public Management', *International Journal of Public Sector Management*, 11 (6), 440–50.

Constable, N. (1997) *Maid to Order in Hong Kong: Stories of Philipina Workers*, Ithaca, NY: Cornell University Press.

Cook, D. (1996) *The Culture Industry Revisited: Theodor W. Adorno on Mass Culture*, Lanham, MD: Rowman and Littlefield Press.

Cooke, M. (1994) *Language and Reason: A Study of Habermas's Pragmatics*, Cambridge, MA: MIT Press.

Coulmas, F. (2000) 'The Nationalization of Writing', *Studies in the Linguistic Sciences*, 30 (1), 47–60.

Crombie, I., Irvine, L., Elliott, L. and Wallace, H. (2003) *Understanding Public Health Policy: Learning from international comparisons. A Report to NHS Scotland Commissioned and funded by the Public Health Institute of Scotland*, Dundee: University of Dundee.

Crystal, D. (1988) *The English Language*, London: Penguin.

—— (1997) *English as a Global Language*, Cambridge: Cambridge University Press.

Csordas, T. (1990) 'Embodiment as a Paradigm for Anthropology', *Ethos*, 18, 5–47.

Curtis, B. (1995) 'Taking the State Back Out: Rose and Miller on Political Power', *British Journal of Sociology*, 46 (4), 575–89.

Dahl, G. (1999) 'The Anti-Reflexivist Revolution: On the Affirmation of the New Right', in M. Featherstone and S. Lash, *Spaces of Culture*, London: Sage, pp. 175–93.

Dahl, R. A. (2000) *On Democracy*, London: Yale University Press.

Dalby, S. (2000) 'A Critical Geopolitics of Global Governance', paper presented at the International Studies Association 41st Annual Convention, Los Angeles.

Daly, J. L. (1989) *The Greenhouse Trap*, New York: Bantam.

Danaher, K. (1997) *Corporations Are Gonna Get Your Momma: Globalization and the Downsizing of the American Dream*, Monroe, ME: Common Courage Press.

Daniels, P. W. (1991) 'A world of services', *Geoforum*, 22 (3), 359–76.

d'Argemir, D. and Pujadas, J. J. (1999) 'Living in/on the Frontier: Migration, Identities and Citizenship in Andorra Comas', *Social Anthropology*, 7 (3), 253–64.

Davies, M. (ed.) (1993) *Women and Violence: Realities and Responses Worldwide*, London: Zed Books.

Davison, E. and Cotton, S. R. (2003) 'Connection discrepancies: Unmasking further layers of the digital divide', *First Monday*, 8 (3). Available at: http://www.firstmonday.dk/issues/issue8_3/davison (accessed 28 April 2006).

Day, G. (1980) 'Strategic Market Analysis: Top-down and bottom-up approaches', working paper #80–105, Marketing Science Institute, Cambridge, Massachussets.

Deacon, B., Hulse, M. and Stubbs, P. (1997) *Global Social Policy: International Organisations and the Future of Welfare*, London: Sage.

Deacon, T. (1997) *The Symbolic Species: The Co-evolution of Language and the Brain*, London: Allen Lane.

Dean, M. (1995) 'Governing the Unemployed Self in an Active Society', *Economy and Society*, 24 (4), 559–83.

—— (1999a) *Governmentality: Power and Rule in Modern Society*, London: Sage.

—— (1999b) 'Risk, calculable and incalculable', in D. Lupton (ed.), *Risk and Socio-Cultural Theory: New Directions and Perspectives*, Cambridge: Cambridge University Press, pp. 131–59.

Deffeyes, K. S. (2003) *Hubbert's Peak: The Impending World Oil Shortage*, Princeton, NJ: Princeton University Press.

Delanty, G. (2000) *Citizenship in a Global Age: Society, Culture, Politics*, Buckingham: Open University Press.

Deleuze, G. (1990) *Negotiations*, trans. M. Joughin, New York: Columbia University Press.

Deleuze, G. and Guitarri, F (1984) *AntiOedipus, Capitalism and Schizophrenia 1*, trans. Robert Hurley, Mark Seem and Helen R. Lane, London: Athlone.

Deleuze, G. and Guitarri, F. (1987) *A Thousand Plateaus: Capitalism and Schizophrenia 2*, trans. B. Massumi, Minneapolis, MN: University of Minnesota Press.

Derrida, J. (1994) *Force de loi. Le "fondement mystique de l'autorité"*, Paris: Galilée.

—— (1998) 'Faith and Knowledge: The Two Sources of Religion Within the Limits of Pure Reason', in J. Derrida and G. Vattimo (eds), *Religions*, Stanford, CA: Stanford University, pp. 1–78.

Derudder, B. (2006) 'On Conceptual Confusion in Empirical Analyses of a Transnational Urban Network', GaWC Research Bulletin 167 (Z). Available at: http://www.lboro.ac.uk/gawc/rb/rb167.html (accessed 10 March 2006).

Desmond, J. (1997) *Meaning in Motion: New Cultural Studies of Dance*, Durham: Duke University Press.

—— (1999) *Staging Tourism: Bodies on Display from Waikiki to Sea World*, Chicago, IL: University of Chicago Press.

—— (2000) *Dancing Desires Choreographing Sexualities on and Off the Stage*, Madison, WI: University of Wisconsin Press.

De Soto, H. (1989) *The Other Path*, New York: Basic Books.

—— (2000) *The Mystery of Capital: Why Capitalism Triumphs in the West and Fails Everywhere Else*, New York: Basic Books.

Dichter, T. W. (2003) *Despite Good Intentions: Why Development Assistance to the Third World Has Failed*, Amherst, MA: University of Massachusetts Press.

Diehl, P. F. (ed.) (2001) *The Politics of Global Governance: International Organizations in an Interdependent World*, 2nd edn, Boulder, CO: Lynne Rienner Publishers.

Dijkstra, J. J., Liebrand, W. B. G. and Timminga, E. (1998) 'Persuasiveness of Expert Systems', *Behaviour and Information Technology*, 17 (3), 155–63.

Dirlik, A. (1998) *The Postcolonial Aura: Third World*, Boulder, CO: Westview Press.

Donaldson, L. (ed.) (1994) *Contingency Theory*, Aldershot: Dartmouth.

Doner, R. (1992) 'Limits of State Strength: Toward an Institutionalist View of Economic Development', *World Politics*, 44, 398–431.

Donnelly, J. (2003) *Universal Human Rights in Theory and Practice*, Ithaca, NY: Cornell University Press

Dos Santos, T. (1971) 'The Structure of Dependence', in K. T. Fann and D. C. Hodges (eds), *Readings in U.S. Imperialism*, Boston, MA: Porter Sargent, pp. 225–36.

Douglas, M. and Isherwood, B. (1979) *The World of Goods: Towards an Anthropology of Consumption*, London: Allen Lane.

Douglas, M. and Wildavsky, A. (1982) *Risk and Culture: An Essay on the Selection of Technical and Environmental Dangers*, Berkeley, CA: University of California Press.

Downs, A. (1957) 'An Economic Theory Of Political Action In A Democracy', *Journal of Political Economy*, 65 (2), 135–50.

Dreyfus, H. and Dreyfus, S. (1985) *Mind Over Machine: The Power of Human Intuition and Expertise in the Era of the Computer*, New York: Free Press.

Driver, S. and Martell, L. (2002) *Blair's Britain*, Cambridge: Polity Press.

Drori, G. S. (2005) 'United Nations' Dedications: A World Culture in the Making?' *International Sociology*, 20 (2), 175–99.

Drucker, P.F (1969) *The Age of Discontinuity: Guidelines to Our Changing Society*, London: Heinemann.

Dryzek, J. S. (2001) *Deliberative Democracy and Beyond: Liberals, Critics, Contestations*, Oxford: Oxford University Press.

DuBois, W. E. B. (1961) *The Soul of Black Folks: Essays and Sketches*, New York: Fawcett.

du Gay, P. and Pryke, M. (2002) *Cultural Economy*, London: Sage.

Du Gay, P. (2003) "The Tyranny of the Epochal: Change, Epochalism and Organizational Reform", *Organization* 10(4): 663-84.

Duménil, G. and Levy, D. (2001) 'Costs and Benefits of Neoliberalism. A Class Analysis', *Review of International Political Economy*, 8 (4), 578–607.

Dunning, J. (1991) 'The Eclectic Paradigm of International Production: A Personal Perspective', in C. R. Pitelis and R. Sugden (eds), *The Nature of the Transnational Firm*, London: Routledge.

Dunning, J. H. (1997) *Alliance Capitalism and Global Business*, London and New York: Routledge, pp. 117–36.

Eade, J. (1997) *Globalization as Local Process*, London: Routledge.

Eco, U. (1985) *Travels in Hyperreality*, trans. W. Weaver, San Diego, CA: Harcourt Brace Jovanovich.

Elliott, J. A. (1999) *An Introduction to Sustainable Development*, London: Routledge.

Estes, R. (1988) *Trends in World Social Development: Social Progress of Nations, 1970–86*, London: Praeger.

Evans, B. E. (2005) '"The Grand Daddy of English": US, UK, New Zealand and Australian students' attitudes toward varieties of English', in N. Langer and W. Davies (eds), *Linguistic Purism in the Germanic Languages*, Berlin: De Gruyter, pp. 240–51.

Ewald, F. (1991) 'Insurance and Risk', in G. Burchell, C. Gordon and P. Miller (eds), *The Foucault Effect: Studies in Governmentality*, Chicago, IL: University of Chicago Press, pp. 197–210.

Fairbrother, P. and Hammer, N. (2005) 'Global Unions: Past Efforts and Future Prospects', *Relations Industrielles/Industrial Relations*, 60 (3), 405–31.

Fairclough, N. (2000) *New Labour, New Language*, London: Routledge.

Falk, R. (1995) *On Humane Governance: Toward a New Global Politics*, Cambridge: Polity Press.

Farr, J. (2004) 'Social Capital: A Conceptual History', *Political Theory*, 32 (1), 6–33.

Fazal, S. and Tsagarousianou, R. (2002) 'Transnational Cultural Practices and Communicative Spaces', *Javnost/The Public*, IX (1), 5–18.

Featherstone, M. (ed) (1990) *Global Culture: Nationalism, Globalisation and Modernity*, London: Sage.

—— (1995) *Undoing Culture: Globalization, Postmodernism and Identity*, London: Sage.

Feifer, M. (1985) *Going Places*, London: Macmillan.

Feinberg, M. and Tokic, D. (2004) 'ITC investment, GDP and Stock Market Values in Asia-Pacific NIC and Developing Countries: Some Preliminary Results', *Journal of the Asia Pacific Economy*, 9 (1), 70–84.

Felice, W. F. (1999) 'The Viability of the United Nations Approach to Economic and Social Human Rights in a Globalized Economy', *International Affairs*, 75 (3), 563–98

Feree, M. and Hess, B. (1995) *Controversy and Coalition: The New Feminist Movement across Three Decades of Change*, New York: Simon and Schuster.

Fern Haber, H. and Weiss, G. (eds) (1999) *Perspectives on Embodiment: The Intersections of Nature and Culture,* London: Routledge.

Feyerabend, P. (1975) *Against Method*, London: Verso.

—— (1987) *Farewell to Reason*, London: Verso.

Finlayson, A. (1999) 'Third Way Theory', *Political Quarterly*, 2 (3), 271–80.

Fischer, C. (1991) 'Ambivalent Communities: How Americans Understand Their Localities,' in A. Wolfe (ed.), *America at Century's End,* Berkeley, CA: University of California Press, pp. 79–90.

Fishman, J. (1991) *Reversing Language Shift: Theory and Practice of Assistance to Threatened Languages*, Clevedon: Multilingual Matters.

Foucault, M. (1973) *The Order of Things: An Archaeology of the Human Sciences*, New York: Vintage.

—— (1977a) 'Nietzche, Genealogy, History', in P. Rabinow (ed.), *The Foucault Reader*, New York: Pantheon, pp. 76–100.

—— (1977b) *Discipline and Punish: the Birth of the Prison*, trans. A. Sheridan, London: Allen Lane.

—— (1990) *The History of Sexuality Volume 1: The Will to Knowledge*, trans. R. Hurley, London: Penguin.

——— (1991) 'Governmentality', in G. Burchell, C. Gordon and P. Miller (eds), *The Foucault Effect: Studies in Governmentality*, Chicago, IL: University of Chicago Press, pp. 87–104.

Frank, A. G. (1988) 'The Development of Underdevelopment', in C. K. Wilber (ed.), *The Political Economy of Development and Underdevelopment*, 4th edn, New York: Random House, pp. 109–20.

——— (1992) 'Third World War: a Political Economy of the Gulf War and the New World Order', *Third World Quarterly*; 13, 267–82.

——— (2004) 'Globalizing "Might is Right": Spaghetti Western Law of the West is No Solution', *Development and Change*, 35 (3), 607–12.

Freeman, M. (2002) *Human Rights: an Interdisciplinary Approach*, Cambridge: Polity Press.

Freud, S. (1989) *Civilization and Its Discontents*, trans. and ed. by James Strachey, New York: W.W. Norton.

Friedman, T. (2000) *The Lexus and the Olive Tree*, New York: Anchor Books.

Friedmann, J. (1986) 'The world city hypothesis', *Development and Change*, 17, 69–83.

Friedmann, J. and Wolff, G. (1982) 'World City Formation: An Agenda for Research and Action', *International Journal of Urban and Regional Research*, 3, 309–44.

Fromm, E. (2001) *The Fear of Freedom*, London: Routledge.

Froud, J., Haslam, C., Johal, S. and Williams, K. (2000) 'Shareholder Value and Financialization: Consultancy Promises, Management Moves', *Economy and Society*, 29 (1), 80–110.

Frow, John (1997) *Time and Commodity Culture: Essays in Theory and Postmodernism*, New York: Oxford University Press.

Fuentes, A. and Ehrenreich, B. (1981) *Women in the Global Factory*, Boston, MA: South End Press.

Fukuyama, F. (1989) 'The End of History?' *The National Interest*, 16, 3–18.

——— (1992) *The End of History and the Last Man*, New York: Free Press.

——— (1995) 'Social Capital and the Global Economy', *Foreign Affairs*, 74 (5), 89–103

Fuller, S. (1999) *Governance of Science: Ideology and the Future of the Open Society*, Philadelphia, PA: Open University Press.

G8 Information Centre (2005) Available at: http://www.g7.utoronto.ca/ (accessed 28 March 2005).

Galloway, A. (2004) *Protocol: How Control Exists after Decentralization*, Cambridge, MA: MIT Press.

Gareis, S. B. and Varwick, J. (2005) *The United Nations: An Introduction*, Basingstoke: Palgrave.

Garrett, P., Evans, B. E. and Williams, A. (forthcoming) 'What Does the Word 'Globalisation' Mean to you? Comparative Perceptions and Evaluations in Australia, New Zealand, the USA and the UK', *Journal of Multilingual and Multicultural Development*.

Gasper, D. (1996) 'Needs and Basic Needs: A Clarification of Meanings, Levels and Different Streams of Work', *Working Paper Series No. 210*, The Hague: Institute of Social Studies.

Gellner, E. (1983) *Nations and Nationalism*, Oxford: Blackwell.

George V. and Wilding, P. (2002) *Globalization and Human Welfare*, Basingstoke: Palgrave.

Gerreffi G. and Korzeniewicz, M. (eds) (1994) *Commodity Chains and Global Capitalism*, Westport, CT: Praeger.

Ghai, Y. P. (2002) 'Constitutional Asymmetries: Communal Representation, Federalism, and Cultural Autonomy', *The Architecture of Democracy*, 1 (9), 141–71.

Giddens, A. (1984) *The Constitution of Society: Outline of the Theory of Structuration*, Cambridge: Polity Press.

—— (1990) *The Consequences of Modernity*, Cambridge: Polity Press.

—— (1991) *Modernity and Self Identity: Self and Society in the Late Modern Age*, Cambridge: Polity Press.

—— (1992) *The Transformation of Intimacy. Sexuality, Love and Eroticism in Modern Societies*, Cambridge: Polity Press.

—— (1994a) 'Living in a Post-Traditional Society', in U. Beck, A. Giddens and S. Lash (eds), *Reflexive Modernization: Politics, Tradition and Aesthetics in the Modern Social Order*, Cambridge: Polity Press.

—— (1994b) *Beyond Left and Right: The Future of Radical Politics*, Cambridge: Polity Press.

—— (1998) *The Third Way: The Renewal of Social Democracy*, Cambridge: Polity Press.

—— (1999) *Runaway World: How Globalization is Reshaping Our Lives*, London: Profile.

—— (ed.) (2001) *The Global Third Way Debate*, Cambridge: Polity Press.

Giddens, A. and Pierson, C (1998) *Conversations with Anthony Giddens: Making Sense of Modernity*, Cambridge: Polity Press.

Gienow-Hecht, J. C. E. (2000) 'Shame on US? Academics, Cultural Transfer and the Cold War', *Diplomatic History*, 24 (1), 465–535.

Girvan, N. (1976) *Corporate Imperialism: Conflict and Expropriation: Transnational Corporations and Economic Nationalism in the Third World*, New York: Monthly Review Press.

Gleick, J. (1993) *Chaos: Making a New Science*, London: Abacus.

Global Unions (2006) Available at: www.global-unions.org (accessed 28 April 2006).

Goetz, K. H. and Hix S. (2000) 'Introduction: European Integration and National Political Systems', *West European Politics*, 23 (4), 1–26.

Goffman, E. (1963) *Behavior in Public Places: Notes on the Social Organization of Gatherings*, New York: Free Press/MacMillan.

—— (1969) *The Presentation of Self in Everyday Life*, London: Allen Lane.

Goldberg, M. M. (1941) 'Qualification of the Marginal Man Theory', *American Sociological Review*, 6, 52–58.

Goldstein-Gidoni, O. (2005) 'The Production and Consumption of "Japanese Culture" in the Global Cultural Market', *Journal of Consumer Culture*, 5 (2), 155–79.

Graddol, D. (1997) *The Future of English? A Guide to Forecasting the Popularity of the English Language in the 21st Century*, London: British Council.

—— (2006) *English Next*, London: British Council.

Gramsci, A. (1971) *Selections from the Prison Notebooks*, New York: International Publishers.

Gray, A. and Jenkins, B. (1994) 'Public Administration and Government 1992–93', *Parliamentary Affairs*, 47 (1), 1–22.

Gray, J. (1998) *False Dawn: The Delusions of Global Capitalism*, London: Granta.

Green, A. W. (1947) 'A Re-examination of the Marginal Man Concept', *Social Forces*, 26, 167–71.

Greenaway, H. D. S. (1992) 'War in Yugoslavia', *Boston Globe*, 3 December, p. 19.

Greer, G. (2004) *Whitefella Jump Up: the Shortest Way to Nationhood*, London: Profile Books.

Griffin, C. E. (1994) 'Drugs, Democracy and Instability in a Microstate: The Challenge to Democracy in St. Kitts and Nevis', *North-South: Magazine of the Americas*, 3 (1), 32–37.

Grumet, M. (1990) 'Show and Tell: a Response to the Value Issue in Alternative Paradigms for Inquiry', in E. G. Guba (ed.), *The Alternative Paradigm Dialogue*, London: Sage.

Guan, X. (2001) 'Globalization, inequality and social policy: China on the threshold of entry into the World Trade Organization', *Social Policy and Administration*, 35 (3), 242–57.

Gugler, J. (ed.) (2004) *World Cities Beyond the West: Globalization, Development and Inequality*, Cambridge: Cambridge University Press.

Gupta, A. and Ferguson, J. (1992) 'Beyond Culture: Space, Identity and the Politics of Difference', *Cultural Anthropology*, 7 (1), 6–23.

Gupta, J. (2002) *Our Simmering Planet*, London: Zed Books.

Gwynne, B. and Kay, C. (2004) *Latin America Transformed: Globalization and Modernity*, London: Arnold.

Haas, P. M. (1992) 'Epistemic Communities and International Policy Coordination', *International Organization*, 46 (1), 1–35.

Haas, P. M. (ed.) (2003) *Environment in the New Global Economy*, Cheltenham: Edward Elgar Publishing.

Habermas, J. (1975 [1973]) *Legitimation Crisis*, trans. T. McCarthy, Boston, MA: Beacon Press.

—— (1987a) *The Philosophical Discourse of Modernity*, trans. F. Lawrence, Cambridge: Cambridge University Press.

—— (1987b) *The Theory of Communicative Action, Vol. 2: Lifeworld and System a Critique of Functionalist Reason,* Boston, MA: Beacon Press.

—— (2001) *The Postnational Constellation*, trans. M. Pensky, Cambridge: Polity Press.

Hall, S. (1998) 'The Great Moving Nowhere Show', *Marxism Today*, November/December, pp. 9–14.

Halpern, D. (2001) 'Moral Values, Social Trust and Inequality – Can Values Explain Crime?' *British Journal Criminology*, 41, 236–51.

Hamelink, C. J. (1983) *Cultural Autonomy in Global Communications*, New York: Longman.

Hammer, N. (2005) 'International Framework Agreements: Global Industrial Relations between Rights and Bargaining', *Transfer*, 9 (4), 511–30.

Hannerz, U. (1989) 'Culture Between Center and Periphery: Toward a Macroanthropology', *Ethnos*, 54, 200–16.

—— (1990) 'Cosmopolitans and Locals in World Culture', *Theory, Culture and Society*, 7, 2–3.

—— (1992) *Cultural Complexity*, New York: Columbia University Press.

—— (1996) *Transnational Connections*, London: Routledge.

—— (2002) 'Flows, Boundaries and Hybrids: Keywords in Transnational Anthropology', in A. Rogers (ed.), *Transnational Communities Programme Working Paper Series*. Available at: http://www.transcomm.ox.ac.uk/working%20papers/hannerz.pdf (accessed 19 March 2006).

Hardt, M. and Negri, A. (2000) *Empire*, Cambridge MA: Harvard University Press.

Harris, J. (2005) 'Emerging Third World Powers: China, India and Brazil', *Race and Class*, 46 (3), 7–27.

Harrod, J. and O'Brien, R. (eds) (2002) *Global Unions? Theory and Strategies of Organized Labour in the Global Political Economy*, London: Routledge.

Harvey, D. (1990b) *The Condition of Postmodernity, An Enquiry Into The Origins Of Cultural Change,* Cambridge, MA: Blackwell.

Havemann, P. (2000) 'Enmeshed in the Web? Indigenous People's Rights in the Network Society', in R. Cohen and M. Shirin (eds), *Global Social Movements*, London: The Athlone Press, pp. 18–32.

Hawkins, V. (2002) 'The Other Side of the CNN Factor: the Media and Conflict', *Journalism Studies*, 3 (2), 225–40.

Hay, C. (1999) *The Political Economy of New Labour*, Manchester: Manchester University Press.

Hayek, F. (1945) 'The Use of Knowledge in Society', *The American Economic Review*, 35 (4), 519–30.

Heath, J. (2005) *The Efficient Society: Why Canada is as Close to Utopia as it Gets*, Toronto: Penguin.

Held, D. (1980) *Introduction to Critical Theory: Horkheimer to Habermas*, London: Hutchinson.

—— (1995) *Democracy and the Global Order: from the Modern State to Cosmopolitan Governance*, Cambridge: Polity Press.

Held, D., Goldblatt, D. and Perraton, J. (1999) *Global Transformations: Politics, Economics, Culture*, Cambridge: Polity Press.

Held, D. and McGrew, A. (2002) *Globalization/Anti-Globalization*, Cambridge: Polity Press.

Held, D. and McGrew, A. (2003) *The Global Transformations Reader: An Introduction to the Globalisation Debate*, Cambridge: Polity Press.

Helleiner, E. (1995) 'Explaining the Globalization of Financial Markets: Bringing States Back In', *Review of International Political Economy*, 2 (2), 315–41.

Heller, M. (ed.) (1988) *Codeswitching: Anthropological and Sociolinguistic Perspectives*, Berlin: Mouton de Gruyter.

Herman, E. S. and Chomsky, N. (1988) *Manufacturing Consent: the Political Economy of the Mass Media*, New York: Pantheon Books.

Herman, E. S. and McChesney, R. W. (1997) *The Global Media,* London: Cassell.

Hicks, N. and Streeton, P. (1979) 'Indicators of Development: the search for a Basic Needs Yardstick', *World Development*, July, pp. 567–80.

Hilhorst, D. (2003) *The Real World of NGOs, Discourses, Diversity and Development*, London: Zed Books.

Hines, C. (2000) *Localization: A Global Manifesto*, London: Earthscan Publications.

Hirst, P. and Thompson, G. (1996) *Globalization in Question: The International Economy and the Possibilities of Governance*, Cambridge: Polity Press.

Hoad, D, (2002) 'The World Trade Organisation, Corporate Interests and Global Opposition: Seattle and After', *Geography*, 87 (2), 148–54.

Hobsbawm, E. (1990) *Nations and Nationalism since 1780. Programme, Myth, Reality*, Cambridge: Cambridge University Press.

Hodson, R. (1997) *Research in the Sociology of Work, Volume 6: The Globalization of Work*, Greenwich, CT: JAI Press.

Hoekman, B. and Holmes, P. (1999) 'Competition Policy, Developing Countries and the WTO', *World Economy*, 22 (6), 875–93.

Hoffmann, S. (2004) 'Thoughts on Fear in Global Society', *Social Research*, 71 (4), 1023–36.

Hogan, J. P. (ed.) (2005) *Cultural Identity, Pluralism, and Globalization*, Council for Research in Values and Philosophy Series 7 (13), Washington, DC: Council for Research in Values and Philosophy.

Holston J. and Appadurai, A. (1996) 'Cities and Citizenship,' *Public Culture*, 8, 187–204.

Hombach, B. (2000) *The Politics of the New Centre*, Oxford: Oxford University Press.

Homer-Dixon, T. F. (2001) *Environment, Scarcity and Violence*, Princeton, NJ: Princeton University Press.

Hondagneu-Sotelo, P. (2001) *Domestica: Immigrant Workers Cleaning and Caring in the Shadows of Affluence*, Berkeley, CA: University of California Press.

Hood, C. (1991) 'A Public Management for all Seasons', *Public Administration*, 69 (1), 3–20.

Hooker, B. and Little, M. O. (eds) (2000) *Moral Particularism*, Oxford: Clarendon.

Horkheimer, M. and Adorno, T. (2002) *Dialectic of Enlightenment: Philosophical Fragments*, trans. E. Jephcott, Stanford, CA: Stanford University Press.

Houghton, J. (2004) *Global Warming: The Complete Briefing*, Cambridge: Cambridge University Press

Howes, D. (1996) *Cross Cultural Consumption: Global Markets, Local Realities*, London: Sage Publications.

Huntington, S. (1993) 'The Clash of Civilizations?', *Foreign Affairs*, 72 (3), 22–49.

—— (1996) *The Clash of Civilizations and the Remaking of World Order*, New York: Simon and Schuster.

Hymer, S. (1976) *The International Operations of National Firms: A Study of Direct Foreign Investment*, Cambridge, MA: MIT Press.

Ignatieff, M. (2003) *Human Rights as Politics and Idolatry*, Princeton, NJ: Princeton University Press.

Inglehart, R. (1977) *The Silent Revolution: Changing Values and Political Styles Among Western Publics*, Princeton, NJ: Princeton University Press.

—— (1990) *Culture Shift in Advanced Industrial Society*, Princeton, NJ: Princeton University Press

International Ecotourism Society. (2006) Available at: http://www.ecotourism.org (accessed 28 April 2006).

Iriye, A. (2004) *Global Community: The Role of International Organizations in the Making of the Contemporary World*, Berekely:, CA University of California Press.

Jameson, F. (1991) *Postmodernism, or the Cultural Logic of Late Capitalism*, Durham: Duke University Press.

—— (2000) 'Globalization And Political Strategy', *New Left Review*, 4, 49–68.

Janowitz, M. (1967) *The Community Press in an Urban Setting; the Social Elements of Urbanism*, Chicago, IL: University of Chicago Press.

Jaspers, K. (1953) *The Origin and Goal of History*, New Haven, CT: Yale University Press.

Jencks, C. (1989) *What is Post-modernism?* London: Academy Editions.

Johnson, C. (2004) *The Sorrows of Empire: Militarism, Secrecy, and the End of the Republic,* New York: Metropolitan Books.

Johnson, S. (1997) *Interface Culture: How New Technology Transforms the Way We Create and Communicate*, New York: Basic Books.

Jones, M. (2001) 'The Contradictions of Globalisation', *Journal of Australian Political Economy*, 48, 5–22.

Jordan, L. and Van Tuijl, P. (2000) 'Political Responsibility in Transnational NGO Advocacy', *World Development*, 28 (12), 2051–65.

Jordan, T. and Taylor, P. (2004) *Hacktivism and Cyberwars: Rebels With a Cause?*, London: Routledge.

Juergensmeyer, M. (2003) *Terror in the Mind of God: The Global Rise of Religious Violence*, Berkeley, CA: University of California Press.

Kachru, B. (1992) *The Other Tongue: English Across Cultures*, Urbana, IL: University of Illinois Press.

Kahn, P. W. (2005) *Putting Liberalism in Its Place*, Princeton, NJ: Princeton University Press.

Kant, I. (1983) *Perpetual Peace, and Other Essays on Politics, History, and Morals*, trans. T. Humphrey, Indianapolis, IN: Hackett Publishing Co.

Kaplinsky, R. (1998) 'Globalisation, Industrialisation and Sustainable Growth: the Pursuit of the nth Rent', *IDS Discussion Paper 365,* Institute of Development Studies University of Sussex. Online. Available at: http://www.ids.ac.uk/ids/bookshop/dp/dp365.pdf (accessed 3 April 2006).

Kaplinsky, R. and Fitter, R. (2004) 'Technology and Globalisation: Who Gains When Commodities are De-commodified?', *International Journal of Technology and Globalisation*, 1 (1), 5–28.

Kariuki, M. S. and Smith, N. J. (2004) 'Are Export Processing Zone (EPZ) Employers Gender Sensitive? An Analysis of Gender Employer-Employee Labour Relations in Kenyan Garment EPZs', *Journal of Social Development in Africa*, 19 (2), 69–89.

Kauffman, S. A. (1993) *The Origins of Order: Self-Organization and Selection in Evolution*, Oxford: Oxford University Press.

Keane, J. (2002) 'Cosmocracy A global System of Governance or Anarchy?' *New Economy*, 9 (2), 65–67.

—— (2003) *Global Civil Society?* Cambridge: Cambridge University Press.

Kellner, D. (1983) 'Critical theory, Commodities and Consumer Society', *Theory, Culture and Society*, 1(3), 64–84.

—— (1984) *Herbert Marcuse and the Crises of Marxism*, London: Macmillan.

—— (1989) *Jean Baudrillard: From Marxism to Postmodernism and Beyond*, Cambridge: Polity

Kelsey, J. (1995) *The New Zealand Experiment: a World Model for Structural Adjustment?*, Auckland, N.Z.: Auckland University Press.

Kennedy, P., Messner, D. and Nuscheler, F. (eds) (2002) *Global Trends and Global Governance*, London: Pluto Press.

Keohane, R. O. and Nye, J. S. (eds) (1972) *Transnational Relations and World Politics,* Cambridge, MA: Harvard University Press.

Keynes, J. M. (1971), *A Tract on Monetary Reform: The Collected Writings of John Maynard Keynes*, London: MacMillan St Martins Press.

—— (1997) *The General Theory of Employment, Interest, and Money*, New York: Prometheus Books.

Kiel, L. D. and Elliott, E. W. (eds) (1997) *Chaos Theory in the Social Sciences: Foundations and Applications*, Ann Arbor, IL: University of Michigan Press.

Killick, T. (1995) *IMF Programmes in Developing Countries: Design and Impact*, London: Routledge.

Kingdon, J. (1995) *Agendas, Alternatives and Public Policies*, New York: Longman.

Kingfisher, C. (2002) *Western Welfare in Decline: Globalisation and Women's Poverty*, Philadelphia, PA: University of Pennsylvania Press.

Kingsnorth, P. (2003) *One No, Many Yeses: A Journey to the Heart of the Global Resistance Movement,* London: Free Press.

Kitzinger, J. (1999) 'Researching Risk and the Media', *Health, Risk and Society,* 1 (1), 55–69.

Klein, N. (2001) *No Logo*, London: HarperCollins.

—— (2002) *Fences and Windows: Dispatches from the Front Lines of the Globalization Debate*, London: Flamingo.

Klotz, A. and Lynch, C. M. (forthcoming) *Constructing Global Politics: Strategies for Research in a Postpositivst World,* Ithaca, NY: Cornell University Press.

Knopp, L. (2004) 'Ontologies of Place, Placelessness, and Movement: Queer Quests For Identity and Their Impacts on Contemporary Geographic Thought', *Gender, Place and Culture: A Journal of Feminist Geography*, 11 (1), 121–34.

Knorr Cetina, K. (1999) *Epistemic Cultures: How the Sciences, Make Knowledge*, Cambridge, MA: Harvard University Press.

—— (2005) 'Complex Global Microstructures: The New Terrorist Societies', *Theory, Culture and Society*, 22 (5), 213–34.

Knox, P. L. and Taylor, P. J. (eds) (1995) *World Cities in a World-System*, Cambridge: Cambridge University Press.

Kontra, M., Phillipson, R., Skutnabb-Kangas, T. and Varady T. (eds) (1999) *Language, a Right and a Resource: Approaching Linguistic Human Rights*, Budapest: Central European University Press.

Koop, C. E., Pearson, C. E. and Schwarz, M. (2002) *Critical Issues in Global Health*, San Francisco, CA: Jossey-Bass.

Kopytoff, I. (1986) 'The Cultural Biography of Things: Commoditization as Process', in A. Appadurai (ed.), *The Social Life of Things*, New York: Cambridge University Press.

Korten, D. C. (2001) *When Corporations Rule the World*, San Francisco, CA: Berrett-Koehler Publishers.

Korten, S. (1990) *Getting to the 21st Century: Voluntary Action and the Global Agenda*, West Hartford, CT: Kurnarian Press.

Korzybski, A. (1958) *Science and Sanity: An Introduction to Non-Aristotelian Systems and General Semantics*, Lakeville, CT: Institute of General Semantics.

Kristensen, P. H. and Zeitlin J. (2004) *Local Players in Global Games: The Strategic Constitution of a Multinational Corporation*, Oxford: Oxford University Press.

Kristol, I. (1978) *Two Cheers For Capitalism*, New York: Basic Books.

Kumar, K. (1995) *From Post-industrial to Post-modern Society*, London: Blackwell.

Laclau, E. and Mouffe, C. (1985) *Hegemony and Socialist Strategy: Towards a Radical Democratic Politics,* trans. W. Moore and P. Cammack, London: Verso.

Laing, R. D. (1960) *The Divided Self: An Existential Study in Sanity and Madness*, Harmondsworth: Penguin.

Lakoff, G. and Johnson, M. (1999) *Philosophy in the Flesh: The Embodied Mind and Its Challenge to Western Thought*, New York: Basic Books.

Landry, R. and Allard, R. (eds) (1994) 'Ethnolinguistic vitality', *Special issue of the International Journal of the Sociology of Language,* 108.

Lane, R. E. (1966) 'The Decline of Politics and Ideology in a Knowledge-able Society', *American Sociological Review,* 31 (5), 649–62.

Langford, W. (1999). *Revolutions of the Heart: Gender, Power and the Delusions of Love*, London: Routledge.

Larner, W. (2000) 'Neo-liberalism: Policy, Ideology, Governmentality', *Studies in Political Economy,* 63, 5–25.

—— (2002) 'Neoliberalism and Tino Rangatiratanga: Welfare State Restructuring in Aotearoa/New Zealand', in C. Kingfisher (ed.), *Western Welfare in Decline: Globalisation and Women's Poverty*, Philadelphia, PA: University of Pennsylvania Press, pp. 147–63.

Larner, W. and Walters, W. (2004a) 'Globalisation as Governmentality', *Alternatives*, 29 (24), 495–514.

Larner, W. and Walters, W. (eds) (2004b) *Global Governmentality*, London: Routledge.

Lash, S. (1994a) 'Reflexivity and Its Doubles: Structure, Aesthetics, Community', in U. Beck, A. Giddens and S. Lash (eds), *Reflexive Modernization: Politics, Tradition and Aesthetics in the Modern Social Order*, Cambridge: Polity Press, pp. 110–73.

—— (1994b) 'Expert-systems or Situated Interpretation? Culture and Institutions in Disorganized Capitalism' in U. Beck, A. Giddens and S. Lash (eds), *Reflexive Modernization: Politics, Tradition and Aesthetics in the Modern Social Order*, Cambridge: Polity Press, pp. 198–215.

—— (2002) *Critique of Information*, London: Sage.

Lash, S. and Urry, J. (1987) *The End of Organized Capitalism*, Cambridge: Polity Press.

Lash, S. and Urry, J. (1994) *The Economics of Sign and Space*, London: Sage.

Latouche, S. (1996) *The Westernisation of the World*, Cambridge: Polity Press.

Latour, B. (1993) *We Have Never Been Modern*, trans. C. Porter, Cambridge, MA: Harvard University Press.

—— (1999) *Pandora's Hope: Essays on the Reality of Science Studies*, Cambridge, MA: Harvard University Press.

Latour, B. and Porter, C. (2004) *Politics of Nature: How to Bring the Sciences into Democracy*, Cambridge: Cambridge University Press.

Lawson, L. (2003) 'Globalisation and the African state', *Commonwealth and Comparative Politics*, 41 (3), 37–58.

Lechner, F. J. (1984) 'Ethnicity and Revitalization in the Modern World System', *Sociological Focus*, 17 (3), 243–56.

Lee, M. J. (ed.) (2000) *The Consumer Society Reader*, Oxford: Blackwell.

Lefebvre, H. (1971) *Everyday Life in the Modern World*, London: Allen lane.

Legett, J. (2001) *Carbon War*, London: Routeldge.

Levine, R. (1997) *A Geography of Time: The Temporal Misadventures of a Social Psychologist*, New York: Basic Books.

Lévi-Strauss, C. (1994 [1969]) *The Raw and the Cooked*, London: Cape.

Levitt, T. (1983) 'The Globalization of Markets', *Harvard Business Review*, 61 (3), 92–102.

Lewis, B. (1990) 'The Roots of Muslim Rage', *The Atlantic Monthly*, 266, 47–60.

Lewis, J. (1991) *The Ideological Octopus: Explorations into the Television Audience*, New York: Routeldge.

Lewis, J. (2001) 'The Decline of the Male Breadwinner Model: Implications for Work and Care', *Social Politics*, 8 (2), 152–81.

Lewis, M. and Wigen, K. (1997) *The Myth of Continents: A Critique of Metageography*, Berkeley, CA: University of California Press.

Ling, L. (2000) 'Hypermasculinity on the Rise, Again: a Response to Fukuyama on Women and World Politics', *International Feminist Journal of Politics*, 2 (2), 277–85.

Linklater, A. (1998) *The Transformation of Political Community: Ethical Foundations of the Post-Westphalian Era*, Columbia, SC: University of South Carolina Press.

Littrell, M. and Dickson, M. (eds) (1999) *Social Responsibility in the Global Market: Fair Trade of Cultural Products*, London: Sage.

Livingston, S. (1997) '"Clarifying the 'CNN Effect'": An examination of media effects according to the type of military intervention', *Research Paper R-18*, Cambridge, MA: Joan Shorernstein Centre of Press, Politics and Public Policy.

Loye, D. (1978) *The Knowable Future: a Psychology of Forecasting and Prophecy*, New York: Wiley.

Lupton, D. (1999a) *Risk*, London: Routledge.

—— (ed.) (1999b) *Risk and Sociocultural Theory: New Directions and Perspectives*, New York: Cambridge University Press.

Lyons, J. (2005) 'Think Seattle, Act Globally: Speciality Coffee, Commodity Biographies and the Promotion of Place', *Cultural Studies*, 19 (1), 14–34.

Lyotard, J.-F. (1984) *The Postmodern Condition: a Report on Knowledge*, trans. G. Bennington and B. Massumi, Manchester: Manchester University Press.

Macarov, D. (2003) *What the Market Does to People: Privatization, Globalization and Poverty*, London: Zed Books.

McArthur, T. (2001) 'World English and World Englishes: Trends, Tensions, Varities, and Standards', *Language Teaching*, 34 (1), 1–20.

MacBride, S. and Roach, C. (1989) 'The New International Information Order', in E. Barnouw (ed.), *International Encyclopeadia of Communications*, Oxford: Oxford University Press.

MacCannell, D. (1999) *The Tourist. A New Theory of the Leisure Class,* Berkeley, CA: University of California Press.

McCormick, J. (2002) *Understanding the European Union: A Concise Introduction,* London: Macmillan Reference.

McCorquodale, R. and Fairbrother, R. (1999) 'Globalization and Human Rights', *Human Rights Quarterly*, 21 (3), 735–66.

Machin, D. and van Leeuwen, T. (2005) 'Language Style and Lifestyle: the Case of a Global Magazine', *Media Culture Society*, 27, 577–600.

McIntyre, W. D. (1998) *British Decolonization, 1946–1997: When, Why and How Did the British Empire Fall?*, Basingstoke: Macmillan.

Maclennan, D. and Pryce, G. (1996) 'Global Economic Change, Labour Market Adjustment and the Challenges for European Housing Policies', *Urban Studies*, 33 (10), 1849–65.

McLuhan, M. and Fiore, Q. (1967 [2005]), *The Medium is the Message*, Corte Madera, CA: Gingko.

McLuhan, M. and Fiore, Q. (1968 [2001]), *War and Peace in the Global Village*, Corte Madera, CA: Gingko.

Makimoto, T. and Manners, D. (1997) *Digital Nomad*, Chichester: Wiley.

Malhotra, K. (2000) 'NGOs Without Aid: Beyond the Global Soup Kitchen', *Third World Quarterly*, 21 (4), 655–68.

Mallaby, S. (2005) *The World's Banker: A Story of Failed States, Financial Crises and the Wealth and Poverty of Nations*, New Haven, CT: Yale University Press.

Mandel, E. (1969). *An Introduction to Marxist Economic Theory*, New York: Pathfinder Press.

Mann, M. (1986) *The Sources of Social Power, Vol. I: From the Beginning to 1760 AD,* Cambridge: Cambridge University Press.

—— (1993a) *The Sources of Social Power Vol. II: The Rise of Classes and Nation-States, 1760–1914*, Cambridge: Cambridge University Press.

—— (1993b) 'Nation-states in Europe and Other Continents: Diversifying, Developing, Not Dying', *Daedalus*, 122 (3), 115–40.

—— (1997) 'Has Globalization Ended the Rise and Rise of the Nation-state?', *Review of International Political Economy*, 4 (3), 472–96.

Marchand, M. H., Reid, J. and Berents, B. (1998). 'Migration, (Im)mobility, and Modernity: Toward a Feminist Understanding of the "Global" Prostitution Scene in Amsterdam', *Millennium*, 27 (4), 955–81.

Marcuse, H. (1972) *One-Dimensional Man*, London: Abacus.

Marker, M. (2003) 'Indigenous Voice, Community, and Epistemic Violence: The Ethnographer's "Interests" and What "Interests" the Ethnographer', *International Journal of Qualitative Studies in Education*, 16 (3), 361–75.

Markowitz, F. (2004) 'Talking about Culture: Globalization, Human Rights and Anthropology', *Anthropological Theory*, 4 (3), 329–52.

Marske, C. E. (1991) *Communities of Fate: Readings in the Social Organization of Risk*, Lanham, MD: University Press of America.

Marty, M. E. and Appleby, R. S. (eds) (1995) *Fundamentalisms Comprehended*, Chicago, IL: University of Chicago Press.

Marwick, A. (1998) *The Sixties: Cultural Revolution in Britain, France, Italy, and the United States, c. 1958–1974*, Oxford: Oxford University Press.

Marx, K. (1972 [1867]) *Das Kapital: Kritik der Politischen Okonomie*, Berlin: Dietz Verlag.

—— (1976 [1867]) *Capital: Volume 1: A Critique of Political Economy*, London: Penguin.

Maslow, A. H. (1970) *Motivation and Personality*, New York: Harper and Row.

Massey, D. (1993) 'Power-Geometry and a Progressive Sense of Place', in J. Bird, B. Curtis, T. Putnam, G. Robertson and L. Tickner (eds), *Mapping the Futures: Local Cultures, Global Change*, London: Routledge, pp. 59–69.

—— (1994) *Space, Place, and Gender*, Minneapolis, MN: University of Minnesota Press.

Mattern, J. B. (2004) 'Why "Soft Power" Isn't So Soft: Representational Force and the Sociolinguistic Construction of Attraction in World Politics', *Millennium: Journal of International Studies*, 33 (3), 583–612.

Matthews, J. T. (1997) 'Power Shift', *Foreign Affairs*, 76 (1), 50–66.

May, S. (2001) *Language and Minority Rights: Ethnicity, Nationalism and the Politics of Language*, New York: Longman.

Mehmet, O., Mendes, E. and Sinding, R. (1999) *Towards A Fair Global Labour Market – The Role of International Labour*, London: Routledge.

Mellor, W. (1920) *Direct Action*, London: Leonard Parsons.

Memmi, A. (1965) *The Colonizer and the Colonized*, trans H. Greenfeld, New York: Orion Press.

Merleau-Ponty, M. (1981) *Phenomenology of Perception*, trans. C. Smith, London: Routledge.

Merriman, P. (2004) 'Driving Places: Marc Augé, Non-Places, and the Geographies of England's M1 Motorway', *Theory, Culture and Society*, 21 (4–5), 145–67.

Merrin, W. (2002) 'Implosion, Simulation and the Pseudo-Event: A Critique of McLuhan', *Economy and Society*, 31 (3), 369–90.

Meyer, J. W. (1980) 'The World Polity and the Authority of the Nation-State', in A. Bergesen (ed.), *Studies of the Modern World-System*, New York: Academic Press, pp. 109–37.

Meyer, J. W., Boli, J., Thomas, G. M. and Ramirez, F. O. (1997) 'World Society and the Nation-State', *American Journal of Sociology*, 103 (1), 144–81.

Michaud, J. (1997) 'Economic Transformation in a Hmong Village of Thailand', *Human Organization*, 56 (2), 222–32.

Mies, M. (1986) *Patriarchy and Accumulation on a World Scale: Women in the International Division of Labour*, London: Zed Books.

Mies, M. and Bennholdt-Thomsen, V. (1999) *The Subsistence Perspective*, London: Zed Books.

Miles, S. (1998) *Consumerism: As a Way of Life*, London: Sage.

Miller, D. (1984) *Anarchism*, London: Dent.

Miller, J. J. (1998) *The Unmasking of Americans: how Multiculturalism has Undermined the Assimilation Ethic*, New York: Free Press.

Milroy, J. and Milroy, L. (1999) *Authority in Language: Investigating Standard English*, London: Routledge.

Mishra, R. (1999) *Globalization and the Welfare State*, Cheltenam: Edward Elgar.

Mittelman, J. H. (2000) 'Globalization: Captors and Captive', *Third World Quarterly*, 21 (6), 917–29.

Moghadam, Valentine M. (2005) *Globalizing Women: Transnational Feminist Networks*, Baltimore, MD: John Hopkins University Press.

Moller Okin, S., Cohen, J., Howard, M., Sloan, R. and Nussbaum, M. C. (1999) *Is Multiculturalism Bad for Women?*, Princeton, NJ: Princeton University Press.

Monbiot, G. (2000) *Captive State: the Corporate Takeover of Britain*, Basingstoke: Macmillan.

Montserrat, G. (1996) *Nationalisms: The Nation-State and Nationalism in the Twentieth Century*, Cambridge: Polity Press.

Moore, H. L. (1995) 'The Future of Work', *British Journal of Industrial Relations*, 33 (4), 657–78.

Morley, D. and Robins, K. (1995) *Spaces of Identity*, London: Routledge.

Morrow, V. (1999) 'Conceptualising Social Capital in Relation to the Well-Being of Children and Young People: a Critical Review', *The Sociological Review*, 47 (4), 744–65.

Moseley, A. and Norman, R. (2002) *Human Rights and Military Intervention*, Aldershot: Ashgate.

Mouffe, C. (ed.) (1979) *Gramsci and Marxist Theory*, London: Routledge.

—— (1999) *The Challenge of Carl Schmitt*, London: Verso.

Mudambi, R. (ed.) (2003) *Privatization and Globalization: The Changing Role of the State in Business*, Cheltenham: Edward Elgar.

Mulhern, F. (2000) *Culture/Metaculture*, New York: Routledge.

—— (2002) 'Beyond Metaculture', *New Left Review*, 16, 86–104.

Mythen, G. (2004) *Ulrich Beck: A Critical Introduction to the Risk Society*, London: Pluto Press.

Nandy, A. (1988) *The Intimate Enemy: Loss and Recovery of Self Under Colonialism*, Oxford: Oxford University Press.

Nederveen-Pieterse, J. (1995) 'Globalisation as Hybridization', in M. Featherstone, S. Lash and R. Robertson (eds), *Global Modernities*, London: Sage, pp. 45–68.

—— (2004) 'Neoliberal Empire', *Theory, Culture and Society*, 21, (3), 119–40.

Negroponte, N. (1995) *Being Digital*, New York: Borzoi-Knopf.

Neill, M. (2001) 'Rethinking Class Composition Analysis in Light of the Zapatistas', in Midnight Notes (ed.), *Aurora of the Zapatistas: Local and Global Struggles of the Fourth World War*, Brooklyn, NY: Autonomedia, pp. 119–43.

Nicholson, L. and Seidman, S. (eds) (1995) *Social Postmodernism: Beyond Identity Politics*, Cambridge: Cambridge University Press.

Nolan, P. and Lenski, G. (1999) *Human Societies: An Introduction to Macrosociology*, New York: McGraw-Hill College.

279

Norberg, J. (2003) *In Defense of Global Capitalism*, Washington DC: Cato Institute.

Norris, C. (1992) *Uncritical Theory: Postmodernism, Intellectuals and the Gulf War*, London: Lawrence and Wishart.

Norris, P. (1996) 'The Nolan Committee: Financial Interests and Constituency Service', *Government and Opposition*, 31 (4), 441–48.

—— (2001) *Digital Divide: Civic Engagement, Information Poverty and the Internet Worldwide*, Cambridge: Cambridge University Press.

Norris, S. and Jones, R. H. (2005) *Discourse in Action: Introducing Mediated Discourse Analysis*, London: Routledge.

Nossal, K. R. (1998) *The Patterns of World Politics*, Scarborough: Prentice Hall.

Notes from Nowhere (ed.) (2003) *We Are Everywhere: The Irresistible Rise of Global Anti-capitalism*, London: Verso.

Nussbaum, M. C. (1996) *For Love of Country: Debating the Limits of Patriotism*, Boston, MA: Beacon Press.

Ó Tuathail, G. and Dalby, S. (1998) *Rethinking Geopolitics*, London: Routledge.

O'Brien, M., Penna, S. and Hay, C. (eds) (1998) *Theorising Modernity: Reflexivity, Environment and Identity in Giddens' Social Theory*, New York: Longman.

OECD (Organisation for Economic Co-operation and Development) (2005) *Modernising Government: The Way Forward*, Paris: OECD.

Offe, C. (1985) *Disorganized Capitalism: Contemporary Transformations of Work and Politics*, trans. J. Keane, Cambridge: Polity Press.

O'Flaherty, M. (1996) *Human Rights and the UN: Practice Before the Treaty Bodies*, London: Sweet and Maxwell.

—— (1990) *The Borderless World: Power and Strategy in the Interlinked Economy*, New York: Harper Collins.

Ohmae, K. (1996) *The End of the Nation State: the Rise of Regional Economies*, London: HarperCollins.

Ougaard, M. (2003) *Political Globalization: State, Power, and Social Forces*, New York: Palgrave Macmillan.

Overbeek, J. (1999) *Free Trade Versus Protectionism: A Sourcebook of Essays and Readings*, New York: Edward Elgar Publishing.

Owusu, F. (2003) 'Pragmatism and the Gradual Shift From Dependency to Neoliberalism: the World Bank, African Leaders and Development Policy in Africa', *World Development*, 31 (10), 1655–72.

Park, R. E. (1928) 'Human Migration and the Marginal Man', *American Journal of Sociology*, 5, 881–93.

Partnerships and Participation. (2006) Available at: http://www.partnerships. org.uk/part/ (accessed 28 April 2006).

Paul, T. V., Ikenberry, G. J. and Hall, J. A. (eds) (2003) *The Nation-State in Question*, Princeton, NJ: Princeton University Press.

Payer, C. (1991) *Lent and Lost: Foreign Credit and Third World Development*, London: Zed Books.

Peck, J. and Yeung, H. (2003) *Remaking the Global Economy: Economic Geographical Perspectives*, London: Sage.

Pecora, V. P. (ed.) (2001) *Nations and Identities: Classic Readings*, Malden, MA: Blackwell.

Peet, R. and Born, B. (2003) *Unholy Trinity: the IMF, World Bank, and the WTO*, London: Zed Books.

Pestieau, P. (2005) *The Welfare State in the European Union: Economic and Social Perspectives*, Oxford: Oxford University Press.

Peters, J. and Wolper, A. (eds) (1995) *Women's rights, Human Rights: International Feminist Perspectives*, London: Routeldge.

Petersen, A. (1997) 'Risk, Governance and the New Public Health', in A. Petersen and R. Bunton (eds), *Foucault, Health and Medicine*, London: Routledge, pp. 189–206.

Peukert, H. (2004) 'Max Weber: Precursor of Economic Sociology and Heterodox Economics?' *The American Journal of Economics and Sociology*, 63 (5), 987–1020.

Phillipson, R. (1992) *Linguistic Imperialism*, Oxford: Oxford University Press.

—— (2003) *English-only Europe? Challenging Language Policy*, London: Routledge.

Philpott, D. (2001) *Revolutions in Sovereignty: How Ideas Shaped Modern International Relations*, Princeton, NJ: Princeton University Press.

Pierson, C. (2004) *The Modern State*, London: Routledge.

Pijl, K. van der (1998) *Transnational Classes and International Relations*, London: Routledge.

Piore, M. and Sabel, C. (1984) *The Second Industrial Divide: Possibilities for Prosperity*, New York: Basic Books.

Plender, J. (2003) *Going Off the Rail: Global Capital and the Crisis of Legitimacy*, Chichester: Wiley.

Plessner, H. (1974) *Diesseits der Utopie*, Munich: Suhrkamp.

Policy Hub. (2005) Available at: http://www.policyhub.gov.uk/ (accessed 28 March 2005).

Pollitt, C. and Bouckaert, G. (2004) *Public Management Reform: A comparative analysis*, Oxford: Oxford University Press.

Pollock, A. M. (2004) *NHS plc: the Privatisation of Our Healthcare*, London: Verso.

Popper, K. (1945) *The Open Society and its Enemies*, London: Routledge.

—— (1959) *The Logic of Scientific Discovery*, London: Hutchinson and Co.

—— (1982) *Postscript to the Logic of Scientific Discovery*, London: Hutchinson and Co.

—— (1983) *Realism and the Aim of Science: Postscript to the Logic of Scientific Discovery Volume I*, London: Routledge.

Portes, A. 1998. 'Social Capital: Its Origins and Applications in Modern Sociology', *Annual Review of Sociology*, pp. 1–24.

Powelson, J. (1998) *The Moral Economy*, Ann Arbor, MI: University of Michigan Press.

Pratt, N. (2004) 'Bringing Politics Back in: Examining the Link Between Globalization', *Review of International Political Economy*, 11 (2), 311–36.

Pryke, M. (2002) 'The White Noise of Capitalism: Audio and Visual Montage and Sensing Economic Change', *Cultural Geographies*, 9 (4), 472–77.

Pusey, M. (2003) *The Experience of Middle Australia: The Dark Side of Economic Reform*, Cambridge: Cambridge University Press.

Putnam R. D. (2000) *Bowling Alone: The Collapse and Revival of American Community*, New York: Simon and Shuster.

Putnam, R. D., Leonardi, R. and Nanetti, R. Y. (1993) *Making Democracy Work: Civic Traditions in Modern Italy,* Princeton, NJ: Princeton University Press.

Raikes, P., Jensen, M. F. and Ponte, S. (2000) 'Global Commodity Chain Analysis and the French filière Approach: Comparison and Critique', *Economy and Society,* 29 (3), 390–417.

Ralston Saul, J. (2005) *The Collapse of Globalism*, London: Atlantic Books.

Ramet, S. P. (2004) 'Explaining the Yugoslav Meltdown, 2: A Theory about the Causes of the Yugoslav Meltdown: The Serbian National Awakening as a "Revitalization Movement"', *Nationalities Papers*, 32 (4), 765–79

Rampton, B. (1999) 'Sociolinguistics and Cultural Studies: New Ethnicities, Liminality and Interaction', *Social Semiotics*, 9 (3), 355–74.

Ray, M. and Jacka, E. (1996) 'Indian Television: An Emerging Regional Force', in J. Sinclair, Jacka, E. and Cunningham, S. (eds), *New Patterns in Global Television*, New York: Oxford University Press, pp. 83–100.

Reck, H. U. (1993) 'Sign Conceptions in Everyday Culture from the Renaissance to the Present', *Semiotica*, 96 (3–4), 199–229.

Reich, R. B. (1992) *The Work of Nations*, New York: Vintage Books.

Relph, E. (1976) *Place and Placelessness*, London: Pion.

Richards, P. (2005) 'The Politics of Gender, Human Rights, and Being Indigenous in Chile', *Gender and Society*, 19 (2), 199–220.

Richmond, A. H. (1994) *Global Apartheid: Refugees, Racism, and the New World Order*, Oxford: Oxford University Press.

Ricoeur, P. (1965) 'Universal Civilization and National Cultures', in P. Ricoeur (ed.), *History and Truth*, Evanston, IL: Northwestern University Press, pp. 271–84.

Ridley, F. F. and Wilson, D. (eds) (1995), *The Quango Debate* (Hansard Society Series in Politics & Government), Oxford: Oxford University Press.

Riese, U. (1995) 'Henry Adams and the Question of Posthistoire', *History of European Ideas,* 20 (1–3), 621–25.

Rifkin, J. (1991) *Biosphere Politics: A New Consciousness for a New Century*, New York: Crown.

Ritzer, G. (1993) *The McDonaldization of Society,* Thousand Oaks, CA: Pine Forge Press.

—— (1997) *The McDonalization Thesis*, London: Sage.

Roach, C. (1997) 'Cultural Imperialism and Resistance in Media Theory and Literary Theory Media', *Culture and Society*, 19 (1), 47–66.

Roach, S. (2005) 'Decisionism and Humanitarian Intervention: Reinterpreting Carl Schmitt and the Global Political Order', *Alternatives: Global, Local, Political,* 30 (4), 443–60.

Robbins, B. (1992) 'Comparative Cosmopolitanism', *Social Text*, 31/32 (10:2–3), 169–96.

Roberts, P. (2005) *The End of Oil: The Decline of the Petroleum Economy and the Rise of a New Energy Order*, London: Bloomsbury.

Roberts, J. T. and Thanos, N. D. (2003) *Trouble in Paradise: Globalization and Environmental Crises in Latin America*, London: Routledge.

Robertson, A. H. and Merrills J. G. (eds) (1996) *Human Rights in the World: An Introduction to the Study of the International Protection of Human Rights*, Manchester: Manchester University Press.

Robertson, R. (1988) 'The Sociological Significance of Culture: Some General Considerations', *Theory, Culture and Society*, 5 (1), 3–23.

—— (1992) *Globalization: Social Theory and Global Culture*, London: Sage, pp. 15–30.

—— (1995) 'Glocalization: Time-Space and Homogeneity-Heterogeneity', in M. Featherstone, S. Lash and R. Robertson (eds), *Global Modernities*, London: Sage.

Robertson, S. (2002) 'The Politics of Re-Territorialization: Space, Scale and Teachers as a Professional Class', *Currículo sem Fronteiras*, 2 (2), xvii–xxxiv.

Robins, K. (1997) 'What in the World's Going on?' in P. du Gay (ed.), *Production of Culture/Cultures of Production*, London: Sage, pp. 11–67.

—— (2003) 'Encountering Globalization', in D. Held and A. McGrew (eds), *The Global Transformations Reader*, Cambridge: Polity Press, pp. 239–45.

Robinson, W. I. (2004) *A Theory of Global Capitalism: Production, Class, and State in a Transnational World*, Baltimore: Johns Hopkins University Press.

—— (2005) 'Global Capitalism: the New Transnationalism and the Folly of Conventional Thinking', *Science and Society*, 69 (3), 316–28.

Robinson, W. I. and Harris, J. (2000) 'Towards A Global Ruling Class?: Globalization And The Transnational Capitalist Class' *Journal of Science And Society*, 64 (1), 11–54.

Rodrik, D. (1997) *Has Globalization Gone Too Far?*, Washington, DC: Institute for International Economics.

Rose, M. (1990) *Lives on the Boundary*, New York: Penguin.

Rose, N. (1996a) 'The Death of the Social? Re-figuring the Territory of Government', *Economy and Society*, 25 (3), 327–56.

—— (1996b) 'Governing "advanced" liberal democracies', in A. Barry, T. Osbourne and N. Rose (eds), *Foucault and Political Reason: Liberalism, Neo-liberalism, and Rationalities of Government*, Chicago, IL: University of Chicago Press, pp. 37–64

—— (1999) *Powers of Freedom: Reframing Political Thought*, Cambridge: Cambridge University Press.

Rosen, M. (1996) *On Voluntary Servitude: False Consciousness and the Theory of Ideology*, Oxford: Polity Press.

Rosenau, J. N. (2003) *Distant Proximities: Dynamics Beyond Globalism*, Princeton, NJ: Princeton University Press.

Rosenberg, J. (2000) *The Follies of Globalisation Theory*, London: Verso.

Rossi, P. H., Freeman, H. E. and Lipsey, M. W. (1999) *Evaluation: A Systematic Approach*, Thousand Oaks, CA: Sage.

Roszak, T. (1969) *The Making of a Counter-Culture,* New York: Doubleday.

Roudometof, V. (1997) 'Preparing for the 21st Century', *Sociological Forum*, 12 (4), 661–70.

Ruggie, J. G. (1998a) 'What makes the world hang together?', *International Organization*, 52 (4), 855–86.

—— (1998b) *Constructing the World Polity*, New York: Routledge.

Sachs, J. (2005) *The End of Poverty: Economic Possibilities for Our Time*, London: Penguin.

Safran, W. (1991) 'Diasporas in Modern Societies: Myths of Homeland and Return', *Diaspora*, 1 (1), 83–99.

Said, E. W. (1978) *Orientalism*, London: Routledge.

Sassen, S. (1996) *Transnational Economies and National Migration Policies*, Amsterdam: Institute for Migration and Ethnic Studies, University of Amsterdam.

—— (1999) *Globalization and its Discontents*, New York: New Press.

—— (2001) *The Global City: New York, London, Tokyo*, Princeton, NJ: Princeton University Press.

—— (2002) *Global Networks, Linked Cities*, New York: Routledge.

Sayer, A. (1997) "The dialectic of culture and economy", in R. Lee and J. Wills (eds), *Geographies of Economies*, London: Edward Arnold, pp. 16–26.

—— (2000) 'Moral Economy and Political Economy', *Studies in Political Economy*, 61, 79–104.

—— (2003 [2000]) 'Developing the Critical Standpoints of Radical Political Economy', Lancaster: Department of Sociology, Lancaster University. Available at: http://www.comp.lancs.ac.uk/sociology/papers/Sayer-Critical-Standpoints-of-Radical-Political-Economy.pdf (accessed 12 April 2006).

—— (2004) *Moral Economy*, Lancaster: Department of Sociology, Lancaster University. Available at: http://www.lancs.ac.uk/fss/sociology/papers/sayer-moral-economy.pdf (accessed 3 April 2006).

Schierup, C.-U. (ed.) (1998) *Scramble for the Balkans Nationalism, Globalism and the Political Economy of Reconstruction*, Basingstoke: Palgrave.

Schiller, H. I. (1971) *Mass Communications and American Empire*, Boston, MA: Beacon Press.

Schiralli, M. (1999) *Constructive Postmodernism: Toward Renewal in Cultural and Literary Studies*, Westport, CT: Greenwood Press.

Schlosser, E. (2002) *Fast Food Nation*, London: Penguin.

Schmitt, C. (1976) *The Concept of the Political*, New Brunswick, NJ: Rutgers University Press.

Scholte, J. A. (1997) 'Global capitalism and the state', *International Affairs*, 73 (3), 427–52.

—— (2000) *Globalization: A Critical Introduction*, New York: St. Martin's Press.

—— (2005) *The Sources of Neoliberal Globalisation*, Geneva: United Nations Research Institute for Social Development (UNRISD).

Scott, A. J. (ed.) (2001) *Global City-Regions: Trends, Theory, Policy*, Oxford: Oxford University Press.

Scriven, M. (1991) *Evaluation Thesaurus*, Newbury Park, CA: Sage Publications.

Seers, D. (1981) *Dependency Theory: A Critical Reassessment*, London: Pinter.

Sen, A. (2002) 'Does Globalization Equal Westernization?' *The Globalist*, March 25. Available at: http://www.theglobalist.com/DBWeb/StoryId.aspx?StoryId = 2353 (accessed 28 April 2006).

Shapiro, E. (1991) 'Fear of Terrorism is curbing travel', *New York Times*, 28 January, Section A, p. 1.

Shaw, M. (1994) *Global Society and International Relations:Sociological Concepts and Political Perspective*, Cambridge: Polity Press.

Sheil, C. (ed.) (2001) *Globalisation: Australian Impacts*, Sydney: University of New South Wales Press.

Sheller, M. and Urry, J. (2000) 'The City and the Car', *International Journal of Urban and Regional Research*, 24, 737–57.

Sheller, M. and Urry, J. (2003) 'Mobile Transformations of "Public" and "Private" Life', *Theory, Culture and Society*, 20 (3), 107–25.

Shils, E. (1981) *Tradition*, Chicago, IL: University of Chicago Press.

Shiva, V. (1997) *Biopiracy: The Plunder of Nature and Knowledge*, Cambridge, MA: South End Press.

Simpson, G. R. (1990) 'Wallerstein's World-Systems Theory and the Cook Islands: A Critical Examination', *Pacific Studies*, 14 (1), 73–94.

Sinclair, J., Jacka, E. and Cunningham, S. (eds) (1996) *New Patterns in Global Television*, New York: Oxford University Press.

Singer, P. (1993) *Practical Ethics*, Cambridge: Cambridge University Press.

—— (2000) *Marx: A Very Short Introduction*, Oxford: Oxford Paperbacks.

—— (2004) *One World: The Ethics of Globalization*, New Haven, CT: Yale University Press.

Singh, K. R. (2002) 'Geo-Strategy of Commercial Energy', *International Studies*, 39 (3), 259–88.

Singham, A. and Hune, S. (1987) 'The Non-Aligned Movement and World Hegemony', *The Black Scholar*, 18 (2), 48–57.

Sklair, L. (1995) *Sociology of the Global System*, Baltimore, MD: Johns Hopkins University Press.

—— (1999) 'Competing Conceptions of Globalization', *Journal of World Systems Research*, 2, 143–63.

—— (2002) *Globalization: Capitalism and Its Alternatives*, Oxford: Oxford University Press.

Skutnabb-Kangas, T. and Phillipson, R. (eds) (1995) *Linguistic Human Rights: Overcoming Linguistic Discrimination*, Berlin: de Gruyter

Slaughter, A. M. (2000) 'Governing the Global Economy through Government Networks', in M. Byers (ed.), *The Role of Law in International Politics: Essays in International Relations and International Law*, Oxford: Oxford University Press, pp. 177–205.

Smart, M. A. (2004) 'Defrosting Instructions: a Response', *Cambridge Opera Journal*, 16 (3), 311–18.

Smith, A. (1981) *The Ethnic Revival in the Modern World*, Cambridge: Cambridge University Press.

Smith, A. D. (2001) *Nationalism: Theory, Ideology, History*, London: Polity Press

Smith, D. (1992) 'Feminist Reflections on Political Economy', in M. Connelly and P. Armstrong (eds), *Feminism in Action: Studies in Political Economy*, Toronto: Canadian Scholars Press, pp. 1–23.

Smith, J. and Johnston, H. (2002) *Globalization and Resistance: Transnational Dimensions of Social Movements*, Lanham, MD: Rowman and Littlefield.

Smith, M. P. (2001) *Transnational Urbanism: Locating Globalization*, Malden, MA: Blackwell.

Snow, D. M. (2004) *National Security for a New Era: Globalization and Geopolitics*, New York: Pearson/Longman.

Sorkin, M. (ed.) (1992) *Variations on a Theme Park: the New American City and the End of Public Space*, New York: Hill and Wang.

Soros, G. (2000) *Open Society: The Crisis of Global Capitalism Reconsidered*, London: Little, Brown.

Speth, J. G. (ed.) (2003) *Worlds Apart: Globalization and the Environment*, Washington, DC: Island Press.

Spivak, G. C. (1985) 'Can the Subaltern Speak?: Speculations on Widow Sacrifice', *Wedge*, 7/8, 120–30.

—— (1988) 'Can the Subaltern Speak?', in C. Nelson and L. Grossberg (eds), *Marxism and the Interpretation of Culture*, Chicago, IL: University of Illinois Press, pp. 271–313.

Starr, A. (2005) *Global Revolt: A Guide to the Movements Against Globalization*, London: Zed Books.

Stehr, N. (1994) *Knowledge Societies*, London: Sage.

Steiner, H. J. and Alston, P. (1996) *International Human Rights in Context: Law, Politics, Morals,* Oxford: Clarendon Press.

Stevens, P. (2005) 'Oil Markets', *Oxford Review of Economic Policy*, 21 (1), 19–41.

Stewart, I. (1990) *Does God Play Dice? The Mathematics of Chaos*, London: Penguin.

Stiglitz, J. (2002) *Globalization and its Discontents*, London: Penguin.

Stokke, O. S., Hovi, J. and Ulfstein, G. (eds) (2005) *Implementing the Climate Regime – International Compliance*, London: Earthscan.

Stonequist, E. V. (1935) 'The Problem of Marginal Man', *American Journal of Sociology*, 7, 1–12.

Storey, J. and Bacon, N. (1993) 'Individualism and Collectivism: into the 1990s', *International Journal of Human Resource Management*, 4 (3), 665–85.

Strang, D. (1990) 'From Dependency to Sovereignty: An Event History Analysis of Decolonization 1870–1987', *American Sociological Review*, 55, 846–60.

Strange, S. (1994) *States and Markets*, London: Blackwell.

—— (1996) *The Retreat of the State: the Diffusion of Power in the World Economy*, Cambridge: Cambridge University Press.

—— (1998) *Mad Money*, Manchester: Manchester University Press.

Surber, J. P. (1998) *Culture and Critique: An Introduction to the Critical Discourses of Cultural Studies*, Boulder, CO: Westview Press.

Swyngedouw, E. (1996) 'Neither Global Nor Local: Globalisation and the Politics of Scale', in K. Cox (ed.), *Spaces of Globalisation. Reasserting the Power of the Local*, Surrey, UK: Guildford Press.

—— (2004) 'Globalisation or "Glocalisation"? Networks, Territories and Rescaling', *Cambridge Review of International Affairs*, 17 (1), 25–48.

Tarnas, R. (1991) *The Passion of the Western Mind: Understanding the Ideas That Have Shaped Our World View*, New York: Harmony.

Taylor, P. J. (1996) *The Way the Modern World Works: World Hegemony to World Impasse*, Chichester: Wiley.

—— (2004) *World City Network: A Global Urban Analysis*, London: Routledge.

Tennant, M. (2004) 'History and Social Policy: Perspectives from the Past', in B. Dalley and M. Tennant (eds), *Past Judgement: Social Policy in New Zealand*, Dunedin, New Zealand: Otago University Press, pp. 9–22.

Terranova, T. (2000) 'Free Labor: Producing culture for the digital economy', *Social Text*, 18 (2, 63), 33–58.

Thomas, H. (1995) *Globalisation and Third World Trade Unions: The Challenge of Rapid Economic Change*, London: Zed Books.

Thomas, R., Mills, A. J. and Helms–Mills, J. (eds) (2004) *Identity Politics at Work: Resisting Gender, Gendering Resistance*, London: Routledge.

Thompson, E. P. (1971) 'The Moral Economy of the Eighteenth Century Crowd', *Past and Present*, 50, 76–136.

—— (1991) *Customs in Common*, London: Merlin.

Thompson, P. and Warhurst, C. (eds) (1998) *Workplaces of the Future*, Basingstoke: Macmillan Business

Tilly, C. (1990) *Coercion, Capital, and European States, AD 990–1990*, Cambridge, MA: Blackwell.

Todd, L. (1990) *Pidgins and Creoles*, London: Routledge.

Toffler, A. (1970) *Future Shock*, London: Bodley Head.

Tomlinson, J. (1991) *Cultural Imperialism: a Critical Introduction*, London: Pinter.

—— (1996) 'Cultural Globalisation: Placing and Displacing the West', *European Journal of Development Research*, 8 (2), 22–35.

—— (1999) *Globalization and Culture*, Cambridge: Polity Press.

Tönnies, F., (2001 [1887]) *Community and Civil Society*, Cambridge: Cambridge University Press.

Tornell, A. and Westermann, F. (2005) *Boom-Bust Cycles and Financial Liberalization*, Cambridge, MA: MIT Press.

Tsagarousianou, R. (2004) 'Rethinking the Concept of Diaspora: Mobility, Connectivity and Communication in a Globalised World', *Westminster Papers in Communication and Culture*, 1 (1), 52–66.

Tumber, H. and Palmer. J. (2004) *Media at War: The Iraq Crisis*, London: Sage.

Tunstall, J. (1977) *The Media Are American: Anglo-American Media in the World*, London: Constable.

Tunstall, J. and Machin, D. (1999) *The Anglo-American Media Connection*, Oxford: Oxford University Press.

Turner, B. (1984) *The Body in Society*, Oxford: Basil Blackwell.

Turner, B. S. (1990) *Theories of Modernity and Postmodernity*, London: Sage.

Turner, S. (1998) 'Global Civil Society, Anarchy and Governance: Assessing an Emerging Paradigm', *Journal of Peace Research*, 35 (1), 25–42.

Turner, V. (1974) *Dramas, Fields, and Metaphors: Symbolic Action in Human Society*, Ithaca, NY: Cornell University Press.

UNCTAD (United Nations Conference on Trade and Development). (2004) *World Investment Report 2004: the Shift Toward Services*, World Investment Report Series, Geneva: United Nations.

United Nations. (2006) Available at: www.UN.org (accessed 28 April 2006).

United Nations Development Fund for Women. (2006) Available at: www.unifem.org (accessed 28 April 2006).

United Nations Development Program. (2006) Available at: www.undp.org (accessed 28 April 2006).

United Nations Environment Programme. (2006) Available at: www.unep.org (accessed 28 April 2006).

United Nations, Women Watch. (2006) Available at: www.un.org/women-watch (accessed 28 April 2006).

Urban, G. (2001) *Metaculture: How Culture Moves through the World*, Minneapolis, MN: University of Minnesota Press.

Urry, J. (1990) *The Tourist Gaze: Leisure and Travel in Contemporary Societies*, London: Sage.

—— (2000) 'Mobile Sociology', *British Journal of Sociology*, 51 (1), l85–203.

—— (2002a) *Global Complexity*, Cambridge: Polity Press.

—— (2002b) 'The Global Complexities of September 11th', *Theory, Culture and Society*, 19 (4), 57–69.

—— (2004) 'The "System" of Automobility', *Theory, Culture and Society*, 21 (4/5), 25–39.

Van Den Berghe, P. (1994) *The Quest for the Other: Ethnic Tourism in San Cristobal, Mexico*, Seattle, WA: University of Washington Press.

Vargas, V. (2003) 'Feminism, Globalization and the Global Justice and Solidarity Movement', *Cultural Studies*, 17 (6), 905–20.

Verkaaik, O. (2003) 'Fun and Violence. Ethnocide and the Effervescence of Collective Aggression', *Social Anthropology*, 11 (1), 3–22.

Vines, D. and Gilbert C. L. (eds) (2004) *The IMF and its Critics: Reform of Global Financial Architecture*, Cambridge: Cambridge University Press.

Vink, M. (2002) 'What is Europeanization? And Other Questions on a New Research Agenda', paper presented at the Second YEN Research Meeting on Europeanisation, University of Bocconi, Milan, 22–23 November 2002. Available at: http://www.essex.ac.uk/ecpr/standinggroups/yen/paper_archive/2nd_yen_rm_papers/vink2002.pdf (accessed 28 March 2005).

Vreeland, J. R. (2003) *The IMF and Economic Development*, Cambridge: Cambridge University Press.

Wachtel, H. (2000) 'Tobin and Other Global Taxes', *Review of International Political Economy*, 7 (2), 335–52.

Wade, R. H. (2004) 'Is Globalization Reducing Poverty and Inequality?', *International Journal of Health Services*, 34 (3), 381–414.

Wagnleitner, R. (1994) *Coca-Colonization and the Cold War: The Cultural Mission of the US in Austria after the Second World War*, Chapel Hill, NC: The University of North Carolina Press.

Walby, S. (2002) 'Feminism in a Global Era', *Economy and Society*, 31 (4), 533–57.

Wallerstein, I. (1974) *The Modern World-System: Capitalist Agriculture and the Origins of the European World-Economy in the 16th Century*, New York: Academic Press.

—— (1980) *The Modern World-System II: Mercantilism and the Consolidation of the European World Economy, 1600–1750*, New York: Academic Press.

—— (1989) *The Modern World-System III: The Second Era of Great Expansion of the Capitalist World Economy, 1730–1840,* New York: Academic Press.

—— (2004) *World-Systems Analysis: An Introduction*, Durham: Duke University Press.

Wang, H. (2004) 'Regulating Transnational Flows of People: an Institutional Analysis of Passports and Visas as a Regime of Mobility', *Identities: Global Studies in Culture and Power,* 11 (3), 351–76.

Ward C. (2004) *Anarchism: A Very Short Introduction*, Oxford: Oxford University Press.

Warschauer, M. (2004) *Technology and Social Inclusion: Rethinking the Digital Divide*, Cambridge, MA: MIT Press.

Waterman, P. (2002) 'Reflections on the 2nd World Social Forum in Porto Alegre: What's Left Internationally?' *Working Papers Series*, no 362, The Hague: Institute of Social Studies.

Weaver, D. (2001) *Ecotourism*, Sydney, Australia: John Wiley and Sons.

Weber, M. (1954) *Max Weber on Law in Economy and Society,* Cambridge, MA: Harvard University Press.

Weiss, J. (2002) *Industrialisation and Globalisation: Theory and Evidence from Developing Countries*, London: Routledge.

Weiss, T. G. and Gordenker, L. (1996) *NGOs, the UN, and Global Governance*, Boulder, CO: Lynne Reinner Publishers.

Weiss, T. G. and Thakur, R. (forthcoming) *The UN and Global Governance: An Idea and its Prospects*, Bloomington, IN: Indiana University Press.

Weiss, T. G., Forsythe, D. P. and Coate R. A. (2004) *The United Nations and Changing World Politics*, Oxford: Westview Press.

Werbner, P. and Yuval-Davis, N. (eds) (1999) *Women, Citizenship and Difference*, London: Zed Books.

Weschler, L. (1999) *Boggs: a Comedy of Values*, Chicago: University of Chicago Press.

Wheeler, M. (2000) 'Globalization of the Communications Marketplace', *Harvard International Journal of Press/Politics*, 5 (3), 27–44.

Whisman, V. (1996) *Queer by Choice: Lesbians, Gay Men and the Politics of Identity,* London: Routledge.

White, S. (1998) 'Interpreting the Third Way: Not One Road But Many', *Renewal*, 6 (2), 17–30.

Williams, K. (1998) *Get Me a Murder a Day! A History of Mass Communication in Britain*, London: Arnold.

Wills, J. (2002) 'Bargaining for the Space to Organize in the Global Economy: A Review of the Accor-IUF Trade Union Rights Agreement', *Review of International Political Economy,* 9 (4), 675–700.

Wilson, D. (1995) 'Quangos in the Skeletal State', *Parliamentary Affairs*, 48 (2), 181–91.

Windmuller, J. P. (2000) 'The International Trade Secretariats', in M. E. Gordon and L. Turner (eds), *Transnational Cooperation Among Labor Unions*, Ithaca, NY: ILR Press, pp. 102–19.

Wolf, M. (2004) *Why Globalisation Works*, New Haven, CT: Yale University Press.

Woo–Cumings, M. (ed.) (1999) *The Developmental State*, Ithaca, NY: Cornell University Press.

Woodcock, G. (1986) *Anarchism: a History of Libertarian Ideas and Movements*, Harmondsworth: Penguin.

Woodiwiss, A. (2002) 'Human Rights and the Challenge of Cosmopolitanism', *Theory, Culture and Society*, 19 (1–2), 139–55.

Woodward, D. (1998) *Drowning by Numbers: the IMF, the World Bank and North-South Financial Flows*, London: Bretton Woods Project.

World Bank (2006) Available at: www.worldbank.org (accessed 28 April 2006).

World Trade Organization (2006) Available at: www.wto.org (accessed 28 April 2006).

Yan Kong, T. (2004) 'Neo-liberalization and Incorporation in Advanced Newly Industrialized Countries: A View from South Korea', *Political Studies*, 52 (1), 19–42.

Young, R. (1990) *White Mythologies*, London: Routledge.

Youngs, G. (2001) 'The Political Economy of Time in the Internet Era: Feminist Perspectives and Challenges', *Information, Communication and Society*, 4 (1), 14–33.

Ziya, O. (1991) 'The Logic of the Developmental State: Review Article', *Comparative Politics*, 24 (1), 109–26.

INDEX

communities of fate **36**, 98–99, 146–47, 184, 211–12

communities of limited liability **36**

community based organization (CBO) 179

community participation **37**, 91–92, 101–2, 114, 116; *see also* active citizen/citizenship

community, concept of 101

complex systems 22

complexity theory 22, **37–38**

confluent love **38–39**

constitutions 125; *see also* nation state

constructivism 174

consumerism 11, **39–40**, 53, 90, 153, 154, 158, 168, 197, 200, 225–26, 226

consumption rituals **40**

consumption; *see* consumerism

contingency theory **41**

convergence thesis **41–42**; *see also* homogenization

convergence, government/institutional 41, 84–86

core-periphery model **42**, 157–58, 252–53

corn laws (UK) 19

corporate anorexia 73

corporatism 42–43

cosmocracy **43**

cosmopolis **43**, 242

cosmopolitan democracy **43–45**

cosmopolitanism 43, **45**, 124; discrepant **70**

counter culture **45–46**, 142–44, 197

counter hegemony **46–47**, 116; *see also* hegemony

counter narratives **46**, 61, 102, 103, 116, 139, 243

creolization **48**

crimes against humanity 24; *see also* human rights

critical geopolitics 103

cultural autonomy **48**

cultural capital **49**, 53, 147–48, 217, 229

cultural convergence; *see* homogenization

cultural defence plea **50**, 241

cultural dumping **50**; *see also* cultural imperialism

cultural economy **50–51**, 197

cultural entrepreneurs **52**; *see also* symbolic analysts

cultural fate **52–53**, 114

cultural genocide 82, 147–48

cultural heritage **53**

cultural imperialism 4, 29, 30, **53–54**, 77, 106, 110–12, 124, 160, 161–62, 163–64, 244

cultural integration **54**

cultural landscape 29, **54–55**, 55

cultural relativism 210

cultural storage 53, **55**

cultural synchronization **56**

culturalism **56**

culturalization thesis 51

culture industry **57**

culture of civility **57–58**

culture, discourse about 164

culturecide 82

currency exchange and speculation 19, 134, 233–34

cyberactivism **58–59**

Dalby, S. 103

Day, G. 158

de Soto, H. 87–88

Dean, M. 4, 119

debt relief 7, **59**

decionism **59**

decolonization **59–60**, 221

decommoditization **60**

de-governmentalisation **61**, 118–19

Delanty, G. 23, 218

demand led economies 242–43

democracy 3, 5, 17, 43, 43–45, **61–65**, 79, 84, 112–13, 220–22, 222

democratic deficit 85, 107–8

Robertson, R. 124, 128, 229–30, 249
Rose, N. 23, 61, 119, 204

Said, E. 186–87
SAP (structural adjustment program) 7, 134–35; *see also* International Monetary Fund
Sartre, J. P. 52
Sassen, S. 247
Schmitt, C. 59
Scholte, J. A. 110
Schröder, G 230–32
SDR (special drawing rights) 134–35 *see* international monetary fund
Seattle 7, **213,** 253–54 *see also* antiglobalization
security council 239; *see also* United Nations
semi-periphery countries **213–14,** 252–53; *see* world systems theory, core-periphery model
September 11 22, 72; *see also* terrorism, fundamentalism
service work 183, **214,** 242–43
sherpas 99
shrimp-turtle case (WTO) 88
simulacrum 9–10, 129–30, 199, 202, **214**
Singer, P. 45, 184
skeptics, of globalization 122, 128, 134, 142, 183, **214–15,** 234, 236
Sklair, L. 235, 237
Smith, Adam 19, 150–51
social capital 25, **215–17,** 229; bonding 216; bridging 216
social exclusion 135, 203–4, 215–17
social movements 6–8, 64, 213, **217–18**
social policy 190–93
social styles 153
social welfare 176, 176–77
socialism 242–43
socialist world government 253
societies of control **218–19**

soft power 52, 54, 120
sovereignty 171–72, **219–20,** 222–23 *see also* nation state, state
space, thick and thin 189
special economic zone *See* Export Processing Zone
speed of life 233
Spivak, G.C. 81, 224–25
spontaneous consent 121
Star TV 111
Starbucks 213
state **220–22;** indigenous 138
statist paradigm 220–22, **222–23;** world 223
Stiglitz, J. 135
Strange, S. 173
structuralism 205
structuration theory 208, **223–24,** 251
subaltern 81, **224–25**
subsistence perspective 13, **225–26**
supermodernity **226;** *see also* reflexive modernization
supply chain 105
surplus value 168, **227**
sustainable development 180, **227–28**
sweatshop 7, 87
swinging voters 12, 20–21
symbolic analysts 196, 212, **228–29,** 238
symbolic capital 215–17, **229**
symbolic tokens 3
synopticon 156

television 28, 110–12 *see also* global media
tempo of life 233
territorialization (de- and re-) 102, 107, 205–6, 206, **229–30**
territory, of state *see* nation state, state, sovereignty
terrorism 97, 99, 176, 240; cells 165; war on 232
thin places 189
third way 21, 37, 179, **230–32**